ENTREPRENEURIAL HACKS: PRACTICAL INSIGHTS FOR BUSINESS BUILDERS

Karl R. LaPan

authorHOUSE

AuthorHouse™
1663 Liberty Drive
Bloomington, IN 47403
www.authorhouse.com
Phone: 833-262-8899

© 2021 Karl R. LaPan. All rights reserved.

No part of this book may be reproduced, stored in a retrieval system, or transmitted by any means without the written permission of the author.

Published by AuthorHouse 05/04/2021

ISBN: 978-1-6655-2455-1 (sc)
ISBN: 978-1-6655-2453-7 (hc)
ISBN: 978-1-6655-2454-4 (e)

Library of Congress Control Number: 2021908777

Print information available on the last page.

Any people depicted in stock imagery provided by Getty Images are models, and such images are being used for illustrative purposes only.
Certain stock imagery © Getty Images.

This book is printed on acid-free paper.

Because of the dynamic nature of the Internet, any web addresses or links contained in this book may have changed since publication and may no longer be valid. The views expressed in this work are solely those of the author and do not necessarily reflect the views of the publisher, and the publisher hereby disclaims any responsibility for them.

THIS BOOK IS DEDICATED
TO THE THREE MOST INFLUENTIAL WOMEN IN MY LIFE—
MY GRANDMOTHER, MARY MARGARET
WHO TAUGHT ME DETERMINATION;
MY MOTHER, ROBERTA WHO INSPIRED ME TO
BE THE BEST VERSION OF MYSELF, AND
MY WIFE, KELLY WHO ENCOURAGES ME TO FINISH
STRONG—AS A DAD, HUSBAND, AND SON.

Thank you to the Foellinger Foundation for funding my Inspire Grants and allowing me time and space to self-discover, discern, and help me be a more effective and adaptive leader.

The proceeds from this book will be invested in The Dr. Daryl R. Yost Fund so we can celebrate business builders and build more inclusive prosperity. This is something Daryl believed in and was passionate about making happen.

The famous American Psychiatrist and author, M. Scott Peck wrote, "Our finest moments occur when we are deeply uncomfortable, unhappy and unfulfilled. For it is only in such moments, propelled by our discomfort, that we are likely to step out of our ruts and start searching for different or truer ways." This is a terrific call to action for many of the courageous and passionate business builders I have encountered over the last 20 years.

MY CALL TO ACTION

A Call to Action (CTA) is a "marketing term for any device designed to prompt an immediate response or encourage an immediate sale." My call to action is simple for you—**Choose to be better. Choose to do better. Choose to seek out people who make you better. Choose to deliver better results.**

For the last 20 years, I have dedicated my professional career to the advancement of entrepreneurship and innovation. Throughout my experiences at the Northeast Indiana Innovation Center (The NIIC), I have been able to interact with thousands of business builders, entrepreneurs, innovators, scientists, economic developers, educators, foreign governments, entrepreneurial support organizations, service providers, and leading thinkers. From these experiences, I have been inspired and encouraged. I wrote this book to highlight the lessons learned, insights, and connections I have made to assist business builders in building, growing, and scaling successful and sustainable ventures. I used to think a score was a long time—but not anymore. Time flies when you are having fun and feeling like you are making a difference.

My sincere hope and aspiration from the strategic and intentional economic and community development work I have done are to lay a strong foundation for raising the confidence, capability, and competence of today's business builders. I have been inspired and often impressed by the obstacles, barriers, and opportunities existing for business builders who see around corners, challenge the status quo, face ridicule, and rise above adversity to make a difference. It is no wonder why very few people choose entrepreneurship as a career option, but those that do seldom regret it.

Over the last 20 years, I have come to internalize what it means to be an entrepreneur and a business builder. To me, an entrepreneur is someone who possesses three interrelated competencies:

- Sees opportunities that are of value to others;
- Creates and captures value; and
- Manages and navigates uncertainty and risks.

- Sees opportunities
- Captures value
- Manages uncertainty

Let's unpack this definition because it is essential to understanding the mindset I am trying to convey in this book:

- **Sees opportunity that is of value to others** reinforces the notion that it is not enough to see a problem or to have a problem. You have to see a problem that other segments or groups of people have.
- **Creates and captures value** reminds us that a sustainable and successful venture must have a viable business model—a way to make money.
- **Manages and navigates uncertainty and risks** drives the entrepreneurial obsession with navigating key commercialization challenges that might get in the way of a successful product or business launch. Through resiliency, grit, and tenacity, the business builder thrives in chaos and excels in the complexities of operationalizing their dreams.

Along the journey, business builders have taught me many valuable lessons. Some of the most powerful lessons I have learned about working with Founders can be captured in three significant domains:

Entrepreneurial Mindset

- To meet people where they are, not where you want them to be (don't try to fix people but work to bring out their best);
- To give more than you get in relationships (relationships can often be asymmetrical, and that is ok);

- To not move entrepreneurs to a level or place, they are not ready to go (don't intervene where someone is not prepared to go); and
- If you have met one entrepreneur … you have met *one* entrepreneur (each is unique, rare, special, and has their own unique story).

Entrepreneurial Bias for Action

- To encourage everyone to take the next step in their entrepreneurial journey, even if it means not moving forward with their venture (success is not mine to determine, it is the business builder's dream and their choices);
- To learn, laugh, lean-in, and love in everything you do—to be passionate, inspired, and committed (if you are not having fun, get out); and
- Work with what you have, not what you don't have (the glass is half full, not half empty), and always have a bias for action.

Entrepreneurial Resiliency

- To always be on your A-game—vociferous lifelong learner, connecting dots, gleaning insights, and aspiring to be at the pinnacle of your craft (the only thing you have, as a coach, to offer is your gifts and talents—sharpen the saw);
- Never give up (if it is important to you, never let anyone undermine you or your dream or your potential success); and
- To be relentless, driven, and intensely focused on your goal (grit is passion and perseverance in action and separates the committed entrepreneur with the mythological entrepreneur).

Throughout my professional career, I have been blessed with great mentors and bosses who always worked to better me, inspire me, and challenge me. These individuals made me into who I am today. I am genuinely grateful to the many professional colleagues and others (Ted, Mark, Carol, Larry and Daryl) and many of my previous bosses—Mel, John, Bruce, Bill, Michael, Ken, and Mark, Larry, who believed in me, encouraged me, bet on me, invested in me, and expected a lot from me. Most of all, they challenged me to always strive to be better and to be excellent in anything I do.

I would be remiss in not recognizing the two primary people responsible for me in the role I have played over the last two decades, the two people who selected me for this extraordinary opportunity and journey—Mike and Eric. Their passion and support have not wavered or dampened while I have been in this role. Just the opposite; their intellect, intensity, passion, and commitment have been a guidepost for me as The NIIC has evolved and grown. Thank you both for all you have done to advance and shape the entrepreneurial community and me.

Finally, I return to my introductory comments in the Call to Action (CTA). My hope is this book will inspire you to <u>be better</u>. I hope that you choose better. Only through *better* leadership, *better* innovation, *better* customer experiences, *better* learning opportunities, *better* citizenship, *better* engagement with our calling, and *better* relationships can we truly become the **best version of ourselves**. This is my goal for all of us, including myself.

Remember, the words of T.S. Eliot—and his challenge to us all to continuously seek answers, to engage in self-discovery along our journey, and to see things with new eyes and new perspectives when writing our own story. He wrote:

"We shall not cease from exploration, and the end of all our exploring will be to arrive where we started and know the place for the first time."

Be Better!

[signature]

Karl R. LaPan
President and CEO—The NIIC (www.Theniic.org)
May 2021

About The NIIC:

> 2020 was the 20th anniversary of the Northeast Indiana Innovation Center (NIIC). The NIIC is a place dedicated to growing the hometown team—creating higher quality, higher-paying jobs, and companies in Northeast Indiana. We accomplish this by providing business builders and entrepreneurs with the tools, support, and business development services to increase their chances of success and to accelerate their growth faster than they might do on their own.

Entrepreneurial Hacks – All Good Things Come in Three's

My Three Best Pieces of Career Advice from Mentors and Bosses

1. "Results, not effort, get rewarded."
2. "Business loyalty is 24 hours deep, and on Fridays, we are even."
3. "An excuse is a lie stuffed with a reason. No excuses."

My Three Biggest Myths About Founders' Blind Spots

1. My idea is amazing; it will change everything.
2. Entrepreneurs are their own bosses.
3. Entrepreneurs take significant risks.

My Three Biggest Myths About Funding an Entrepreneurial Venture

1. There is a massive amount of money out there to fund good ideas.
2. It is fast and easy to raise money if you have a good idea.
3. Raising money is more important than finding paying customers.

My Three Biggest Insights From Graduate School

1. Organizations mirror the dysfunction of their leaders.
2. You can't move someone further than they are prepared to go.
3. Behavioral change is a function of (awareness of the need for change + willingness to change) multiplied by the burning platform for change [crisis or opportunity].

My Three Biggest Business Principles and Practice

1. Jeff Bezos from Amazon.com schedules his most important meetings at 10 am.
2. Apple's Steve Jobs had a finite capacity of brainpower to make well thought out decisions (he wore the same thing every day—black turtleneck, blue jeans, and New Balance sneakers)—the average person makes 35,000 decisions a day.
3. Warren Buffet said, "Price is what you pay. Value is what you get."

My Three Best Business Books That Have Stood the Test of Time

1. **Good to Great** by Jim Collins
2. **Leadership is an Art** by Max DePree
3. **Competitive Strategy, and Competitive Advantage** by Michael Porter

My Three Best Career Insights

1. Learning agility is the number one most essential asset (you must also have depth in two disciplines, breadth across disciplines/functions, and obtain transferable and marketable skills).
2. Take the career assignments no one else wants and make something of it (it will help you get noticed, promoted, and build your skillset).
3. Find and place someone mature strategically in your organization to be your sounding board. It is lonely at the top!

My Three Favorite Business Quotations

1. "The purpose of a business is to create a customer." — Peter Drucker
2. "If you look closely, most overnight successes took a long time." — Steve Jobs
3. "When you're curious, you find lots of interesting things to do. And one thing it takes to accomplish something is courage." — Walt Disney

My Three Examples of Bad Advice

1. **Partner with everyone.** (The advice should be: Go into projects with partners who mutually invest in each other's outcomes and success.)
2. **Hire slow. Fire fast.** (The advice should be: Hire slow. Fire Faster. Things are unlikely to get better—so fire sooner. Second chances rarely work out when your gut says the person is a bad fit.)
3. **Shrink your way to greatness.** (The advice should be: Cost management can only go so far. At some point, you have to invest in something market-facing every day to create an enduring company.)

My Three Most Influential Bible Verses

1. Be watchful, stand firm in the faith, act like men, be strong. ~ **1 Corinthians 16:13**
2. To whom much is given, much is required. ~ **Luke 12:48**
3. Now faith is the assurance of things hoped for, the conviction of things not seen. ~ **Hebrews 11:1**

My Three Most Inspirational Public Figures in My Life

1. Saint John Paul II
2. President Ronald Reagan
3. Steve Jobs

My Three Pet Peeves About Startups

1. Hockey stick projections pulled out of thin air with little to no basis in reality.
2. No skin in the game but wanting everyone else to invest.
3. Lack of commitment and follow-through. Always have a reason for falling short.

My Best Three Pieces of Advice I have Read in Commencement Speeches

1. Adapt, adjust, and revise. (Alan Alda)
2. Don't settle. Live your own life. Take the unbeaten path. (Steve Jobs)
3. You might want to change fields, so focus on skills. (Sallie Krawcheck)

CONTENTS

Introduction xxi

Chapter 1 1
   i. Building a Culture of Innovation 1
   ii. Creativity Starts Here 3
   iii. Leaning into the Future of Work 4
   iv. Think Different: Marketing Lessons from Apple 6
   v. Hiring? Think Selection and Look for These Three Things 8
   vii. What Constitutes a Culture Powered by Learning Agility? ... 10
   viii. Three Ways to Take Corporate Innovation to the Next Level 14
   ix. Don't Fear Automation: How Business Builders Can Embrace It 16
   x. Opportunity Risk Assessment: Going Beyond the Numbers 17
   xi. Three Habits of Innovative Business Leaders 19
   xii. Do's of Business Model Innovation 20
   xiii. Innovation and Entrepreneurship: A Look at Drucker's Powerful Approach 22

Chapter 2 29
   i. Managing Uncertainty 30
   ii. A Case for Cultivating an Empathy-Driven Culture 32
   iii. How to Go from Good to Great: Start by Removing These Distractions 34
   iv. Protect Your Peace: Three Habits to Embrace 37
   v. Redefining Success Through the Lens of Vulnerability 39
   vi. Employee Health and Wellness: It's Good for Business! 41
   vii. Ask for Help! 43

- viii. Rethinking Balance 44
- ix. Dealing with Imposter Syndrome 46
- x. Resilience and Reinvigorating Yourself 48
- xi. Taming the Loneliness Monster 50
- xii. The Power of "Why" 52

Chapter 3 58
- i. What Does It Mean to Be a People-Centric Organization? ... 58
- ii. Technology Is Not a Substitute for Quality Relationships & Human Interactions 60
- iii. Finding a Business Partnership That Is Right for You 62
- iv. Time for a Culture Shift? Try These Three Tips 66
- v. How to Win Friends and Influence People (Online) 67
- vi. Take Your Communication to the Next Level 68
- vii. Authenticity Sells: How to Craft an Intentional Customer Experience 70
- viii. Cut the Jargon 72
- ix. Three Universal Lessons About Entrepreneurship 73
- x. Honesty Is Always the Best Policy 75

Chapter 4 80
- i. Time to Recalibrate? 80
- ii. Recession-Proof Your Business 82
- iii. Why Veterans Make Good Business Builders 84
- iv. Stuck? Here's How to Get Unstuck 86
- v. Three Ways to Overcome Founder's Syndrome 87
- vi. The Understated Introvert Advantage 89
- vii. Firing on all Cylinders: Ways to Push Forward 90
- viii. Got Grit? 92
- ix. Hypothesize, Experiment, Learn, and Pivot 94
- x. Resilience: The Key to Coping with Failure 96
- xi. Lean into Failure with These Tips 98
- xii. How to Weather Economic Ups and Downs 99

Chapter 5 106
  i. Crowdfunding: Is It for you? 107
  ii. Lessons from the Campaign Trail–The Advocacy Imperative 110
  iii. An Entrepreneurial Mandate—The Business Case for Indiana 112
  iv. What Makes a Great Pitch? Start Here 114
  v. Lessons from Shark Tank 117
  vi. Is Your Venture Really Investment Worthy? 119
  vii. How to Invest in Yourself on a Budget 121
  viii. Early Stage Investing Trends 123
  ix. Three Ways to Bootstrap Your Business 124
  x. Are You Getting What You're Worth? 126
  xi. One Form of Exit—Sell the Business 128

Chapter 6 135
  i. Stronger Together: The Case for Entrepreneurial Networks 136
  ii. Trade Shows Done Right 137
  iii. Tips for Meeting with Legislators 139
  iv. Cultivate and Invest in These Relationships: Self, Team, and Network 140
  v. Three Ways to Network Your Way to Success 142
  vi. Tap into Your Network to Grow as an Entrepreneur 144
  vii. Meeting Madness: Cut the Clutter (Or Another C Word of Your Choosing!) 146
  viii. Seven Seconds Matter: Hacking the Formula for Good First Impressions 148
  ix. Women Seeking Mentors: Questions to Ask 149
  x. Three Tips to Help You Master the Art of Networking ... 151
  xi. Growing Beyond a Solo-Entrepreneur 153

Chapter 7 161
  i. Case Study: Planet Fitness and Knowing Your Niche 161
  ii. Plant-Based Power: Lessons from Natural Foods Disrupters ... 163
  iii. A Marketing Case Study: Earth Day 50 Years Later 165
  iv. A Call to Action on Rural Entrepreneurship 166

- v. Launching a Venture? Some Potential Pitfalls 169
- vi. Tips for Nonprofit Business Builders 170
- vii. Your Product Demo Sucks (And How to Fix It) 172
- viii. Carving Out Your Niche: Re-defining Success on YOUR Terms 173
- ix. Gravitas. Personal mojo. Stick-to-itiveness. Vulnerability. 173
- x. Three Lessons Entrepreneurs Can Learn from Food Trucks..... 175
- xi. Marketing Failures and Lessons Learned 177
- xii. Three Practical Lessons from Running a Lemonade Stand... 179

Chapter 8 184
- i. The Truth About Competitive Advantage........................... 185
- ii. Thinking Big: How to Penetrate a National Market 186
- iii. "Would You Like Fries with That?" What Business Builders Can Learn From These Chain Successes 189
- iv. Discounting 101: Good or Bad for Business? 191
- v. Don't Get Burnt: Three Lessons from the Fyre Festival 193
- vi. Success on Tap: What Business Builders Can Learn from Craft Breweries 195
- vii. Relish the Competition or Fear Them? 197
- viii. The Midwest Advantage 199
- ix. Three Lessons from Popular Super Bowl Ads..................... 200
- x. Do's of Product Innovation... 202
- xi. Don'ts of Product Innovation 204

Chapter 9 211
- i. Stay on Top of Your A-Game... 212
- ii. The Importance of Delegating 213
- iii. Rethinking Busyness 215
- iv. Don't Leave Change Management to Chance..................... 216
- v. Staying Grounded: Beware of Carpetbaggers and False Prophets 218
- vi. Growing Pains: Three Missteps to Avoid............................ 221
- vii. Habits of Highly Effective Business Builders 222

viii. Avoiding "Low Battery" Entrepreneurial Burnout: Practical Tip 224
ix. Surviving—and Even Thriving—After Five Years 226
x. From Side Hustle to Full-Time Entrepreneur: Is This Really What You Want? 227
xi. Growth Mode: Navigating Choppy Waters 230
xii. Know When to Fold 'Em 233

Chapter 10 239
i. Understanding the Entrepreneur Mindset 240
ii. Lean into Curiosity 241
iii. Goal Setting 243
iv. The Stoic Leader 244
v. The Morally Courageous Leader 248
vi. Want a More Entrepreneurial Organization? Start Here 251
vii. The Minimalist Organization 252
viii. A Grateful Mindset 254
ix. Work Smarter Not Harder: Three Classic Mindsets to Avoid 256
x. Are You Sabotaging Your Success? 258

Chapter 11 264
i. A Pipeline of Female Founders 264
ii. #GoalCrushing: Three-Must-Have Ingredients for Success 266
iii. Vision and Values … So What? 268
iv. Hacking Creativity: Start with Solitude 269
v. Perseverance Is a Slice of Grit 271
vi. Three Ways to Embrace Change in Your Business 273
vii. How to Foster a Culture of Entrepreneurship at Your Company 274
viii. Banish "The Mondays": How to Stay Engaged at Work 276
ix. Konmari Method: Spark Joy for Business Success 278
x. Three Lessons from the Founding Fathers 279
xi. Success, Significance, and Legacy 281

20 Years of Insight 289
    i.   Lessons Learned From 20 Years at The NIIC 289
    ii. Life Lessons Learned from My Mother 294

Conclusion 309
Endnotes 315

INTRODUCTION

As human beings, we've been wired to expect and appreciate that good things come in threes—from entertainment to science, from religion to marketing, the "rule of three" even has its own Latin phrase "*Omne Trium Perfectum.*" Translated as "everything that comes in threes is perfect, or, every set of three is complete," three is the minimal requirement for a pattern, something our brains are more likely to remember and grasp.

Genies, fairy tales, wise men, even the American Constitution (Life, Liberty, and the Pursuit of Happiness) present information in trio. Public service announcements (Stop, Drop, and Roll), advertising and marketing campaigns, even music and sports (Gold, Silver, Bronze) are more memorable in the pattern of three.

As business builders, whether it's merging three ideas together or having a foundation of three key elements—the likelihood of success is greater in threes. The following chapters are broken down into subsections, each with their own set of three main points. Consider these the building blocks for building an effective business in the most impactful way.

CHAPTER 1

INNOVATION

Creativity, innovation, and a culture of agility are three essential aspects of breakout businesses. With this comes a necessity to process failure, "because there is inevitable failure in creativity," as Walt Disney CEO Bob Iger says.

Neil Armstrong assures us as well, "there can be no great accomplishments without risk." To go beyond what any other company has done, you must be willing to take a risk, and think outside the box. Here are my thoughts on how your company should approach breaking out from the norm.

i. Building a Culture of Innovation

Everyone benefits from building a culture of intrapreneurship at the workplace. It's just that sometimes business owners don't know where to begin when it comes to encouraging innovation on the job. Here's some food for thought on the topic:

1) Let go (Get the right people on the bus and in the right seats). Does your staff consult with you on every major decision? Do you have your hands in all the projects being completed at the moment? Are you the only one steering the ship? If any or all of these are true, you probably need to consider relinquishing some control for the sake of your employees' development. Although it's scary at first to step aside, eschewing micromanaging for a more hands-off approach can allow for some fresh air and new ideas that might help you lap the competition.

2) Embrace an entrepreneurial mindset (Be change-ready and resilient). Clinging to old systems and methodologies just because that's the way it has been done is a recipe for stagnancy. Always ask why you are doing something. How does it further an end goal? You should be wary of entrenched traditions (legacy beliefs—if McDonald's is questioning whether it should serve hamburgers and french fries, what sacred cows should you be reassessing?). Encourage the team to always question basic operating principles and to engage in creative destruction techniques. Adaptability is key.

3) Make room for 'pivots' (Embrace learning, mistakes, do-overs are badges of honor). If your employees equate making mistakes with a mark of shame and don't have the confidence to fail forward, smarter, they will never take the risks necessary for personal and professional growth. Reward the process of experimentation (trial and error) even when the errors, at times, might outnumber successes. This is known as failing forward. Be candid about your own missteps so they see you're being authentic and sincere.

At the end of the day, your number one goal should be to inspire relevance. Imitation is the greatest form of flattery, so always run faster than your competitors and become the market leader. Hold regular strategic and brainstorming sessions in which team members present their creative ideas for discussion and funding. Make investments in innovation a core component of your strategic plan.

As management guru, Peter Drucker said, "All organizations need one core competency: innovation."

ii. Creativity Starts Here

Creativity is not something exclusive to artists types. Business builders across any discipline can benefit from harnessing the power of creativity. After all, without creativity and commercialization of good ideas, most companies would not grow or be relevant. One of the things I learned at the Disney Customer Experience Summit is, "creative processes must not end when business processes begin; the two are interdependent."

Let's look at three strategies around creativity that can serve you and your organization[1]:

1) Brainstorm, Ideate, and Generate Ideas

Creative thinking is not a straight, linear trajectory. Innovators adapt the solution to the problem, not the other way around that can be counterproductive. What pain points need to be addressed? Creative product owners/business builders take an objective approach when accounting for user behaviors and preferences while being open-minded to more efficient ways of doing things. They put all options on the table before making a determination. They know that the most straight-forward one isn't necessarily the best.

2) Collaborate

While some experts posit that collaborators need to be like-minded and partnerships free of conflict, that's not a recipe for growth. When you align forces with someone at odds with your position, it can help refine/cement your own beliefs and values. Sometimes we need people to challenge our assumptions to help us get the creative juices flowing.

3) Unplug and Pause

Our brains (and bodies) aren't made for being "on" 24/7 and around people at all hours of the day. There's a reason your brain can feel like mush after a long day at the office. We need downtime to recover mentally and physically, but also arrive at innovative solutions. It's the reason why so many artists and writers practice their craft in solitude. The brain needs time to process the day's events, and that requires hitting the "pause button" and retreating to your personal space. Find time every day to pursue a creative endeavor, take a walk or allow your mind to wander.

---

iii. Leaning into the Future of Work

The nature of how we work has changed in the last decade. Remote work has become the new norm, a reality that companies must embrace if they are looking to attract the best and the brightest. As PwC's global survey of CEOs[2] revealed, the availability of talent is one of the top three threats to the growth of global organizations. I would opine and add any organization regardless of size, location or business type.

That said, forward-thinking companies know that if they want to stay relevant, they need to be open to flexible work arrangements where it doesn't impair or adversely impact their customers or the work culture. Not only can this make you attractive from a recruiting and retention perspective, but companies can also experience cost savings. This setup allows for allocating more resources to innovation and growth.

However, innovative and creative firms still need the community-building, connections and camaraderie that comes from working, learning and laughing together. There is no substitute for human interactions albeit with AI, machine learning and advancement in robotics, there may be less of it in the future!

Still, this is nothing to leave to chance. Companies with the most robust flexible work programs share some common characteristics:

1) Leadership is on board and engaged.

HR may have hiring power, but you need to align your leadership team on where they stand when it comes to hiring virtual talent. Otherwise, you risk internal division and tensions. Members of the "old guard" may not be as comfortable with nontraditional work arrangements and, therefore, might need more education on how to manage and integrate them into the company.

The onus then falls on managers to go to bat for their remote staff. If you don't quantify or qualify their value, it's easy for leaders to have the "out of sight, out of mind" mentality. However, when those in authority see them as a crucial part of the team, they treat virtual employees or contingent workers to maximize their organizational value and impact. Not every job in a company can be done remotely.

2) They invest in communication tools.

Communication is critical to teams, whether on-site, virtual, or a combination of the two. Fortunately, technological advances like Skype, Slack, Zoom, Remote Desktop access, Dropbox and the like have made it possible to collaborate and interface in real-time with no disruption to workflow.

3) They are culture driven.

While culture is intentional, when done right, it's something all team members can intuitively sense. It is important to not take an out of sight out of mind approach but rather ensure your organizational processes value and integrate your entire organization—remote workers, contingent workers, and full-time in the office workers.

Team meetings via video and occasional in-person meetings and company retreats are means to that end. If you've succeeded in creating and fostering a blended team with virtual talent, you'll find that the dynamic feel natural when they do meet in person.

No matter how work is being done, or on what platform communication takes place, remote work is no substitute for physical space. Studies and experience both show that it is not an "all or none" but a hybrid when it comes to remote versus onsite work. Remote workers need to feel respected, valued and appreciated. Their efforts need to be connected and aligned to the organizational culture and the delivery of services in a seamless and meaningful way. Often, companies need access to professional space, external accountability to make sure they are working on and not just in their business, and the credibility and clout that comes with working with a business incubator or an accelerator.

---

iv. Think Different: Marketing Lessons from Apple

I confess I have a love-hate relationship with my Apple products. Sometimes it totally botches what I write, sometimes my iPhone dials a number when I hang up too fast after a call, sometimes it skips letters when I write a text, but no matter what, Apple continues to release a new model every single year.

While its innovations have clearly disrupted the market over a long period of time (iPhone, iPad, streaming services, Apple Watches, and a plethora of other products and services), over the years, I think the company's success lies more in its marketing efforts than in the technology itself. I have to admit I am often jealous of what Samsung has done, but for interoperability purposes I keep my iPhone, iMac, and iPad, not ditching them for the better battery life, the 5G readiness, and the wireless charging options that makes Samsung the success it is!

Think about it for a moment. Almost everything Apple releases succeeds, and the media responds accordingly. Moreover, from a financial standpoint, the company reached a record high[3] of $275 Billion in 2020. Apple's annual revenue quadrupled in the last ten years. They are clearly one of the Big 4 tech stocks—GAFA (Google, Apple, Facebook, and Amazon).

All of this stems from the fact that the company has found a way to marry design with utility in a way that reaches consumers. It's more than a transaction—Apple has cultivated a tight-knit community of loyal brand ambassadors. How do they do it? It starts with the right marketing mix. Here are a few lessons you can take away from Apple's infiltration into the mainstream.

1) Keep your unique value proposition front and center.

Apple does not compete on price. You'll almost certainly pay more—sometimes a lot more—for an Apple product than another one on the market. How is this sustainable? While other companies focus on a single standout feature in their marketing, Apple sells the entire solution bundle (product, apps, streaming services), and their customer base keeps coming back for more.

The "Apple experience" begins with comparing different product versions, trying out products in the retail store, actually buying the item, receiving it, unboxing, and setting up. The company has been intentional in crafting and refining each one of these elements. They all are supposed to speak to the customer's sensibilities in some way. In other words, the anticipation and excitement around the product (their packaging, unveiling, keynotes around product launches) become synonymous with the brand, which further drives sales.

2) Simplicity sells.

Apple embraces the mantra that simplicity is the ultimate sophistication. Their products are synonymous with sleek and minimal design. They also have short and memorable names. Think of the "App Store." Why over-complicate things? Tech can learn a lot from this strategy of approachable simplicity.

3) Build a community.

It's no accident that Apple has created such an enthusiastic fan base. Have you heard someone rave about their PC lately? Not likely. It's like a cool kid's club everyone wants to join—the brand personality is fresh, fun, friendly, and above all things, *different*.

Look no further than the "Think Different"[4] ad campaign. This is an excellent example of how Apple showed customers that the brand understands them and is *like* them.

Bottom Line: Apple has cracked the code when it comes to moving consumer electronics. However, the idea here isn't to mimic Apple. Instead, look to the company (and others) to find creative ways to do the same in your business, while embracing the power of a consistent marketing mix.

---

v. Hiring? Think Selection and Look for These Three Things

Innovation isn't something that just happens by accident—it has to be cultivated in an organization. The most innovative companies have committed to and followed through with a strategic approach to not hiring but selecting, engaging, and retaining their talent.

Disney World in Orlando is the largest single site employer in the U.S., so they know a thing or two about people. What they found is you don't hire, you select. Selection is one of the five levers of their highly revered people engagement strategies (communications, training, care, selection, and culture).

Here are three intangibles to consider when recruiting to build your own culture of innovation.

1) Hire for Attitude, Train for Skill[5] / Follow the 51% Rule.

Carol Quinn's book *Don't Hire Anyone Without Me* spends a lot of time on attitude. Over the years, it has become increasingly more difficult to find "right-fit" talent. In her book, Carol makes the point that, "As a general rule, the attitude that is hired is the attitude that remains." Further, she shares that the attitude that she is talking about is "the attitude that is conducive to achieving maximum performance and results."

Does the candidate see things as they are or what could be? The most progressive companies hire visionaries—people who aren't comfortable with the status quo. Do those you're hiring want to build something great, or simply collect a paycheck?

In his book, *Setting the Table*, the successful restauranteur Danny Meyers follows the 51% rule. Select based on 51% emotional skills and 49% technical skills. Emotional skills include things like empathy, intellectual curiosity, kindness and optimism, and self-awareness. These are proven traits of high-performance employees who are integral to customer loyalty and profitability. These traits "tip" the scale.

2) Foster Meaningful Connections and Relationships.

Relationships are the currency of business. The true definition of a collaboration is that we mutually invest in each other's outcomes. Sounds easy? But it is really hard to do. Too many organizations measure collaboration in quantity not quality. Go deep with a few rather than go wide with many. What kinds of connections do your prospective team members bring with them? What kind of untapped potential might they have in terms of social capital?

3) Persevere Against the Odds.

Despite popular beliefs, successful entrepreneurs are strategic about risk taking. They evaluate contingencies, develop plan B and C, and are willing to take calculated risks. Do your prospective teammates have experience leading through uncertain times, or do they shudder at the thought of uncharted waters? Risk savvy people tend to be more innovative because they aren't as afraid of what's on the other side as they have already assessed and mitigated the probable risks.

Mistakes happen. Are those you're hiring able to reset and take another step forward following a setback? Most of the products on the market today would not be possible had someone given up after a few attempts. Look for "grit" as Angela Duckworth describes in her book of the same title, otherwise known as passion and perseverance.

While a quality candidate might embody only a few of these traits, don't get discouraged. Just as it is rare to find a unicorn in start-ups, the same is true in finding a unicorn in a person. I firmly believe these soft skills cannot be taught but they can be "honed and refined" over time. They are innate—a form of emotional intelligence or as Meyers calls it, Hospitality Quotient (HQ).

---

vi. What Constitutes a Culture Powered by Learning Agility?

Companies today place a strong emphasis on culture, workplace flexibility, and perks as points of difference in bolstering talent attraction and retention. But there's another driver that's often overlooked—and that is the importance of an adaptive and agile learning[6] culture.

I have been fascinated since the 1990s in the "learning organization." One of the first books to influence my thinking was Peter Senge's *Five Disciplines of Learning Organizations* (written in the 1990s and revised in 2006). He provocatively stated, "One-third of 500 companies will disappear within 15 years, and the average lifetime for the largest enterprises is approximately 40 years." His "call to arms" shaped and sharpened my focus on personal mastery and goal achievement. His systems thinking really resonated and drove many of the professional and personal development opportunities I took advantage of in my own self-improvement journey.

Fast forward to LinkedIn's 2019 Workforce Learning Report[7], which made a strong case for investing in employee development at a corporate level. The report highlighted that 94% of employees said that they would stay at a company longer if it invested in helping them learn.

So how can companies empower employees to do so? It comes down to timing and supporting them when it matters the most, like during onboarding, career discussions, and advancement.

Here are some straightforward ways to integrate professional development into your everyday work environment:

1) Embrace online, and on-demand learning.

According to the Workforce Learning Report, all generations valued self-directed learning experiences as their preferred approach to learning, it's not a surprise that this is highest among digital natives. The report's findings indicated that 43% and 42% for Gen Z and Millennials, respectively, stated a preference for this type of engagement.

Instead of investing your budget into all-day seminars or workshops, decision-makers might instead consider an investment in micro-learning platforms to engage talent.

2) Provide social and interactive learning experiences.

According to the survey, the lion's share of the employees said they value working with instructors and other learners in group settings. Think video and real-time collaboration. Learning doesn't have to occur in a vacuum. Some people don't absorb information well when it's passive and not in a dynamic and collegial environment.

3) Prioritize softened transferrable skills.

Hard skills may be required to succeed in a specific role, but they aren't necessarily what will propel your organization forward. The priority should be on honing interpersonal and critical thinking skills that everyone needs, regardless of industry or job.

Employers should also realize that self-aware employees recognize their limitations and shortcomings. Only a third of the respondents said they "strongly agree" that they are fully equipped skills-wise, to do their job. This means organizations would be well-positioned to integrate skill development into the corporate culture as a means to attract and develop talent.

At the end of the day, remember—engagement starts at the top. Seeing managers engaged in continuous learning sets a powerful example for employees about what it means to prioritize education, training, skill development, and competency building. When managers are involved, their teams are more likely to follow suit. Employees succeed most when managers provide specific guidance, and that applies to learning as well. And the survey stated, three-fourths (75%) of employees said they would take a course upon their manager's recommendation.

---

vii: Launching a Product Has Never Been Easier ... or Is It?

So, you have an excellent idea for a new product? Exciting times are ahead, no doubt. However, you also have your work cut out for you to take yours from concept to reality. Today, there is a strong emphasis on speed to market, cutting development times down and commercializing in ways that are faster, cheaper, better, and smarter. Despite what contemporary models show and say, commercialization is not always a linear and straightforward process.

Learn from the most seasoned entrepreneurs and be prepared to launch, taking into account these three key challenges:

1) Product Development/Commercialization

Developing a product requires the expertise of all types and the scope and scale of the work will vary according to the technical complexity. For example, creating a new hardware product will likely require a small team of product developers. Unless you are the one in five early-stage companies likely to obtain any outside investment, many startups outsource their initial R&D or contract moonlighting workers to complete their first product concepts.

The good news? The gig economy means that freelancers are a valuable resource that innovators of the past did not have at their disposal. The growing base of contract workers will no doubt be a boon to startups. Bureau of Labor Statistics on the gig economy shows continued growth from 55 million contingent workers in 2017 to 57 million gig workers in the US economy, amounting to a staggering 36% of all US workers.

2) Implementing Market Feedback

The buzz today is customer discovery and validation. The idea is to get out of the product development lab and into real-time customer feedback and to integrate the learnings quickly and seamlessly in the product development process. Many business builders are not receptive to customer feedback and fight the input every step of the product development cycle. Remember, the idea is to solve someone else's problem or pain, not your own.

Target market feedback can be golden when incorporated into the product. However, it can be a time and resource-intensive process. The software can allow you to release a simple version quickly (minimum viable product), gather feedback, and integrate it into the next version.

Still, the fact remains that it's nearly impossible to know what consumers want to buy until you have a viable product. However, physical products require a considerable investment of time and effort in navigating the complexities of developing, prototyping, pre-producing, and manufacturing the product before you can gather substantive market and use-case feedback.

One workaround is to sell the product before you make it. That might mean pre-selling the product on your website or running a crowdfunding campaign. Both of these strategies will require brand recognition and an interested audience (many of whom are first to try new and innovative things), so start building a following now and follow the best practices rubric for how to make your crowdfunding efforts worthwhile.

3) Cash Flow

Many people that talk about producing a product want to build their manufacturing plants. Given the capital intensity, the sizable investment, the unlikely ability to reach scale, most business builders should look at contract manufacturing to meet their needs and redirect their limited cash to other aspects of their product's value chain.

Once manufacturing is live, cash flow can be a real challenge. Many factors are at play—redesigning the product for manufacturability, paying the production in advance, having to order a minimum quantity of the product and have inventory on hand, and navigating the working capital challenges of getting paid 30-90 days after shipment. All of these factors put pressure and strain on the business builder. Some business builders have been successful at getting attractive payment terms (especially if they have pre-existing relationships in the industry) and others have relied upon factoring or angel investors to provide the funding to navigate the difficulties of the working capital cycle. Please don't underestimate how much time it might take to build a credible distribution and supply chain for your product.

---

viii. Three Ways to Take Corporate Innovation to the Next Level

Talk about innovation is cheap. How do you actually create a culture in which innovative (transformative and disruptive not just incremental) thinking is the norm? Here are a few factors I believe are critical to curating an innovation-driven mindset in the workplace:

1) An organizational commitment to continuous innovation

"Kaizen" is a phrase first introduced by the Japanese in a manufacturing setting. It means a commitment to continually evolving and improving. It means never being satisfied with the status quo because there's always room to do better.

How can you inspire employees to adopt this mindset? Start by asking them after meetings or project events, "What did you learn?" The question will prompt them to stop and think about what's working and what's not.

This will no doubt put them on a trajectory of continuous improvement. The Northeast Indiana Innovation Center commits to the ISO 9001:2015[8] quality system because it focuses on risk-based monitoring and continuous innovation as core principles of our operating system.

2) Mission (not just metric)-driven strategy

Achieving outcomes should be a byproduct of fulfilling your organizational mission, not the other way around. For the company to be successful, employees need to have a deeper understanding of priorities and why they matter in the context of the organization's higher calling and purpose. Measuring program impact is critical to understanding and achieving meaningful outcomes.

3) Fail FORWARD faster

Employees need to feel at home by taking calculated risks without the fear of repercussions in the workplace. Yet, too often in the business world, we expect employees to execute correctly the first time around. This creates an environment in which people feel gun shy, and innovation is stifled or only focused on incremental improvements. What would happen if you created a nurturing culture and a common language around failure?

No matter what strategy you implement, innovation comes from intellectual curiosity and keeping discovery mode "on." Don't operate in silos—innovation doesn't belong to a single department or position. It's all around us. Think in terms of "Big I" innovation and "Little I" innovation. There are different kinds of changes. For example, your accounting department may be able to inspire ways to elevate customer service and vice versa. Sometimes the best insight comes from people with a fresh and different perspective. When people all come together toward a focused mission, great things happen.

ix. Don't Fear Automation: How Business Builders Can Embrace It

In 2017, I gave a talk on the power of technology to dislocate 80 million jobs from workplace automation, how pharmacists could be displaced by vending machines, how self-driving vehicles could transform transportation, and the related distribution and logistics.[9] I ended my talk with three core engagement principles—committing to long-term creative destruction strategies, leveraging culture building, and embracing and leaning into the automation wave. These principles take advantage of the promise and potential of automation versus the "dark side" of automation.

What is the future of innovation and the business world in general? Undoubtedly, automation will play a role. But what might that look like? Here's a look at three ways the dynamics will likely change:

1) Automation means time savings + speed

Automation is poised to help business builders focus more on the end deliverables. With processes streamlined through technology, companies can dedicate more time to innovation and less on administrative items that can be time sucks. For example, open source is democratizing access to software and making it easier for startups to go further faster. With these systems gaining steam, going from idea to execution will be significantly less time intensive.

2) Virtual work will still leverage place-based options

The Bureau of Labor Statistics identified that up to 24% of U.S. workers conducted some or all of their work from home in 2015[10] (most current data available) and this number is expected to grow. Post COVID, companies today more than ever are open to nontraditional work setups. Emerging technologies such as VR virtual conferencing mean it's only a matter of time before more convenient and customizable options are available for business builders. This means business builders will be able to source talent and capabilities exponentially, but placemaking will still be a catalyst.

3) Faster validation and cheaper sources of capital

The most experienced business builders know that products don't go to market overnight. The validation process can take months or years. However, as the world gets smaller, feedback is being driven by online crowd-sourced communities like GoFundMe and Kickstarter. This means a business builder can discern whether or not to pursue an idea in a fraction of the time it took a few years ago and the funding required to prove its validity is likely cheaper. What's more, this means by the time a product is formally introduced, there's often already a community of support behind it.

---

x. Opportunity Risk Assessment: Going Beyond the Numbers

Too often, innovators sort and evaluate their ideas as they develop them. The better method is to inventory all of your ideas before you start to evaluate them. By prematurely conducting an evaluation of your ideas as you ideate them, you stunt the likely creativity and energy that can come from a robust and innovative idea generation process.

Once you have completed the generative ideation process, and you are evaluating whether or not to move forward with a particular opportunity, business builders would benefit from pausing and thinking through some of the following:

1) Risk-based monitoring

Conducting a basic risk-monitoring audit is helpful. What trends or patterns have marked your business building journey? You might historically like to play it safe, take smaller, calculated bets, or put all your chips on the table. This context will help you determine your tolerance for taking on additional risk. The most important thing is that you should evaluate the post-mortem of how well the risks you took worked out for you. Do you need to change anything in your process? Were there blind spots? Did your gut "trump" your head or vice versa?

You might be tempted to think cheap office space, hanging out at Starbucks, or reimagining a home office is less risky than committing to working with an entrepreneurial support organization that can work with you "hand and glove" and hold you accountable as you grow your business venture. What is the benefit of taking a cheap approach versus if you grow faster, hire faster, get customers faster, find funding faster, and finish your product faster? Are you really managing your risks or just finding a cheap and convenient solution? What is the real opportunity cost? Would you really put all your chips on black double zero or all your winnings on one strategy of doubling down on a hard 11?

2) Trusted advisors in your circle of influence

No person is an island as they say, and your support network matters in risk-taking (and in success in general). If you have a group of trusted advisors, you can probably bet on them to give you a reality check, if needed. Tough love can be precisely what you need to avoid an ugly outcome. Do you have people you can turn to, for "real talk" and whose interest in only your success? If so, vet your opportunities with this key center of influence.

3) Your opportunity lenses

Are you a glass is a half-empty or half-full person? Your outlook can enter into the equation. Those who tend to wear rose-colored glasses would benefit from taking a step back before making a determination as well as getting feedback from a sounding board. On the other hand, a pessimistic viewpoint could mean you have a tendency to evaluate an opportunity as riskier than it might be. Neither extreme can bode well for someone looking to enter into a deal objectively.

xi. Three Habits of Innovative Business Leaders

Were you among the 41% of Americans who started the year with a resolution or two? Sadly, most abandon them for various reasons within the first three months of the year. I am not writing to be critical of your honorable intentions. Instead, I am inviting you to challenge yourself by committing to and implementing lasting change that can have favorable results for your business and you. Consider adopting these three habits of innovative business leaders:

1) Embrace Level 5 leadership

You've likely heard of emotional intelligence and its application to the workplace. Leaders with high EQs know how to keep their egos at bay. An innovative leader is open to hearing ideas that might challenge their beliefs or the status quo, and in the process improve or strengthen the idea. I just completed a 7-day Global Leadership Summit (GLS) Growth Track daily video on EQ. A major ah-hah for me was the two skills most difficult to master—**self-awareness** (only 36% of leaders are able to accurately identify their emotions at the moment) and **social awareness** (too inwardly focused and not outwardly focused in their interactions with other people). Both are essential skills to the notion of Level 5 leaders—simultaneously embracing **Humility + Will**.

2) Don't lose sight of the big picture.

What if Henry Ford had given up after the first prototype? Innovators dust themselves off and see failures as temporary hurdles. Distinguish between activities and results. My first boss told me, "results, not effort, get rewarded." Be vigilant in keeping score but don't be confused by being busy on your to-do list at the expense of getting things done.

3) Listen more talk less.

When someone is speaking, are you truly listening or busy formulating your response? We are all guilty of the latter, from time to time. Good listeners are fully present and know how to make others feel validated and heard. This is critical to team-building and personal trustworthiness. Be present and engaged in your relationships with others. This is a key area for my personal habit development—improvement of my social awareness and having an intentional and outward people focus!

---

xii. Do's of Business Model Innovation

When most people think about innovation, products are often top of mind. However, an important source of innovation potential is business model innovation. Think about the largest fleet of transportation cars not owning any of its cars—Uber. Think about the largest network of lodging opportunities not owning any of its hotels or resorts— Airbnb. Think about Southwest Airlines flying "point to point" and only flying Boeing 737 in their fleet when airlines typically ran a hub and spoke system flying all types of planes. All of these marketplace disruptions reinforce the value and significance of business model innovation.

There has been a movement in the startup world led by the likes of Osterwalder, Reis, Blank, and Maurya to simplify the complexity of disruptive innovation in a 9-block business model canvas, or—a lean canvas. These canvases create, capture, and deliver value for the various customer segments served.

Keep in mind some of these salient best practices for moving your best thinking to the marketplace.

1) Identify your likely customer first—discover and validate.

Get out of the lab and get some hands-on customer research to discover and validate the pain, problem or job-to-be-done. "Fast testing" of your business concept through customer discovery and validation early can save you time, money and resources. Using proven, evidenced-based business search methodologies like The SearchLite[11] can save you a lot of heartburn and headaches later.

2) Seek disruption in the marketplace.

Identify the gaps in the existing product or service delivery value chain and create novel or different ways of transforming that product or service to deliver new value to the end-user or customer. Think about the pain points and how your solution delivers a better experience, a cheaper product, or a more engaging customer experience (and delight) to a customer segment. Experiment, iterate, learn and experiment again (and again and again)!

The profit model is an essential component to business model innovation. What are the ways you create viable profit streams? Think about the razor and the razor blades. What are your razors and razor blades (annuity streams for ongoing and sustainable profit generation)?

3) Pricing drives behavior. How will your business make money?

Think twice about giving something of value away to get initial users. Maurya makes this point very clearly in his book *Running Lean*. Pricing drives behavior. What behavior do you want to drive with your pricing strategy? Think strategically about how best to price and deliver your services.

In addition to these three key elements, it is important to know and delineate your triggers. Entrepreneurs often get caught up in loving their idea, product, or service so much that they forget to establish triggers. Triggers are needed to make sure you are not deluding yourself when the market is sending you important feedback. For example, you have a terrific idea for a new product disruption and need to sell 61 websites to break-even. Establish specific goals, timeframes, and success metrics to help reduce the "noise" in the marketplace and focus your efforts. My first manager at GE once said, "**Results, not effort, get rewarded.**" Knowing the difference between activity and results is key to your success. Don't get trapped into loving your idea so much that you forget to pay attention to the warning signs.

Sustainable competitive advantage is more than a business concept taught in an MBA class. To achieve, it takes market focus, discipline, and execution. Every day companies are trying to unravel your marketplace advantages. So, a constant focus on business model innovation is essential to staying on top of your industry. Every day, creative entrepreneurs and aspiring innovators are trying to eat your lunch.

---

xiii. Innovation and Entrepreneurship: A Look at Drucker's Powerful Approach

One of my favorite management gurus is Peter Drucker. He is known as the "Father of Modern Management." His thoughts about entrepreneurship are timeless. Drucker once said the definition of an entrepreneur is "one who is crazy." If you know anything about the business world in the last 70 years, then you likely know about how consultant and author Peter Drucker has shaped it. Drucker's philosophies still resonate with business owners today.

In closing out this chapter on innovation, I would like to revisit some of the concepts mentioned in his book, "Innovation and Entrepreneurship," which was first published in 1985.

In the book, Drucker lays out some guidelines for how entrepreneurs (and really anyone) should approach innovation.

Do:

1) **Analyze Opportunities** — "Purposeful, systematic innovation begins with the regular analysis of opportunities."
2) **Look, Ask, and Listen** — "Innovation is conceptual and perceptual—look at both numbers and people aspects."
3) **Keep It Simple and Focused** — "It should do one thing (or else it will confuse) and as everything new runs into trouble, if complicated, it cannot be easily fixed."

Don't:

1) **Try to Be Clever** — "Innovations are for ordinary human beings and incompetence is in abundant and constant supply, so anything too clever is almost bound to fail."
2) **Try to Do Too Many Things at Once** — "An innovation needs the concentrated energy of a unified effort behind it — it also requires that people who put it into effect understand each other and this, too, requires a unity, a common core."
3) **Innovate for The Future** — "Innovate for the present! Innovative opportunities sometimes have long lead times, but it is still necessary to focus on projects that, if successful, lead to immediate practical applications."

Also, worth mentioning are the three necessary conditions for innovation, which he says are "obvious but often disregarded."

Necessary Conditions for Innovation

1) **Innovation Is Work.** It requires knowledge, ingenuity, diligence, persistence, and commitment—among other things.
2) **To Succeed, Innovators Must Build on Their Strengths.** The challenge is to look at the big picture but ask which opportunity fits you and the company.
3) **Innovation Is an Effect in Economy and Society.** That means innovation has to be "close to the market, focused on the market, indeed market driven."

In my experience, all these factors are usually taken into account, but usually not with much intentionality.
"Business has only two functions—marketing and innovation."

Chapter 1: Conclusion

To promote and facilitate innovation, you must first lay the foundation and establish a company culture conducive to innovation. Advanced technology, automation, new ideas, and failure all must be embraced. The old ways of doing things are just that—old. Don't be afraid to try new things and break out of old patterns.

Successful innovation builds on strengths and is a constant commitment. Business innovators know that the only constant is change, and that continual evolution goes hand in hand with continual improvement. In the words of Winston Churchill, "To improve is to change; to be perfect is to change often."

Chapter 1: Questions for Consideration

i. Building a Culture of Innovation

Are you furthering a culture of innovation or stifling it? Remember, Drucker was right when he said, "Culture eats strategy for breakfast." How can you promote innovation from within?

ii. Creativity Starts Here

Start now, carpe diem! If you're thinking about taking your organization and culture to a higher level or contemplating how to engage better and maximize team engagement and results, consider outsourcing corporate innovation responsibilities. There's no shame in wanting your organization to experience greater flexibility and potentially faster results.

iii. Leaning into the Future of Work

Has your company embraced this paradigm? If so, what tips do you have for the transition? How has it helped your organization innovate or scale? How do you measure or know if it is working?

iv. Think Different: Marketing Lessons from Apple

What do you do in your business to be unique and generate raving fans? What are the top three most successful businesses in your sector doing to sell more product? How can you take inspiration from their methods, and apply it to your own brand while still maintaining your own unique value add?

v. Hiring? Think Selection and Look for These Three Things

A well-rounded team represents a variety of skillsets and domains of knowledge. Do those you're selecting add value to the bottom line or are they more of the same? Bringing on additional team members means opening yourself up to new inputs and insights that can lead to innovation. People and talent are the drivers of innovation. Are you open to new insights and ideas that challenge your organizational status quo?

vi. What Constitutes a Culture Powered by Learning Agility?

Are any of your employees currently engaged in ongoing education or required courses? How many of your upper level staff are currently learning something in a structured manner? What would be most beneficial for each employee segment to learn? Cues are taken from the top, so consider enrolling in a course or class yourself before you encourage everyone else to do so as well.

vii: Launching a Product Has Never Been Easier … or Is It?

There are high failure rates for new products. We see the successes but not always the failures. Remember, the Microsoft Zune? I bet not! Microsoft lost nearly $290 million on it and sold just over two million of them. Apple sold over 300 million iPods. If you have successfully launched a physical product, what lessons have left a mark on you? What would you do differently if you could start over?

viii. Three Ways to Take Corporate Innovation to the Next Level

Is your company committed to ongoing improvement? Have you made that clear to all your employees? How about your position on failure? Do employees have freedom to fail, or are they afraid to? What steps can you take to make sure the work environment is conducive to innovation?

ix. Don't Fear Automation: How Business Builders Can Embrace It

How can your company capitalize on the time savings from automation? Has your company embraced virtual/remote work? If not, what's holding you back? Have you explored cheaper sources of capital? Looked to fast-track validation? Don't let antiquated ways of doing things hold you back, lean into technology.

x. Opportunity Risk Assessment: Going Beyond the Numbers

Are the risks holding you back bigger than the potential rewards? Remember, fortune favors the bold. As Bill Gates reminds us, "To win big, you sometimes have to take big risks." This doesn't mean take them blindly however; it is still important to weigh them out, and get a second, or third or fourth opinion from trusted advisors or those with experience. How can you tell if you're considering all the facts objectively?

xi. Three Habits of Innovative Business Leaders

Have you mastered social and self-awareness? How can you work on leveraging these as they relate to humility and will? Do you keep the big picture in mind while also listening more and talking less? Which of these habits are you willing to incorporate into your daily routine?

xii. Do's of Business Model Innovation

How are you maintaining your competitive advantage? Do you know, and have you delineated your triggers so that you are not deluding yourself? Who is your ideal likely customer? And how can you disrupt the marketplace while catering to them? Do you have goals and a plan for how your business will make money? Having a plan and pricing structure is crucial.

xiii. Innovation and Entrepreneurship: A Look at Drucker's Powerful Approach

Are you committing any of the "*don'ts*"? If, so what is one actionable step you could take this week to take a more purposeful and systematic approach to innovation?

CHAPTER 2

EMOTIONAL WELL-BEING & SELF CARE

It is far too easy to put yourself last on your never-ending list of things to do/maintain. Running a business while balancing family, friends, and a home can seem like an impossible feat in the best of times. You may not always feel like adding in things like regular self-care, physical exercise, or even a little mindfulness to your already packed schedule. Still, they are an essential part of maintaining overall wellness.

Entrepreneurs wear many hats and are often stretched too thin. Without proper care of your physical body and mind, there will come the point where you simply collapse. To prevent burnout, put yourself first. Without a properly running engine, the train won't go anywhere. Similarly, your business will not go far without a clear and healthy mind at the helm. Be kind to yourself and take the utmost care of your mental state.

Today, more than ever, self-care is a critical component in becoming the best version of yourself. So many distractions and interruptions along with busyness in our lives makes it difficult, and almost impossible to live a well-balanced life. So, when you think of your ideal week, be sure to block out time to put your energy toward the things that matter. Be sure to protect that time because it is so easy to give up on the things that give you energy, purpose and to give in to the tyranny of the urgent.

i. Managing Uncertainty

Life went on hold for much of the world as everyone had to grapple with the implications of COVID-19 pandemic. This destructive, insidious, and silent killer caused our once thriving stock market, economy, and high quality of life to come to a screeching halt. Anxiety is high, as many don't know if we can flatten the curve, will it bring some peace of mind to the devastation caused in its wake. Indeed, the global pandemic is a dire situation, and I don't want to minimize the emotional turmoil, the tremendous loss of life, the loss of community, and the loss of connections caused by social isolation and this disease.

Still, in the face of more questions than answers, we can do what we can as a business community (beyond social distancing and common-sense handwashing) to try to manage our physical health, emotions, and encourage/support each other at the same time.

Here are a few ways to do just that.

1) Embrace rituals.

Even if your routine is off, maybe because of telecommuting, the kids being home from school, and other distractions, you may find comfort in turning to a method. A morning practice, like reading, meditation, or working out, can help create some semblance of order when life seems to change by the hour. Forming and building disciplined habits is key to having rhythm and balance in your life. I gain a lot of my daily rhythm and discipline through my work to master critical concepts from Brian Johnson's *Optimize*[12] mastery program

2) Make space for rejuvenation and action.

Sometimes the greatest gift is newfound time and space. If the pace of work has slowed down (or come to a halt), try to find solace in the fact that work and rest should be a yin and yang relationship. Catch up on sleep and unplug from the media to the extent you can. Meditation, yoga, controlled breathing, or other mindfulness activities can provide some peace of mind and relaxation for you during this overwhelming time so that anxiety, fear, or panic don't close in. I have resumed listening to audiobooks because I am overwhelmed daily at what I listen to on the radio, see on the web, or watch on tv.

Recently, I started listening to one of my favorite books from long ago—*7 Habits of Highly Effective People*[13] by Stephen Covey—to get back to basics and to focus on something I control—my behavior and actions. Paralysis and inaction will only serve to rob you of a better life worth living—the choice is ours.

3) Let ideas flow.

Similar to above, more downtime can mean more space for brainstorming and get out of old thought patterns that may be holding us back. Too often, we're too busy to sit and think about new ways of doing things, and that is a detriment to growth – personally and professionally. So, allow your mind to wander and look for various new ways to connect dots. You just might come up with a great idea!

In addition to these three recommendations, it is always wise, no matter the circumstances, to up the ante on the appreciation. Expressing gratitude and showing empathy to valued customers, employees, partners, and suppliers are good for business, especially in volatile and uncertain times when people's lives are being turned upside down. Paying it forward offers dividends. These dividends include opening up to more and better connections and relationships, as well as improving physical and psychological well-being, well-being, and happiness.

Uncertain times have many people on edge. While we can't predict the future, we can make our mental and well-being a priority.

What are your coping mechanisms, and how are you navigating these uncharted waters as we prepare for a new "normal"?

---

ii. A Case for Cultivating an Empathy-Driven Culture

I talk a lot about EQ (emotional intelligence) and how it, along with business coaching, are critical assets for successful entrepreneurial business builders. But what's often missing from the conversation is why empathy matters.

Empathy is defined as "the feeling that you understand and share another person's experiences and emotions; and the ability to share someone else's feelings."[14] Some might find the two concepts at odds—business and empathy—but I assure you that there's a lot to gain from taking on another's perspective in the context of our professional lives. In a technology-enabled world, the lack of empathy is more and more evident every day.

Empathy is not an elusive, pie-in-the-sky idea. On the contrary, it's a skill that all of us would benefit from putting into daily practice and thereby adding value to our organizations.

Here's how:

1) Understanding customer needs and improving offerings based on consumer feedback can give you as an organization a fresh and novel perspective.
2) Employee relations and morale can benefit from understanding the skills and styles of each person and how that can inform and enhance *human* interactions and, more importantly, human understanding.

3) Empathy-driven leadership can help you understand others while commanding a better understanding of the most positive aspect of yourself.

Applying empathy may seem more intuitive on a one-on-one level, but there's a lot to be gained in making it a part of an organization's DNA. Just how important is empathy at the corporate level? Here's one example. I am a big fan of Amazon's Jeff Bezos, even though I was skeptical of Amazon when it first started. Its business model and inability to generate profits seemed to me to be very defective, but he has made a bold statement about the company's values, and where and how empathy fits into the mix. He has made his email address public and ostensibly reads every note from customers, per his comments made in an April 2018 onstage interview at the George Bush Presidential Center.

Business Insider captured a few of those remarks:

"We have tons of metrics," Bezos explained. "When you are shipping billions of packages a year, you need good data and metrics: Are you delivering on time? Delivering on time to every city? To apartment complexes? ... Whether the packages have too much air in them, wasteful packaging?"

In other words, that feedback can provide a look under the hood. If data seems to contradict customer sentiment, he believes the customers.

"The thing I have noticed is when the anecdotes and the data disagree; the anecdotes are usually right. There's something wrong with the way you measure it," he explained.

In short, company performance can't be isolated to figures related to revenue. The human element matters, and that's where empathy plays a significant and essential role. It allows us better to understand the people whose lives to which we are trying to add value. And in the process, we gain a fresh perspective and insight that can drive more strategic decisions.

The magic of empathy is the connection it helps us form with other people. Some of us are naturally more in tune, while others can be completely oblivious of others' feelings. Most of us fall somewhere in between the two extremes. But empathy, like many skills, can be a process. It's learned, developed, and applied when and where needed. It's informed from and grounded in self-awareness.

Does your organization place a value on empathy? If so, how? Do you embrace empathy? If so, how did you develop the "habit"?

---

iii. How to Go from Good to Great: Start by Removing These Distractions

Time is your enemy, truths all people, including business builders, must acknowledge if they want to achieve something big. Dr. Brené Brown, author, speaker, professor, stated: "Time is precious and an unrenewable resource." Sometimes hitting goals calls for making a tough decision in removing obstacles and barriers (both tangible and intangible) that no longer serve us. While it might be true that entrepreneurship survives on mythology, it is time to insert a heavy dose of reality into the mix. If we don't, our startup rate as a nation will continue to decline. We will continue to produce disposable companies. Neither of these two trends will positively impact our standard of living for the next generation.

Here are a few common distractions that can get in the way of our success.

1) Toxic People

We lack constructive discourse in the U.S. today. People will call you a "glass-half-empty" rather than "glass-half-full" when you give experienced, honest and authentic responses to someone's idea. We are all in love with our thoughts, but there is a pervasive "fake it to you make it" mentality that makes transparency and constructive feedback often not possible. Fierce and crucial conversations are avoided, and many play the victim card and expect they are entitled to something because they perceive they deserve it, but not because they earned it or delivered value.

Today, nobody wants to hear "no." The expectation is if you have an idea, everyone should just tell you what you want to hear or, worse, give you a truck full of money (for free). This lack of accountability in our culture is driving more noise in the entrepreneurial ecosystem, more false starts, more avoidable and premature startup failures (based on trying to prove lousy or defective business models, bad or dumb ideas or professionalizing business plan competition winners who go from contest to contest-winning but never produce a viable business venture).

The reality is we are fostering and perpetuating a culture of startup negligence by not providing honesty and transparency because the truth is there are many great ideas. Still, only a few become a blockbuster success, and even fewer are investable. A great idea might give you admissions to the park, but it doesn't guarantee you are going to ride the attractions. Given business builders are putting their money and reputation on the line, they need to be surrounded with real and authentic advice, not sugar-coated, pie in the sky accolades to make them feel better. Recalling Dr. Brown, she observes and reminds us that "brave leaders are never silent about the hard things." We need more brave leaders.

Surrounding yourself with the right people also means limiting access to those who are wasting your time—business builders must establish and maintain boundaries with relationships. Do you know that friend who always needs a favor? Maybe it's time to tell them "no." That volunteer assignment at your church or synagogue or pet cause? Can you scale back? If these "extras" are getting in the way of your success at work, it may be time to rethink your engagements because your startup needs focus, commitment, and all of your energy. Remember, my first line of this blog, *time is your enemy*. Today, relational boundaries often do get in the way because we are intentionally blurring the lines of accountability and avoiding reality (Jim Collins famously called it *confronting the brutal facts*, and how doing so is an attribute of *Good to Great*[15] companies).

2) Home Office

While some can thrive working from home, many fall prey to the distractions. After all, there will always be housework to do. If the budget allows for it, consider a coworking space. You may find you're more focused away from home, and as a bonus, you'll likely make some connections that could advance your business. To conserve cash, we avoid surrounding ourselves with the tools needed for startup success—access to capital, talent, the right workspaces, and networks. These tools don't come from Starbucks or your garage, where you often experience emptiness, isolation, and loneliness. They come from working with entrepreneurial support organizations, surrounded with people like you.

3) Perfectionism

You never achieve perfection, as it's a moving target. Likewise, there is never a "right" time to start a business. Successful entrepreneurs start companies and projects, knowing that they are works in progress. They embrace a "ready, fire, aim" mentality and a fast test environment (to experiment, iterate, learn, and pivot quickly and cost-effectively) because they know any effort is better than waiting around and potentially missing out because a competitor acted more swiftly. Don't get locked in analysis paralysis, which usually leads to inaction. Fail forward, faster, cheaper, and better.

At the end of the day, when you've whittled away all these distractions, you're left to contend with yourself. Don't let your ego, or self-love, impede your progress. Thinking you have created the best thing since sliced bread will only turn people off. There are many bright and capable people in the world, and they are all trying to get there first—just like you. Letting your ego take the reins will result in disaster. Thinking you know more than subject-matter experts will soon cost you in time, money, and people. It's okay to admit your shortcomings and seek help when it's outside of your domain, expertise, or comfort zone.

Building a successful and sustainable business can be a challenging, rewarding, and exciting way to live your life, to give back to your community, and to create something worthwhile. Avoid the distractions that derail so many business builders so you can fully self-actualize your potential and your probable success.

---

iv. Protect Your Peace: Three Habits to Embrace

Building a business can be intense. It› so easy to sacrifice our well-being for the sake of the bottom line and to keep up appearances. In today's frenzied world, can you ever work hard enough? Often, you might feel like you are firing on all cylinders and giving 150%.

The truth is, there will always be something more to do when you leave the office or workspace. The nature of work has changed in recent years in that so many can work remotely, further exacerbating the problem. We are always "on." The expectations we put on ourselves and others can be unrealistic at best.

How then can you develop healthy habits to safeguard mental well-being? The following are a few best practices that some of the most high-powered people lean on regularly to protect their peace—and thrive!

1) Flex your "no" muscle.

As a respected person in the business community, you will no doubt, get requests for meetings, collaborations, partnerships, strategy sessions, etc. While people may be well-intentioned and it's flattering to be sought out, you're only one person. Spreading yourself thin will do you and your business a disservice.

So, be intentional in your "yeses" and reap the rewards of a less cluttered headspace and more meaningful relationships. Everyone benefits when you show up fully present and your attention is undivided. A culture of overload may be trendy right now, but it's not constructive and may just be toxic.

2) Make your physical well-being a priority and pay attention to your "Wheel of Life."[16]

Late nights and early mornings may be part of the gig, at least initially. However, running on empty will catch up with you sooner than later. The same goes for poor diet and inactivity. Is your body silently (or not-so-silently) screaming for help? Listen to it and follow up with a doctor if you suspect something's not right. Health is wealth, as they say. A focus on physical well-being is a personal goal of mine to do better and more in this category.

The *wheel of life* intention is to strive for balance (not equality, but balance) in your physical, intellectual, emotional/relationships, and spiritual growth (PIES is the pneumonic I came up with to do my weekly inventory to see how in balance these four dimensions are in my life.)

3) Find strength in numbers.

Whether it's catching up one-on-one with a mentor or accountability or business coach, it's essential to have a person or people in whom you can confide. Entrepreneur-centric meetups, workshops, seminars, and fundraisers are all avenues to find like-minded souls. A support network (mastermind, leads, or networking group) can be a powerful force in your professional life.

When all else fails, take a pause and hit the reset button. A pause can be a vacation, attendance at a self-help workshop or conference, taking some quality time to meditate or focus on your mindfulness, going to yoga, or reading a book in solitude. Find your happy place—even if it's just allowing yourself a daily indulgence, guilt-free. Humans aren't made to work 24/7, so don't feel pressure to be superhuman.

v. Redefining Success Through the Lens of Vulnerability

In the business world, success is most often measured by "hardcore" KPI's (key performance indicators)—measures including, but not limited to EBITDA growth[17], quarterly earnings against prior periods, top-line organic growth, the mix of sales by channel, or partner or orders backlog.

However, this performance-driven mindset can come with real costs to mental and physical health. Entrepreneurs especially are feeling the pinch, and the mental health crisis is making headlines. According to *TechCrunch*, entrepreneurs are 50% more likely to report having a mental health condition, with some specific requirements being incredibly prevalent amongst founders like anxiety, depression, and addictions.[18]

There has to be a better way. What if instead of "pushing through," we were more honest with ourselves about our abilities and needs? We might find we enjoy our work and personal lives more when practicing empathy and vulnerability. Consider these three steps:

1) Take Inventory

You might start by reviewing all facets of life—in his book, *The Dream Manager*[19], Matthew Kelly assesses four key dimensions: intellectual, physical, emotional/relationships, and spiritual well-being. Everyone's wheel of life will look different, but for many, its family, marriage, health, leisure, and business. For you, today, which areas are robust, and which ones might need some attention? Similarly, we also must acknowledge that sometimes life will feel "off-balance," and we must tell ourselves that it's only a season of life, and this too shall pass.

2) Register Emotions

Speaking of feelings, it's human nature to want to crush that list of milestones and deliverables, but there's a danger in defining our self-worth by our productivity alone. Again, it's helpful to check-in. How are you feeling? Sometimes slowing down is the best thing we can do for ourselves. Everyone would be well served to regularly ask such questions as what does success look like to you? What things are you excited about daily? What are you most scared of, and need to lean into for your personal growth?

3) Be Honest

Furthermore, business builders need to be at home by showing up authentically at work, regardless of their emotional state. Brad Feld, a managing director of the Foundry Group, spoke to the emotional weight on entrepreneurship in an interview with *Inc.* magazine: "When you are willing to be emotionally honest, he says, you can connect more deeply with the people around you. 'When you deny yourself, and you deny what you're about, people can see through that,' says Feld. '**Willingness to be vulnerable is very powerful for a leader.**'"[20] I would add not just for leaders, but for anyone striving to become a "better version of themselves."

While some fear the consequences of practicing this vulnerability, author and speaker Brené Brown say its part and parcel of blazing your trail. What many eschew or even look down on, Brown insists there is a key to success, real intimacy, and happiness at home and work.

"Entrepreneurship is vulnerable by definition," she told *Foundr*. "**The definition of vulnerability is uncertainty, risk, and emotional exposure**. If you are not experiencing uncertainty, risk, and emotional exposure, you are not an entrepreneur."[21] Brown reminds us that vulnerability is not about being weak, winning, losing, or being insecure. Vulnerability is about courage and strength.

What can you do today to lean into your vulnerability? Who makes you better, and are you surrounding yourself and your business with these people?

vi. Employee Health and Wellness: It's Good for Business!

It is vital for everyone to shine a light on better mental health, wellness, and self-care for entrepreneurs and business builders. To put business builder mental illness in perspective, a 2015 University of California study found that "nearly a full half of people who start a company say they have struggled with some form of mental illness, with a third saying they have a lifetime illness."[22] Business builders, in general, experience more depression, ADHD, substance abuse, and bipolar disorder than their non-entrepreneurial counterparts.

Whether you need resources, information or providers, there are many organizations and groups available to meet you where you are. I hope that you will avail yourself of these resources when needed because education is key to understanding your options and taking action.

It seems nowadays everyone is trying to get more productive hours out of the day. The Internet is flush with self-help articles on the themes of "hacking your workday," "work smarter, not harder," etc. In other words, our society is distracted by technology that is always on, the tyranny of the urgent, and a constant juggling/optimizing of workflow for the sake of getting more done in less time.

But this is the wrong way to go about it. It's a reactive approach. What if you, as a business builder or entrepreneur, employed a proactive approach instead? To establish a results-oriented environment, business builders must create a culture where self-care is encouraged, and part of the organizational culture being built in the workplace. This is most effective when leaders set an example of what that means and follow through.

Following are a few areas in which business builders can focus their energies to inspire productive wellness habits to manage their wheel of life better[23]:

1) Physical Health

Lack of sleep can be detrimental to one's health in so many ways. Do you routinely work late, only to come in before the sun rises? Sleep deprivation will catch up eventually. The same goes for poor nutrition and lack of exercise. Discipline and adopting effective physical health behaviors is essential to achieving optimum physical well-being.

2) Intellectual Health

Effective leaders are naturally curious and always wanting to expand their understanding of topics both in and outside their fields. Whether it's trade journals, conferences, seminars, or other forms of continuing education, set specific goals for your lifelong learning and for new skills that grow your capabilities.

3) Emotional & Spiritual Health

No workplace is immune from problems. How do you, as a business builder, respond to conflict, challenge, or any adverse situation? Again, employees look to leaders for examples of grace under pressure. A workplace culture that addresses conflict head-on is healthier than those that avoid it. As a business builder, how do you work on cultivating your emotional intelligence (especially self-awareness) to engage in meaningful and fierce conversations (this is a terrific book of the same name[24]) with others?

Regardless of religious beliefs, you can find a higher meaning in your everyday work. Many see that their vocation is part of a higher calling from their Creator. Put simply, leaders who have more than a superficial connection with their work are healthier in all aspects. That sense of grounding can inspire confidence and meaning/purpose among the teams they lead.

If there's one takeaway—it's that paying attention to and incorporating discipline around your self-care and wellness is smart business. Well-being is serious business, and lost productivity is real. So, don't skip your yoga session, your book club, your vacation, or anything you can do to recharge your batteries.

vii. Ask for Help!

The stresses and tolls of starting, building, and growing a business cannot be understated, and often the isolation, loneliness, and peaks and valleys of doing your own thing result in a silent struggle.

While independence, drive, and self-motivation are common traits among business builders, they can also prove to work against us. A form of self-care—asking for help—can be a mixed bag at times. That's because we know we may need to do it for our sanity, but we also fear it exposes our vulnerabilities.

Still, there's a lot to be gained in reaching out for support and assistance. Here are three reasons why asking for help can benefit you, your family, and your organization.

1) Break out of your comfort zone

If you're reached a point where you know you need to ask for help, congratulations! Asking for help is not an easy thing to do, and it requires not only awareness and acceptance of your need, but it also requires you to move out of your comfort zone where you already know everything. You are now operating in the space of growth and development, where things are new, and you are open to guidance. Feeling uncomfortable is good because it means you are moving forward into uncharted territory, not treading water.

2) Tap into the power of experience

Seeking help from an established business builder or an entrepreneurial support organization can prove to be a wise move. Regardless of the nature of the business, the foundations of entrepreneurship, and best practices in business management are universal. Consulting with someone whom you respect can help you advance your ideas and sidestep potential potholes without having to make the same mistakes.

While you might equate asking for help with weakness, it can lead to much more than you might have considered. Growing your network is a byproduct of reaching out for support, encouragement, and inspiration. That's because sometimes the answer is found in talking with diverse people with differing perspectives. There is strength in numbers and connecting to community-building resources is an essential pillar of building a sustainable business.

The reward here is not necessarily the result, but the process itself. Each contact you make can enrich your life and help you get closer to your goals.

3) Learn to listen

The best leaders know that listening is part and parcel of the job. Listening is a critical skill when building and growing a business. Taking a thoughtful "pause" (a time out of sorts) and engaging in reflective thinking often sets the condition for you to do better, and smarter thinking and brainstorming around the business problem, pain, and opportunity.

Asking for help hones active listening skills. What's the point of seeking someone out for advice if you're not going to contemplate it? It's a waste of both of your time. Active listening demonstrates respect and intentionality. It also challenges you to see situations from someone else's perspective, which can be precisely what we need when we feel stuck. Listening can also be what it takes to diffuse a tense situation with a customer, employee, or vendor.

The bottom line here: Asking for help is not a sign of weakness or failure. See it as an opportunity to grow and learn.

viii. Rethinking Balance

It seems nowadays everyone is trying to find balance in life. There's a whole cottage industry built on self-help books on the topic, after all. I wonder if we should consider a different perspective when it comes to juggling all of life's demands. Think about achieving personal and professional satisfaction over a lifetime instead of balance at any given moment.

I'm a firm believer that you must love what you do and do what you love—and the rest will follow. Those who live by this will be successful and content, even when life feels off-kilter.

In his book, *OFF Balance*[25], Matthew Kelly, offers three principles on how best to live to achieve higher levels of personal and professional satisfaction. These principles are:

1) **Each of us is on this planet to become the best-version-of-ourselves** (and as Matthew reminds us, to do so requires the real work of self-discovery).
2) **Virtue is the "ultimate organizing principle"** (and, as Matthew states, virtue is the essence of excellence in both life and business).
3) **Self-control is "central to the best way to live"** (and as Matthew has reflected, there is no success without the ability to delay gratification).

If I'm honest, I love to spend time outside of traditional work hours working to build The NIIC and its brand. It's because I love the people who work hard to develop and sustain the organization and the things for which The NIIC stands. In other words, I don't seek out "balance" in the traditional sense. I find the idea of limiting the time I spend each week helping the organization grow, for the sake of following some prescribed formula, limiting and stifling. I seek, what Matthew Kelly, states are the *real goal*, living your life with high levels of personal and professional satisfaction.

I am not the first person to come to this conclusion. In Malcolm Gladwell's book *Blink*[26], he describes what he calls a "state of flow." This is the ideal state for maximum productivity—where you are energized and fully present. When you're in that zone, the last thing on your mind is balance.

Engagement is the buzz word today. We want client engagement and employee engagement in the workplace. Why? Because people are happier, more productive, and live better when it is evident and present in the workplace.

Flow is when you're the most passionate, productive, and successful version of yourself you can be. And it's fun! If you're spending less than half of your time in your state of flow, I challenge you to reconsider how you can allocate your time to achieve it better—is it saying "no" more? Is it delegating more? Or is it something else? I think the underlying issue most people grapple with when seeking balance is more intentional about how they spend their time. If something doesn't serve you, then it might be time to re-evaluate the nature or mix of your work.

However, if you find significant meaning and fulfillment in something, that is a true gift. Relish in it, and you just might find that choosing "satisfaction" overbalance is the preferred answer. So, how satisfied are you? And more importantly, if you are not highly happy, what are you doing about it?

---

ix. Dealing with Imposter Syndrome

I talk a lot about the nuts and bolts of entrepreneurship, but seldom do I address the emotional/mental side of the peaks and valleys of entrepreneurship. I would be remiss not to touch upon it to some extent.

Have you ever felt like a phony in your personal or professional life? Do you ever feel like you haven't achieved "enough" to consider yourself a subject-matter expert? These thoughts can cloud successful and high achieving entrepreneurial minds in all stages of business venture development.

Blame it on "Imposter Syndrome."

I know this is a strong word, but there was considerable psychological research in the late 1970s and 1980s behind the term. Studies show that between 40-70% of successful people feel like an imposter at one time or another. Please note, imposter syndrome is not a mental disorder—it is merely a feeling that a vast majority will experience at some point in life.

In graduate school, one of my professors in a class said, "99% of all people in the world come from a dysfunctional family, and the other 1% lie about it." The same can be said about imposter syndrome with high-achieving and successful people. Also, this syndrome is highly familiar with successful women (but it is not exclusively a female phenomenon). The key is to realize we are human, and we all make strides to hide or work on our imperfections. Instead of focusing on them, take some time to focus on your strengths/talents, and how you can add value and channel this energy productively.

Take some time and listen to the podcast "Overcoming Imposter Syndrome" by Ben from BrilliantSide[27], and then consider these three ways to get out of your head:

1) Help someone without expecting anything in return.

Seek out, or at least be open to, people who are experiencing problems you might be able to tackle. You might pleasantly surprise yourself with your depth and scope of knowledge and how someone else can apply it. Paying it forward is an excellent thing for your self-worth and making the world, your community, and other people better.

2) Be humble—but not too modest.

It's okay to own your success and acknowledge that we are the masters of our fate. Sure, no success happens in a vacuum, and there are many factors involved that come together to form the whole package that is you. While some people are privy to specific opportunities that others aren't, that doesn't negate the effort put forth. Success is no accident, even if the cards are stacked in your favor. Emotional intelligence focuses on self-efficacy and how we deal with professional mastery and recovery from failures.

3) Learn to embrace it.

A little bit of self-doubt now and then is normal and healthy. Whenever these feelings take over, you are best served to examine and articulate your doubts and anxieties. Sometimes verbalizing your fears, seeking out other's opinions, putting pen to paper may be optimal ways to overcome and find the potential solutions to the problem. There often can be more than one right answer to a problem.

For what it's worth, I have observed that almost every successful person has felt like an impostor at some point—no matter how confident, self-controlled they seem on the surface. Vulnerability and opening yourself to self-disclosure—strengthening relationships and improving self-awareness—is key to professional and personal growth. (Reference an excellent tool for this—the Johari Window.[28])

To get your brain flowing on this issue, BrilliantSide recommends journaling on ways you can increase your self-efficacy in an area where you feel like an impostor.

Remember, small victories add up.

---

x. Resilience and Reinvigorating Yourself

Have you become restless about your brand? Do you have a desire to shake things up, transform yourself, or change something in your life? Educational futurists have predicted that the next generation will have 11-17 careers in a lifetime—no, not jobs but careers. Talk about the need to shake things up. While some might be scared by this prediction, others, like me, are energized by the thought of reinventing myself more than once in my lifetime!

Innovation is not limited to companies. People are constantly reinventing themselves in the marketplace. Taking control of your brand may mean the difference between personal and professional satisfaction and disengagement. Trust me; there is no lack of disengagement in the U.S. workplace. Nearly 80% of American workers are dissatisfied or disengaged in the workplace. This speaks to our personal need for change and to take control of our life, but to do so, we need to know what we want.

Keep in mind these tips for reinventing and re-energizing your brand (and business):

1) Find people who make you better and bring out your personal best.

Maintain your intellectual curiosity by surrounding yourself with other curious, like-minded go-getters.

2) Be intentional about becoming the best version of yourself.

Commit to a personal development plan and a dream list—we all need to dream a little more.

Think about what word or words you want to own as representative of your brand personally. Think Volvo and "safety," Disney and "happiness," and Starbucks and "third place."[29] What is your unique selling proposition?

3) <u>Choose</u> reinvention.

Reinvention is about personal change. You have to break old habits in favor of forming new or different habits. What are you restless about, and what are you open and willing to change? Mental toughness or grit provides some of the staying power necessary to do the hard work of personal reinvention.

It has been said that your passion must be more reliable than your fear to truly succeed. What fears are holding you back? Lean into these fears with your passion.

Remember, for meaningful personal change to occur, you must have the following: **awareness of the need for behavioral change + willingness**

to change x burning platform or significant opportunity for change to increase the likelihood of success.

Is your reinvention driven out of a crisis or opportunity?

---

xi. Taming the Loneliness Monster

Entrepreneurship can be an exciting adventure. You get to work on your passion on your terms (... *sometimes*). However, the same reasons you chose the boss's life may also prove to be a source of frustration or even an emotional roller coaster.

What do I mean by *"taming the loneliness monster"*? Well, many of you know or have realized that starting and running a small business can be a lonely undertaking. You have to consciously seek out ways to combat isolation in your day-to-day routine to combat the ups and downs (stress, anxiety, and too much to do) of building a business. Here are a few ideas:

1) Create an advisory board ... *gain new insights!*

Seek out a few people (three at most to start) you can call on to serve as advisors. They can help brainstorm ideas, consult with you on business matters, or simply act as moral support. Show your appreciation and provide an incentive in the form of a nominal board fee, free or discounted products, or other perks. Be sure to have a plan and know what you want to achieve from the board. Keep in mind; feedback is a gift. Pick one big question you are trying to address at each meeting and build the plan and dialog around it.

If one-on-one attention is more your style, you might consider tapping into the power of a mentor. Many small business centers offer new, and growing entrepreneurial companies access to a network of volunteer mentors and advisors with expertise in fields that match their needs. Mentors should be experienced entrepreneurs, senior-level executives, subject matter experts, and professional service providers. They can assist you by providing advice and guidance with mission-critical business issues, such as financial planning, business development, marketing strategies, human resources, and general management.

When you're ready, cast a wider net, and expand your circle, get feedback from the marketplace. Be sure to catalog your insights and learnings. Challenge your assumptions. Solicit input from experts, customers, suppliers, friends, employees, and trusted advisors. Think about: What's working? What would they like to see changed? Listen more, talk less.

2) Participate in a lead-generating networking group or a business/leadership roundtable ... *get grounded!*

Networking groups are a venue to forge friendships with other business owners while at the same time generating business. Come prepared with an elevator pitch and have plenty of business cards on hand. There is a myriad of networking groups meeting regularly in every community; all you have to do is look. Be sure to set specific metrics of how you will judge your efforts successful and periodically review your ROI.

3) Join an entrepreneur support group ... *get inspired!*

Invite fellow business owners to a monthly session to compare notes and provide constructive feedback. It could be as formal or informal as you want it to be. Take turns featuring one of your companies at each meeting or open the floor to the general discussion.

These are three great ways to network and get outside support, but a strong foundation requires a reliable team *inside* your business. One reason entrepreneurs get stuck in the office is that they are trying to manage everything themselves. Follow this rule of thumb: If it's not directly generating or leading to revenue or customers, you should ask yourself what value-add there is in working on it. Look for people to hire or entrust freelancers with tasks that can be outsourced or managed remotely. This will free you up to spend more time working *on* the business, as opposed to *in* the business.

Remember, you are not alone, scaling and growing are not easy, and that's why only 2% of all U.S. small businesses are the high performance/high growth. Be sure to celebrate the small successes along the way. Keep in mind Richard Branson's words of wisdom: "surround yourself with encouraging people who support your pursuits." The bottom line is to keep people who care about you close to you while you are a business building but make sure you are always facing the brutal facts/reality.

Loneliness can lead to health problems, so find productive outlets to channel your energy and "entrepreneurial firefighting skills."

If you think you are invincible and can do it all, think again by listening to Sheryl Sandberg's UC Berkeley commencement speech.[30] I think you will agree it is a terrific reminder of the importance of **resilience** (learning, growing, and renewal) and leaning into "joy and meaning" because, as Sheryl aptly reminds us, "the hardest days determine who you are."

---

xii. The Power of "Why"

If you have not seen the TED Talk[31] or read the book *Start with Why*[32] you really should. Simon Sinek captures the essence of "people don't buy what you do; they buy why you do it." Often this is the rallying cry of entrepreneurs and would-be entrepreneurs in the recruitment of talent, the launch of an innovative product or service, and exerting their passion for doing something different or for thinking differently.

Entrepreneurs often see around the corner before others do. They connect disparate dots in ways most people don't or can't. This is why, at any one time, only about 11% of adults are engaged in entrepreneurial endeavors.

As entrepreneurs, it's so easy to get caught up in the day-to-day grind. But I challenge you to take a step back for a moment and consider the *why*. Why are you in business? If you can't quickly answer this question, this could provoke some soul-searching.

Here are three reasons you should keep your *why* at the forefront of your mind during day-to-day operations:

1) It's grounding.

Most businesses take longer, cost more, and earn less than you think—at least in the short run—and there can be lots of setbacks along the way. If you're only doing it for a paycheck, it can be easy to abandon ship in the early stages. However, if you have faith in your concept, it's easier to go the distance. You'll likely appreciate your success more, given the humbling journey.

2) You have an end game in mind.

Your "why" is the reason your business has staying power. You create great products or offer exceptional services to your customers because it's critical to your mission. You hire and train quality personnel because it's vital to your purpose. The customer experience is flawless because it's essential to your purpose. These practices aren't a means to an end—they are ends in and of themselves.

3) A sense of purpose is contagious.

Think about your "tribe" for a moment. Why do they support you? They likely love what you do and want to be part of it. The same goes for your workforce, especially Millennials. This generation is known to be socially conscious, and that ethos extends to their work lives. They want to participate in meaningful work in their careers. Since Millennials will dominate the workforce in a few years, having a clear and engaging purpose will become even more critical to attracting talent.

Passion + Persistence + Purpose are three critical ingredients for entrepreneurial success.

Chapter 2: Conclusion

There are many ways to nurture and care for your well-being, which in turn directly impacts your ability to run and maintain your business venture successfully. When you run out of steam or hit a breaking point, that could very well mean the end of your company. To ensure long shelf life, just like any relationship, you must take steps to fortify your mental, physical, and emotional health.

Fear, uncertainty, and isolation are common feelings all entrepreneurs must grapple with at some point. Accepting and addressing these speed bumps head-on will help you become a more grounded and capable business owner. The tough times help shape who we are and are incorporated into our deeper *why*. Remember why you are in business, and how far you've come. Sometimes, we are our own worst enemy. Through imposter syndrome, poor self-confidence, and a focus on the negatives of what we didn't do, we undermine our potential success.

Chapter 2: Questions for Consideration

i. Managing Uncertainty

What are the top three ways that you can mitigate an overwhelming fear of the unknown? Have you taken action today?

ii. A Case for Cultivating an Empathy-Driven Culture

How do you demonstrate empathy for those you work with/for?

iii. How to Go from Good to Great: Start by Removing These Distractions

What are your three biggest distractions? Write them down along with the steps you will take to help eliminate their impact.

iv. Protect Your Peace: Three Habits to Embrace

Have you taken a moment of calm today? Found a second, or two, for Zen? What have you done lately to protect your inner peace? Choose your preferred method and write it on your calendar to ensure you carve out space for this vital activity.

v. Redefining Success Through the Lens of Vulnerability

What steps have you taken to "lean into" your vulnerability? What makes you feel vulnerable, and how can you turn those feelings into an opportunity for growth? Be honest!

vi. Employee Health and Wellness: It's Good for Business!

How are you protecting your mental, physical, and emotional health? How can you also promote well-being in the workplace?

vii. Ask for Help!

When was the last time you got "uncomfortable"? Chances are, you were in a position of being unsure or needing assistance. Think of this as the trigger for you to seek out a professional to help you in this area of uncertainty. Who can you ask for help? With what? Try something small with someone you trust so that next time you need help, you won't hesitate to reach out.

viii. Rethinking Balance

Are you satisfied with your work/life balance? If not, write down actionable steps or a plan to shift things in the right direction. If there is no easy way to adjust, maybe it's time to accept the need for more significant changes, or even a new career.

ix. Dealing with Imposter Syndrome

How can you be more vulnerable and open to increasing your self-awareness? What tips and tips or tricks have you found helpful to silence this voice in your head?

x. Resilience and Reinvigorating Yourself

Without personal reinvention, we can quickly become stagnant and irrelevant. What actions can you take to breathe some fresh air into your brand? Make a list and start now.

xi. Taming the Loneliness Monster

If you have struggled with loneliness as a result of your work, what are some ways you've found to overcome this hurdle? Have you joined a local networking/entrepreneur group? If not, consider attending one at least once, even if you aren't lonely. Broadening your contacts is never a bad idea and can lead to new opportunities.

xii. The Power of "Why"

Why are you in business? What drives you to get up every day and do what you do? Write it down and keep it at the forefront of your mind as you conduct your daily work.

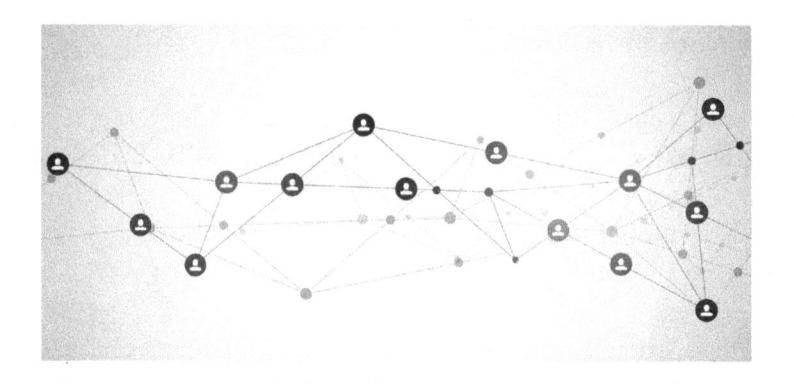

CHAPTER 3

CONNECTION & COMMUNICATION

Strategy and capabilities will only get you so far, and they are only two legs of the corporate transformation triumvirate—the third being culture. All three need to be aligned and designed together. While the first two are more straightforward, culture is an intangible that is harder to pin down. It entails a host of elements, can mean something different to everyone, and grows and evolves.

At its core, culture has to do with people, living breathing humans who understand your company vision, believe in the mission, and are committed to working toward a common goal. Establishing a flexible and innovative culture that empowers individuals to take ownership and responsibility for results will pave the way to an effective and productive institution. The keys to this elusive culture? Nurturing an environment with connection and communication.

i. What Does It Mean to Be a People-Centric Organization?

Human capital, talent, associates, cast members—whatever you call them—they matter to every organization. People are perhaps the most critical piece of the puzzle. And while many businesspeople know this to be intuitively correct, it can be hard to know where to start.

Let's take a look at a few tried and true principles exhibited by some of the world's most people-centric organizations, and how you can apply them to your business.

1) Foster, a culture that engages people.

As Peter Drucker famously said, "culture eats strategy for breakfast." If workers feel appreciated and valued, they tend to feel more confident in taking on new challenges and demands. How can you involve your team members in important decisions and encourage them to speak up when they think it's necessary?

The Walt Disney Company sets the bar high with its employee-centric reputation. In a Disney Institute post, the author describes an incident in which Belle went above and beyond:

"What motivates employees to go above and beyond the call of duty to provide this kind of memorable customer experience? It's not magic, but the method. The theme park team didn't consult a script or take instructions from their manager. They did what they did because Disney has created a culture where going the extra mile (magical moments, take 5's) for customers comes naturally."

If you've ever been to a Disney theme park, you probably have experienced this "magic" firsthand. I have.

2) Re-examine how you define success.

The most plugged-in leaders today know that while the financial aspect of the business is essential, that's ultimately not what motivates workers. It's a sense of common purpose. By identifying and speaking to the core drives of their people, leaders will inspire their teams to assign more significant meaning to their tasks. By being intentional in integrating purpose into your operations, people-centricity will become second nature.

3) Lean into diversity and inclusiveness.

Most breakthroughs don't occur when people come from homogenous backgrounds with similar points of view. On the other hand, a more diverse team—whether gender, ethnicity, cultural, or socio-economic backgrounds, education levels, perspectives, backgrounds, or ages—can all be a boon to innovation.

Break down internal silos to create opportunities for employees from different backgrounds, experiences, and job functions to collide and collaborate. Encourage employees to share different opinions and celebrate people and teams who are willing to push back on the status quo. This type of cross-pollination of ideas and skills can prove to be a recipe for a more robust and forward-thinking organization.

Applying a people-centric approach to process and products is not an option in 2020. It is a *must* to remain relevant in a competitive market. People make a place, so treat them accordingly. In turn, the culture will thrive, innovation will flourish, and your employees will be inspired to make a measurable difference every day.

---

ii. Technology Is Not a Substitute for Quality Relationships & Human Interactions

Not long ago, AI expert Kai-Fu Lee estimated that automation could replace 40% of jobs within fifteen years[33], but wait—is that possible in sales?

There's no question that technology (AI, AR, machine learning, and the like) will continue to transform the industry landscape. But if you think an all-robot sales team is the wave of the future, think again.

Technology is not a substitute for relationships. The human touch is critical to the sales process.

We are all in sales, but looking at successful salespeople, they share some common threads. First, they build strong relationships and have a solid understanding of a client's needs while understanding the value created by their products or services. Second, the most effective salespeople have engaged listeners, empathetic, and storytellers. Today, technology cannot rise to this level—at least not yet. In the future, the most sustainable solutions will need to marry a human's emotional needs with their desire to be efficient and productive.

SnapApp reminds us, "Today, there is an average of 5.4 stakeholders involved in any given sale. On top of that, buyers are much more educated—90%[34] of the buying process is over before a salesperson talks to a lead."[35]

With this in mind, here are some examples in which this can come alive—the 3C's—custom solutions, coordination/collaboration, and connectivity:

1) Custom Solutions

To truly understand customer priorities, businesses need to understand their customer's values, motivations, and pain points. Salespeople must listen carefully and follow up with intelligent questions and innovative solutions to solve their customer's problems.

However, technology presents an opportunity to take this further. AI tools can analyze the findings. Predictive analytics can connect the dots between data to make it into usable information and speed up the sales process. In short, these tools identify patterns that help salespeople discern whether a custom product or a no-frills one is appropriate. Personalization and customization of product and service offerings will be critical to the future.

2) Coordination/Collaboration

The sales cycle doesn't end with the sale. If it's a physical good, it may need to be packaged and shipped. Ultimately, salespeople are responsible for making sure the product arrives when promised or the solution is implemented on time, within budget, and as promised. But sometimes they face delivery and logistical challenges. This is where AI has potential. A robust B2B platform can improve organizational transparency and alignment so that all parties can feel like they are part of a well-oiled team and aligned on their metrics and customer satisfaction goals.

3) Connectivity/Connections

While tools like chatbots are becoming more prevalent in the customer service space, they aren't without flaws, including not being able to detect emotion. While these tools can be useful for front-line communication, they aren't a substitute for human connection. For example, if a customer has a concern that needs to be escalated, they aren't going to ask to speak to a robot but a live human being.

Never underestimate the power of a phone call or face-to-face interaction to strengthen or regain trust and build an essential emotional connection.

Technological advancements will no doubt help organizations enhance, improve, and expand their customer relationships. But we can't overlook the underlying truth that human beings will still need to be part of the equation.

---

iii. Finding a Business Partnership That Is Right for You

A business partnership can solve some problems yet create other challenges and difficulties. Of course, inventorying and weighing the pros and cons is a crucial first step if you're thinking of going this route. Finding the right partner and ensuring the compatibility of the relationship is nothing to rush into, as it often comes with high stakes.

To adequately inform your decision, you need to do your due diligence paying attention to a myriad of influences and insights that can provide valuable clues into whether a partnership is viable and in your best interest. Let's take a look at three pros and three cons you should be sure to consider.

PROS

A partnership may offer many "tangible" benefits for your particular business, such as:

1) Compensating for Weaknesses

Maybe you lack skills or expertise in a specific area. The "right" partner can (and should) accentuate your positives and round out your blind spots and gaps.

For example, you may be great at marketing, but not so good when it comes to keeping the books. You may be a rockstar when it comes to customer service but freeze up at the thought of networking. This may be one of your first considerations when you look at the potential relationship holistically. Where might your business partner help to pick up the slack, better differentiate, or complement what you have to offer?

2) Increased Startup Capital, Cost and Time Savings

A prospective partner may offer more in-depth financial resources necessary to better capitalize on your efforts. He or she may also have connections or a proven track record that could benefit you from a funding perspective. They may be more poised than you to attract potential investors, raise more capital to grow your business, and likely to develop faster and more reliable than you would on your own.

A startup is often resource intensive. Having a business partner would allow you to offset some of that burden, theoretically resulting in more substantial savings than flying solo. Additionally, a partnership can mean you are more strategic and productive with your time since you're better leveraging and focusing your limited resources.

3) Wellness and Self-Care

A partnership may yield psychological benefits. It may allow you to cut back on time spent on the office, knowing someone is invested in the business even when you're not physically present. Work-life balance is underestimated among the entrepreneur community but critical to overall business and personal health. Additionally, the right partner can act as a sounding board, cheerleader, and confidante, all of which are critical throughout the development of a sustainable business.

Business builders are often isolated, lonely, and feel overwhelmed by all the pressure to deliver. They often lack the tools and skills to manage the high highs and low lows of starting, growing, and scaling a sustainable venture.

CONS

There are two sides to every coin, don't forget possible downsides to a business arrangement:

1) Liabilities / Future Complications

In addition to sharing profits and assets, a partnership means partners have to contend with any losses too. This can place a burden on your finances and assets. Your business partner's lousy decision can become your responsibility. That's why it's so important to enter into the relationship with a certain amount of "preparedness" and "triggers" for how to handle difficult and crucial conversations.[36]

At some point down the road, you or your partner may wish to sell the business. This could cause tension if both parties aren't on board with the timing or specifics of the deal. That's why having a formal exit strategy is essential to account for any situations that may call for the partners to move on by buying the other out, selling to a strategic buyer, or winding down the business because goals, needs, and performance justify the action. Having established mechanisms for dealing with potentially tricky situations is paramount to long-term success.

2) Loss of Autonomy / Lack of Stability

Are you willing to answer to someone else when it comes to shared decision making? If you've been a solopreneur for some time, you might find the transition to be a rude awakening. Sometimes, it is a hard and challenging transition from being a "lone ranger" to be an accountable partner.

Even if you have a solid exit strategy spelled out in your partnership agreement, the change in circumstances could mean instability in the business. How comfortable are you with facing uncertainty? I have always believed that one essential business builder skill is managing uncertainty and approaching decision-making from a risk perspective (monitoring, managing, and mitigating risk).

3) Cultural Fit

Too often, we take for granted that if we share similar views, that is sufficient for determining if a partnership is a cultural fit. The reality is that we need to look under the hood and examine our collective core values, experiences, and vision to determine if our union is a right fit on all levels. Don't underestimate the power of culture in unraveling a partnership. Toxic people create toxic workplaces. It is well established that organizations often mirror the dysfunction of their leaders.

In short, a business partnership is a marriage. As with any strong union, it's based on finding the right partner. Don't rush into it and take precautions to maintain the health of the relationship by preparing for adverse outcomes before you sign on the dotted line. You can accomplish this if you and your partnership start from a place of transparency, openness, and mutual respect.

iv. Time for a Culture Shift? Try These Three Tips

Cultural change in any organization must come from the top down. The adage, "the small things are the big things," applies here when it comes to effecting change in a workplace setting.

While culture can seem nebulous or intangible, it does matter. Research shows that talent increasingly cares about culture. That said, if you have a strong one, the bottom line will likely reflect those priorities. Peter Drucker made this point clear when he opined, "Culture eats strategy for breakfast."

The following are three success practices for driving a culture change that will stick:

1) Define a set of desired values and behaviors.

This goes beyond a mission statement, which can be viewed as window dressing. Cut the business jargon and come up with behavioral descriptors for each value you define. Don't stop there. Articulate how those values translate into actionable behaviors at all levels—from entry-level staff to middle managers to executives. At the NIIC (The Innovation Center), we do this every month in our internal culture Happy Hour, where we celebrate our successes and find ways to improve and offer exemplary client and community experiences on our campus every day.

2) Go beyond the surface level.

Take a hard look at your mission, vision, and values, and consider how they inform your HR processes, including hiring, compensation, benefits, and professional development. The most employee-centric companies have a seamlessly married and aligned theory with practice, and it shows.

3) Measure it.

As the saying goes, what gets measured gets managed. Help demonstrate the effectiveness of your efforts by implementing stakeholder surveys and exit interviews to take the temperature of your culture, and NPS (Net Promoter

Score) measures the engagement/loyalty of your clients and customers. Insight gleaned from these tools can identify gaps between desired and actual behavior and help you determine where to target your efforts.

What's next? Organizational assessment tools can provide companies and their leaders with essential insights that you need to create and maintain a high-performing corporate culture. As each company is different, there is no one-size-fits-all solution. Companies should choose the tools that work best for them and try to see the bigger picture. Consistency is also crucial, regardless of the system you adopt.

---

v. How to Win Friends and Influence People (Online)

In 1936, Dale Carnegie published an incredibly valuable and influential best-selling self-help book, *How to Win Friends and Influence People*.[37] An adaptation book with an updated title[38] focuses on the modern age to capitalize on creating a vibrant digital and connected network.

If there's one marketing trend that's had a good run, it's the rise and prevalence of social media influencers. If you're not familiar, this term refers to people who curate robust online personas and develop a significant fan base and audience as a result. In other words, they are the trendsetters ("merchants of cool"), and consumers of all stripes tend to look to them for inspiration and direction on everything from music to nutrition.

So, what does this mean for you? You can learn from their online game and apply it to your marketing strategy. Here are three key themes from the influencer culture to take note:

1) Branding Matters

Instagram is all about the visual appeal by design. That's why influencers have sleek graphics and video that commands attention. The most popular accounts, like Beyoncé, get millions of likes, story views, etc. But don't get so invested in these indicators that you lose sight of consistency. What you push out needs to be on-brand, too. For example, if your brand is playful, you'll want to accompany images with light-hearted captions that invite engagement. More than anything, authenticity resonates with consumers.

2) Be Open to Collaboration

Brands no longer operate in silos in today's world. Everyone—from visual artists to motivational speakers—is collaborating to gain a more significant following, or reach, in return for reciprocity. The key is to find a complementary brand. For example, it makes sense that brands like Spotify and Hulu would align because both products appeal to a similar demographic.

3) Stay Current on Trends

Influencers are usually the first to embrace a new functionality within the app—so-called early adopters. So, naturally, if you want to come across as plugged in online, you need to put in the time to understand the changing landscape.

Like any area of your business, you should always be pushing to take things to the next level. You can't put all your eggs in the proverbial basket that is social media for many reasons. Don't forget about good old-fashioned face time! Events are a great way to connect with your consumer base and get access to inside knowledge. Plus, this is a chance to build trust and inspire confidence, which is always more comfortable in person.

---

vi. Take Your Communication to the Next Level

"What we've got here is a failure to communicate." — Cool Hand Luke

Does your business suffer from this issue? Your product may be great, but if the communication is lackluster, you may have a problem.

According to *Fast Company*, "Powerful, persuasive communication leads to success—personal success, career success, and organizational success."[39] However, to avoid info-whelm, start by evaluating your communications strategy and employing these three crucial tips:

1) Deliver on speed.

Speed is a differentiator and a small business advantage. Without the trappings of an enormous bureaucracy, entrepreneurs can be agile, market smart, and fast-moving. Building this type of intentional culture from inception is critical to long-term success.

Quick response and communication times are dependent on your systems and processes. How do you manage and track customer touchpoints? CRM systems like Salesforce, and customer support platforms like Zendesk and Freshdesk have gained popularity in recent years and can help ensure timeliness and organization.

2) Small talk matters.

Sure, "big talk" is the stuff of business, but small talk has a place, too. Regardless of your industry, you can take the time to chat with your clients as you would with friends or colleagues. People do business with people, not companies, after all. So, anything you can do to set yourself apart can make a huge difference.

Make sure your employees are trained in best practices when handling customer communication. Customers expect transparent, authentic, and open conversations.

3) Under-promise and over-deliver.

No one wants to be "sold." Instead, phrase your ideas as suggestions while outlining the pros, cons, features, benefits, etc. Ask them what they expect from the outset and don't make any promises you can't keep.

Good businesses know the importance of healthy client relationships and have policies and procedures aligned with their customer acquisition and retention strategies. From a bottom-line perspective, it costs four to ten times less to keep a client than to acquire a new one.

A little effort goes a long way, so make a point to invest in high tech, high touch solutions to deepen essential client relationships and to create enduring and memorable interactions.

---

vii. Authenticity Sells: How to Craft an Intentional Customer Experience

There is a reason the average net promoter score in the United States is 10. High quality, world-class customer experiences are an exception, not the rule.

What makes for remarkable customer experiences?

- An emotional connection and interactions to/with the brand;
- Something memorable, "sticky," different, or a "wow" (unexpected); and
- An underlying feeling of acknowledged value and worth (appreciation).

Today, more than ever, people are craving authentic experiences from brands. As a result, the brands commanding the most attention know how to engage customers profoundly and sustainably. The truth is it doesn't matter what you're selling. Deep emotional connections built on insights are king. Think about how few and far between handwritten notes are today!

For example, pizza chain Domino's Pizza has worked to create a great brand experience on all of their different channels, including social media, apps, and websites. Specifically, they offer many personalized messages to their customers, such as push notifications. Customers love the convenience factor, and this drives likely conversions.

What can small businesses do who don't necessarily have the marketing power of a chain like Domino's? You can still apply their best practices. Follow these steps to craft an intentional customer experience and reap the rewards.

1) Engage in Active Customer Discovery and Validation

A vital component of the business model process is the search for the business model. Active and engaged market research is one avenue. If a tight budget constrains you, you could conduct a free or low-cost online survey. The ultimate goal is to dig a little deeper to understand consumer preferences. For example, how does your widget make customers' lives easier, or help them overcome perceived challenges? Using this insight, consider how you might incorporate those intangibles into your business and improve the overall customer experience?

2) Connect the Dots

A novel idea or innovation is one that tests positive on desirability, viability, and feasibility. Once you understand the pain points of your consumer base, it's time to explore possible avenues. Conducting a feasibility study will help you better understand what falls under the scope of your capabilities. For example, do you have the capital to launch a new or improved product line? Do you have the personnel needed to support growth? What partnerships can you leverage? How much will it cost, and what's the related ROI? What is the competition doing? How can you sustain growth?

3) Execute, Execute, and Execute

Once you have determined the next steps, identify key performance indicators, and delegate responsibilities to bring your vision to fruition. Survey your core clientele to ensure the experience is still satisfactory. Too much, too soon, can compromise quality and, ultimately, your reputation.

Remember, a good idea is worth one point, and execution is worth ninety-nine points.

When in doubt, remember that experience-based businesses are designed around people, not products. You can't go wrong with taking a step back to focus on the human element, above all else.

---

viii. Cut the Jargon

Have you ever read a blog or company website and couldn't easily make sense of the message? That is "business speak" at its worst. Jargon is so prevalent in our world that plain English seems like the exception to the rule. We've become used to expressions and buzzwords that didn't exist 10 or 15 years ago.

- *We don't have the bandwidth right now to complete this project.*
- *We need buy-in from executive leadership.*
- *She employs an out-of-the-box approach.*
- *We are streamlining our operation to optimize our divisional synergies better.*

These are some examples of typical *mumbo-jumbo* in the modern corporate world. While some might think loading up an article with buzzwords can help their cause, the fact remains that it has the opposite effect. Effective communicators know this and try to avoid falling into this trap.

Why? Language is supposed to connect, not marginalize people. When done right, words are powerful tools that can motivate and inspire action. However, the names you choose when addressing a colleague or prospective client could work against you. Jargon[40] can be unintelligible words and sentences that distract from the critical point or call to action you are making. You might "lose" the person before you even break through the surface—and that's a shame. An exceptional brand experience needs approachability.

Relationships, the currency of business, are formed when people feel like they can relate to other people or brand personas. However, when businesspeople use jargon, they run the risk of making people think sidelined because they can't follow or engage in the conversation. And no one wants to feel like their intelligence is being insulted or belittled. (This is not a good feeling when you are trying to build rapport.)

The challenge is to think about word choice differently. Simplicity in language does not have to mean your brand is unsophisticated. You can skip the jargon and still come across as professional. Jargon may be interpreted as over-compensating for weakness or insecurity. You have a strong brand, so why detract from it with language that only adds noise?

Remember: You're doing business with people. Write in ways that form a real connection or bond with people, and you'll win the communications game.

---

ix. Three Universal Lessons About Entrepreneurship

Global business travel—gaining new insights, fostering real connections, and forging lifelong relationships—can change you. I've had the pleasure of visiting and observing entrepreneurial communities all across the globe. Through those experiences, I've learned that, despite differences in cultural norms and practices, there are specific insights about entrepreneurship that ring true universally.

Here are my top three:

1) Great ideas come from all corners of the world.

Some people are naive in thinking that innovation only happens in large urban centers on the coasts. But the truth is, there are solid ideas in even the most remote areas. That's because the internet has democratized access to knowledge, talent, and other resources. It's not unusual for cross-cultural teams to work together remotely and achieve better outcomes than they would in isolation. Global inspirations come from seeing around corners, connecting dots, and demonstrating the same passion and perseverance you see from business builders regardless of location.

2) Failure is universal, but it doesn't have to obstruct smart risk-taking.

Every entrepreneur faces de-risking challenges, whether it be product, market, management, financial, regulatory, or market. While some cultures are more tolerant of risk, that doesn't mean they are more poised to succeed. They just might be more at home with it. For example, China is developing an inspiring and progressive startup culture because of their attitude toward risk, as one blogger posits:

"When the Chinese see an opportunity, they will take it. They aren't afraid to fail because they see life as a cycle of events. If they fail, they believe their time will come again."

I have also seen firsthand how the federal government in China also underwrites some of the speculative R&D for startups giving them an edge when they need it most.

3) Connections matter everywhere.

A deep and robust collection of contacts can be instrumental in building and scaling a business anywhere. Again, China offers an example of how entrepreneurs leverage their connections. As Alina Dizik writes in her article, "Good startups have great networks,"[41] the Chinese know how to tap into these social networks.

"Guanxi, a traditional Chinese concept, refers to longtime acquaintances who have a relationship defined by intimacy, obligation, and a high level of trust. In a business context, the Guanxi is a family-like, deeply trusted circle of people who can help grow a business—as opposed to a larger, more professional network where trust and longstanding relationships are not necessarily always present. A guanxi network, says Burt, shares some similarities to what in the US might have been called in the past—the 'old boys' club."

Regardless of your geographic location, you can try your hand at entrepreneurship and business building.

---

x. Honesty Is Always the Best Policy

Brands are built on trust. That is true across every industry. Think for a moment about your favorite products. What keeps you coming back for more? Chances are that the brand's reputation and its promise come into play somehow.

If you want a sense of how important a brand's promise is and how fragile it might be, consider the controversies associated with Honest Co. as a cautionary tale.

The consumer products startup was initially pitched as an alternative to traditional chemical-heavy products on the market, like laundry detergent. According to their website, "(w)hen, we were trying to think of a name for our company; we thought we should choose something that reflected our core values and highest aspirations. The Honest Company was a clear choice."

Yet The Honest Company wasn't so honest after all. The eco-friendly claims were exposed as less than truthful in a *Wall Street Journal* exposé.[42] What followed was a significant product recall and legal trouble. The company ended up reformulating the product in question, but no doubt, the company lost credibility with health and socially conscious consumers who realized the honest company wasn't very honest.

To add insult to injury, imagine the backlash when Founder Jessica Alba announced that the brand would replace its CEO with a former Clorox exec.[43] The image Alba worked so hard to create so quickly eroded by the decision. No doubt in some consumers' minds, the company (and Alba) had sold out.

The lesson here?

Deliver on your promise. The Honest Co. is an egregious example of what happens when you veer off course. For example, if you claim to offer organic, GMO-free products, then provide organic GMO-free products. If you are less than genuine, customers will take notice, and that could have negative repercussions on your bottom line. Failing to deliver on your promise hurts your organization (and the stakeholders involved—employees, suppliers, and communities) just as much as the customer in the end.

Chapter 3: Conclusion

A product or service is just a thing or a capability. Yes, they are an essential part of business, but without clear communication and connection—they are like the cart without the horse. Customers, employees, and business networks must all be leveraged through the power of language and culture. Building a successful business requires a human element in addition to the structure and strategy.

Make sure you are honest, straightforward, authentic, genuine, timely, and empathic. No easy feat to be sure, but if you can manage to strike the right balance, your company and you personally will surely thrive.

Chapter 3: Questions for Consideration

i. What Does It Mean to Be a People-Centric Organization?

Is your workplace people-centric? If not, how can you work to change this? Do you know what drives the people around you? Start there, and work to incorporate the passions and views of those on your team to help draw them in and inspire them.

ii. Technology Is Not a Substitute for Quality Relationships & Human Interactions

How is your company leveraging technology to help humans with 3C's (custom solutions, coordination/collaboration, and connectivity)? Do you have processes in place to ensure your business never loses that "human touch"?

iii. Finding a Business Partnership That Is Right for You

In your experience, what worries you most about finding the "right" partner? How can you mitigate these concerns? Having a list of deal-breakers and makers can help you feel more secure and prepared for when the right person comes along.

iv. Time for a Culture Shift? Try These Three Tips

Is your culture aligned with your brand? Culture must resonate with all stakeholders. How does the brand hold up both internally and externally? Making sure you are on the same page across the board is especially relevant in the Age of the Internet when one bad experience can turn into a viral disaster.

v. How to Win Friends and Influence People (Online)

Does your brand have a consistent strategy for connecting online? What can you do to accelerate this process, while still maintaining authenticity? Push yourself outside of your comfort zone—people are more likely to respond to originality and vulnerability than any stock image or quote.

vi. Take Your Communication to the Next Level

What kind of communications culture do you want to create in your organization? What are the tools that will help make this easier? From software to training, no aspect of communication is too small to consider.

vii. Authenticity Sells: How to Craft an Intentional Customer Experience

What makes your customer's experience remarkable? Start there, craft a plan to optimize, and keep your customer's wants, needs, and feelings central to your entire process.

viii. Cut the Jargon

What words or phrases could you do without in your life? What are your best examples of mumbo-jumbo? Keep an eye out for overused buzzwords that you routinely see in company jargon and eliminate them from use. Think clean, straightforward language for precise and reliable connections.

ix. Three Universal Lessons About Entrepreneurship

Good startups have vast networks that can be called a universal truth about entrepreneurship. No matter where you are, big or small, it's all about who you know. How can you broaden your business network, with the understanding that this is one of the cornerstones of good business? Don't let fear or hesitancy hold you back. Every business owner needs a more extensive network, and smart builders are always open to making new connections.

x. Honesty Is Always the Best Policy

When it comes to business, white lies or half-truths can get you into hot water and begin to erode faith in your brand. It is essential to deliver on all your promises and maintain an honest reputation. It wouldn't hurt to do a little housecleaning/review of all the statements and claims on your marketing and website just to ensure they are all completely genuine. What, in your life, doesn't pass the mother, mirror and newspaper test? What would your mom say if you told her, what do you see if you look in the mirror and what would you think if you say what you did or said on the front page of the newspaper tomorrow?

Adaptability

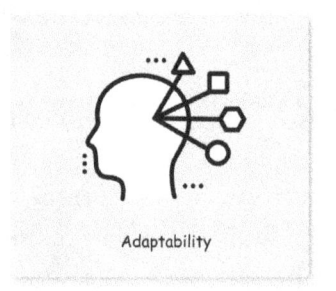

CHAPTER 4

IMPROVISE, ADAPT, OVERCOME

Famous for their tenacity and commitment, marines are trained to improvise, adapt, and overcome until the battle is won. No matter what you're facing, or going up against, there is always a way through. Maybe victory does not look like you thought it would, and that's okay. The field of combat can change daily, from small to large engagements, you have to be ready to assess whatever information you have and make the best choice possible—even if it's merely persevering.

Building and running a business is no small feat; there will be good days and bad. With dedication, pacing, and pure willpower, you are more likely to succeed if you are willing to push through when times get tough. To take the military analogy a little further, with the proper team in place to help support, and carry out your delegations, your business will have more than a fighting chance.

i. Time to Recalibrate?

Pivoting can be expensive, time-consuming, and sometimes over-rated, but so can the consequences of not adjusting the trajectory of your business venture at the optimal time and sometimes re-evaluating your current approach precisely what your enterprise needs to do to ensure future success. But how do you know when it's time?

Here are three telltale signs business builders should watch for as early indicators of the need to reassess, realign, and rethink your venture:

1) You're in a dry spell.

Momentum is everything, so if you're not on a growth, the path you can't hit that next level. "Moving the needle" may require you to shift employees into different roles, allocate resources differently, or explore new adjacent market opportunities. Likewise, growth may also call for innovation in terms of products or services, especially when they add value to your current menu of offerings. Product, process, business model, customer experience, or other innovation methods might just mean new customers, repeat customers, more market share, more significant product differentiation, and new channels. Incorporating customer feedback and leveraging marketing research might lead to new insights and new ways to reimagine your business.

2) The market has changed.

When you first launched, customers might have wanted X, but months or years later, they might wish to Y. The key is to solve pain points and stay relevant. The data frames the story. Stay on top of metrics and key performance indicators like return, service calls, churn rate, etc. to keep up with changing customer needs. As mentioned above, talk to your customers to get a handle on their expectations and experiences. Then revise your plan accordingly so you can better align and connect the dots.

3) You need full-time people in contractor roles.

In the early stages, you might rely on freelancers as the engine of your business. This contingent worker can augment your staff resources, provide you flexibility as you pivot your business model, and fill in significant gaps.

You don't have to trudge through growing pains alone. Mentor networks range from serial entrepreneurs and c-suite executives, to subject matter experts and professional service providers. Their involvement is transactional, typically consisting of one-to-three meetings. Continuing the working relationship afterward may occur if you and your mentor consent to do so.

They'll work with you to guide on mission-critical matters, such as:

- Financial analysis, including investment and access to funding
- Business development and sales strategy
- Marketing strategies
- Human resources
- General management
- Strategic planning
- Partnership agreements
- Networking

Mentorship programs can be found at many small business centers that are flexible and available at your convenience, for every stage of development. The length and frequency at which you seek mentorship are entirely up to you and your mentor.

ii. Recession-Proof Your Business

Depending on whom you listen to, economists, or Fortune 500 CEOs, it seems like a recession might be expected sometime in 2022. That said, it is always best to prepare for the worst. That may look a little different according to the nature of one's business, but I believe there are a few key lessons we can learn from ventures that survived and even grew during the Great Recession of the late 2000s. When I wrote this observation about a recession, it was because of the political and economic climate considerations, little did I know there would be economic collapse because of a pandemic!

1) Do not skimp on marketing and innovation.

As a famous adage says, "When times are good you should advertise. When times are bad, you must advertise." While your knee-jerk reaction may be to cut your marketing budget to curb costs, this is a myopic view. You cannot grow your business without constant brand awareness, and you can't count on your customer base to stick with you—especially if they don't hear from you.

Amazon is an excellent example of a company that did not stave off innovation despite a global economic downturn. The recession struck retail companies, but the e-commerce giant was able to increase sales by nearly 25%! Why? Amazon introduced new products and launched new services, which helped drive revenue. Think about this fact—over 12,200 retail storefronts shuttered in 2020.[44]

2) Prioritize training and professional development.

Training can give you a competitive edge. Your sales force can learn new techniques and your current skills to bring in new business. If you're looking for a sales edge, I highly recommend searching online for a local company that specializes in sales training, professional coaching, and business consulting services to help you and your organization grow, as one-on-one training is often much more effective. If you are more of an autodidact, there are a myriad of books and online courses that can help hone your expertise.

3) Embrace an attitude of "we are in this together."

Be transparent and candid with your employees. If appropriate, show them financial performance metrics and projections. Don't be afraid to lay out specific parameters, like, "we need to increase sales by 15% in the next six months," or, "we need to secure three new customer contracts to diversify our revenue." This transparency may be the extra motivation they need to help your company survive—or even thrive during tough times.

Weathering a potential recession is difficult, but not impossible. Have realistic goals, and plan for the potential downside, ensure management is paying attention to the details, lay out your plans, and execute. Moreover, if you need further inspiration, look to organizations and leaders who have grown despite softness in the market. (For example, Disney after 9/11 is a great role model, and Jack Welch always said the time to build is when others are contracting.)

iii. Why Veterans Make Good Business Builders

Did you know that more than one in ten vets are business owners? While serving and protecting our country, U.S. military personnel learn vital lessons along the way that can be leveraged into civilian life. Naturally, veterans have a natural affinity for entrepreneurship. Here's a look at how military service can help equip individuals for the demands of building a business.

1) Focus, Prioritization, and Extreme Discipline

Business owners have to divide their attention to contend with competing priorities. However, it can be easy to lose focus and traction at the same time. The disciplined nature of the armed forces means they must stay focused to get from Point A to Point B. Therefore, military personnel are particularly adept at silencing distractions, quickly assessing situations, and identifying innovative and viable solutions.

The military tests people on all levels. As a result, there's a certain mental toughness and resilience that becomes incorporated into personal character. It takes a disciplined leader not to give up in a moment of weakness. Commitment is essential when steering a business through tough and turbulent times.

2) Spirit of Collaboration with a Systematic Approach

No man or woman is an island in the military, and the same holds in business. Teamwork builds successful companies. This mantra is something ingrained in those who serve because it can be a matter of life and death. You depend on one another for support. Prominent companies have competent and robust leadership, the bigger the company, the bigger the team.

Working with groups of people successfully also means clear communication. Veterans are at home with processes and procedures. You don't just hop into a jet and take off without running through the proper chain of command, as well as a checklist. That same attitude is a boon to business builders and their ventures, especially when the operation has many levels of intricacy and alliances.

3) Adaptability and Resourcefulness

Change is inevitable in the service—and the business world. In the military, stagnancy is a foreign concept. You're constantly adjusting to a change in circumstances. In the private sector, businesses must pivot when necessary and always look to improve.

Veterans are known to bring to the table a keen ability to find a way to bring a mission to fruition, come hell, or high water. This trait is an essential trait for a business builder to exhibit, as startups are often fraught with obstacles and adversity in the early stages.

By the way, if you're a veteran with a business idea and need help making it a reality, there are resources available. SBA programs provide access to capital and preparation for small business opportunities. They can also connect veteran small business owners with federal procurement and commercial supply chains.[45]

iv. Stuck? Here's How to Get Unstuck

It can happen to the best of us. Our business may be in growth mode for a while, and then we lose momentum for one reason or another. Plateaus happen. Companies are not immune to significant fluctuations in their business cycle. The challenge is knowing how to spot, assess, and plan for these unexpected situations so you can get back on track. The key is both managing the size of the dip and the duration of the decline.

The following are actionable steps (the 3 R's) you can take to reclaim your footing and reduce the adverse impact of the dip.

1) Reframe

Rather than honing-in on Failure, instead, shift your focus to celebrate your organization's wins and find ways to replicate or build off what's worked before. Why reinvent the wheel? Maybe there are some unmined nuggets of wisdom that could come out of this creative exploration.

You also might survey your most loyal clients as to why they keep coming back. It never hurts to express your appreciation. You might cross-sell, upgrade, or add-on to foster goodwill and drive additional incremental sales. While you're at it, ask them to be frank about ways in which you might improve. You could extend this practice to your team if you have employees. Just be sure that any feedback is anonymous so that people don't feel like negative comments could threaten their job security.

My organization began using continuous customer satisfaction and engagement system called Happy or Not. This system gives us real-time feedback on how things are going. In the first five months, we received nearly 10x the client and guest feedback we received in the entire year prior, providing us with useful intelligence on how we are doing.

2) Reconnect

Most people don't wake up as Steve Jobs or Elon Musk, so they don't even know what they don't know. Sometimes our dreams and aspirations only limit us. We believe that our work has value and a strong *why* behind it. In other words, we are untainted by Failure or the expectations we place on ourselves. However, as we advance in our business, we often get caught up in the day-to-day operations and lose touch with this passion that sustains us through the tough times. This often leads us to work in, and not *on* our business.

The antidote? If we can find a way to reconnect with the feelings that caused us to start or build our business in the first place, we may find new ways to resolve long-standing challenges. Perspective is everything.

3) Reflect and Recharge

Take a servant leader's approach. When in doubt, ask yourself, "How can I be of service?" When you feel you're in a creative valley, know that one way out is giving without the expectation of anything in return. Perhaps you become a mentor. What about serving as a keynote speaker at a charity event? Alternatively, maybe you consider how you can better provide, deliver, or reimagine a new service offering to your target audience. By giving back and paying it forward, you will recharge your batteries, likely making yourself a better you—not only for yourself but for the lives of those you come into contact with.

---

v. Three Ways to Overcome Founder's Syndrome

Entrepreneurs and business builders of organizations of all sizes often grapple with a psychological struggle known as Founder's Syndrome, a term used to refer to a leader's resistance to change, difficulty with giving up control, know-it-all mentality, and tendency to withhold information. If left unchecked, it can negatively impact the health and wealth of the Founder and the company, creating toxicity, negativity, and poor morale.

The key is to be self-aware, intentional, reflective, and willing to challenge your assumptions and beliefs.

1) Allow room for introspection and tame your self-worth

Take time and space to look at yourself as separate from your organization, and to examine the reasons you want to stay, as well as the costs and benefits to the company. Waiting just for the sake of self-preservation can be tempting. On the other hand, it is sometimes necessary to exit for the organization.

Sometimes you have to be honest with yourself. If you don't think the organization can survive without you and your leadership, you've probably answered that question because you haven't made sustainability a priority. Your attitude toward innovation and change in general directly impacts the future of the company. Ask yourself whether you care more about organizational legacy or personal self-worth. Find ways to augment your own learning and discovery—workshops, networking groups, self-help seminars, and mentors among all others.

2) Name your fears and address them head-on.

Create a succession plan that touches on all the "what-ifs" related to your potential departure. For example, let's say you are the current public-facing image of the company. What happens when you're no longer in the picture? How will staff adhere to your long-curated messaging to the media and public? Create a living document to provide a framework for public relations and guide future spokespeople with talking points about priorities.

3) Let go—early.

Live in the windshield and not the rearview mirror. While your vision and passion were what launched the business in the first place, you might have to make room for others to lead at some point. Relying on the same thought processes and actions as you did in the beginning, are not necessarily the best thing for the organization or its stakeholders and customers long-term. If you fear the vision would change if you weren't at the helm, perhaps it's time to let innovations unfold while you are still on board.

If all else fails, find strength in numbers. Chances are other founders who are experiencing the same struggles and frustrations. Make a point to aligning yourself with others in the same shoes. Having such support can allow you to be honest before it's too late to change direction.

Or maybe you need some advice about making this transition. Business coaching and mentorship programs may provide some clarity and a roadmap to enable your transformation. Don't hesitate to reach out.

---

vi. The Understated Introvert Advantage

When you think of a business builder, what qualities or personality traits come to mind? Maybe someone who has high energy and can effortlessly work a room, perhaps a Gladwell connector type? The truth is, while the business world can seem to acknowledge and value this sales and relationship orientation, we can't forget the introverts—the reflective, unassuming, thoughtful, and reliable types. Look at Warren Buffet and Bill Gates. They are both natural introverts and are considered by most people's standards to be successful business owners/builders. There are many other examples of introverted leaders who've shown they have what it takes to be robust and successful business builders.

Nearly 51% of the U.S. population's MBTI type[46] is introverted; let's look at why this is the case.

1) They are natural-born creators.

Introverts seek to innovate out of pure motivation to challenge themselves. They don't do it for external validation or glorification. In this way, they don't get as easily discouraged because they don't open themselves up to critique as early on.

2) They tend to be calculated (deliberate and intentional) in their decision making.

Introverts, by their very nature, might be somewhere sitting in quiet and solitude for hours. This isolation means they have the time and bandwidth to plan their next move methodically. Extroverts, however, tend to require a great deal of social interaction to feel fulfilled, which doesn't always allow for as much thoughtfulness in contemplation and planning.

3) They aren't afraid to lean on others for advice.

Introverted types are always looking for the best solutions, even if that means removing their egos from the equation. When building a business of any size, it pays to have the best and brightest people in your circle. Introverts are naturally adept at analyzing the ideas of others, offering thoughtful feedback, and taking into account what others have to offer. They are empathetic, sincere, and authentic (comfortable in their skin).

There are many ways in which our stereotypes and perceived value of what makes a successful business builder are stacked against introverts. However, in the world of business building, introverts can and *often do* thrive.

---

vii. Firing on all Cylinders: Ways to Push Forward

Growth and stagnation are natural parts of the business lifecycle. But what happens when you stay too long in the latter phase? It takes a savvy business owner to know how to ride those often-unpredictable waves.

Here's what engaged business leaders, and I have to say about moving past a plateau.

1) Go on a Fact-Finding Mission

As a business owner, you are often concerned with working in your business, versus *on* your business. This can be very detrimental to business growth, and this cycle of non-stop busyness (activity-based versus results-driven) usually means you are treating symptoms instead of looking at the causes.

For substantial growth to occur, you must peel back the layers and cut to the underlying issues. Is it a human capital problem? An aspect of your product or customer mix? How and what is your customer experience?

One of the things I enjoy doing to stay fresh and sharp is going on listening journeys. Several times during the year, Daryl (my colleague) and I went off to visit and meet with different businesses to learn about what they are doing to stay on top, how they are reinventing themselves, and what their biggest challenges and opportunities are. Once, we visited Airframe Components[47], and Roy, the owner, talked about how he bought the business from his father, challenges in working in a family business and pivoting the business model, how he treats and inspires loyalty with his employees, his inventory management advantage, and how he is expanding to meet the growing needs of his customers. I appreciated Roy for generously sharing his knowledge. I find that benchmarking information and insights are helpful for coaching and advising clients and also as critical inputs when we do our strategic planning about our programs, services, and environmental assumptions (think PEST analysis[48]).

2) Strike a Balance and Do Something Different

You and the team may be working crazy hours, but are you working smart? And how about work-life satisfaction? It is no longer about balance but how *satisfied* you are in the particular aspects of your work and life. If you're not showing up rested and renewed each day, your work suffers and productivity wanes. Make space for recharging your batteries (professional development, networking, reflection time, mastermind, etc.), and your company (… and you, and the bottom line) will benefit.

What does your Bill Gates-type sabbatical[49] or think-week look like for you? How can you recharge, reset and reimagine your venture's future?

3) Analyze and Continuously Improve Processes

Customer dissatisfaction and complaints can result from employee lack of training, turnover, experience, or misunderstanding. You might need to take a hard look at your culture, processes, and procedures and retool as necessary. The best customer experiences are orchestrated, consistent, and the quality of the interactions and engagement measured.

One of the best ways to push forward is simply to be open to change and opportunity. As the Founder, you likely have worn many hats and had your hands in all the aspects of the business during the early phases. However, as your operation grows and evolves, the need to empower and lean on others[50], as well as to trust in their capabilities, becomes even more necessary. Do you need to look at ways to have others step up and lead at the project, strategic business unit, or organizational level?

Plateaus and ruts happen and can be a wakeup call if we pay close enough attention. Be pro-active and willing to troubleshoot and pivot for the sake of your business venture's existence, livelihood, and your sanity.

---

viii. Got Grit?

What does it take to be a successful entrepreneur? Sure, a great idea and funding help. But there's one key element that separates the winners from those with less favorable outcomes. That variable is grit. Call it persistence, stick-to-it-tiveness, or tenaciousness. Grit is a theme that runs through the backstories of some of the most successful entrepreneurs.

1) Anyone can be gritty.

Everyone loves to read accounts of the underdog coming out on top. Often these people were able to rise above their circumstances to achieve greatness. In business, so much of our success hinges on good connections and a strong network of support, among other things. However, grit is an internal quality and not something bestowed on a privileged few. People from the most modest of means or dire circumstances can have grit. It doesn't discriminate on socioeconomic status, skin color, or gender.

2) Grit is passion and perseverance for long-term goals.

Angela Duckworth's book *Grit: The Power of Passion and Perseverance*[51] is worth the read. One of the many insights is to take the assessment she administered at West Point. You can find it here, the **Grit Scale**.[52] Greater self-awareness and reflection are critical aspects of the appraisal—it is no good or bad. It is how you see yourself. If you are unhappy with the result, the good news is grit can change over time, but like anything that can be nurtured or developed, you have to be intentional about it.

I believe grit is what can take aspiring entrepreneurs to the next level. The key is to strike a balance and temper it with patience. People with grit know when to step away from situations and revisit them with a clearer head. It's the difference between being proactive and reactive, or giving up or persisting.

3) Time + Experience + Survival = Grit

Omer Shai, the CMO of Wix.com, said it best in an article[53] for Entrepreneur: "Starting something isn't enough. The ability to persevere and be resilient after that something has been started is the true stamp of an entrepreneur. It's the people who stay the course and continue to invest in developing their enterprise beyond the starting point that should be the model for successful entrepreneurship." Resilience, adaptiveness, perseverance, and courage (one of my favorite words) are proxy words for gritty.

Shai makes an important observation when he talks about the necessary conditions for going beyond the starting point. The challenge is that unlike interpersonal skills, grit is a difficult thing to practice or affect. There aren't many useful exercises to flex your grit muscle. It's more of a case of experiences happening to you that require you to adapt and adjust—and thus become grittier.

How did you score on the grit scale? **I scored a 4.0 out of 5,** putting me in the 65th percentile of American adults. Quite frankly, I was hoping for higher. If you add up the odd-numbered questions and divide by 5, this gives you your passion score; if you add up the even-numbered items and divide by 5, this gives you your perseverance score. I bet one of those two descriptors trumps the other. This is where I will be doing some future self-reflection.

---

ix. Hypothesize, Experiment, Learn, and Pivot

"Failure is simply a cost you have to pay on the way to being right." — Seth Godin

I want to talk about the implications of Failure in professional growth and the development of your venture.

1) An opportunity for growth.

We tend to make Failure a personal thing. It can be hard to put distance between ourselves as entrepreneurs and our shortcomings in business. Put simply, we internalize Failure and tell ourselves negative messages, but smart and savvy entrepreneurs **never let Failure define them**. We can learn a lot from the scientific method when approaching Failure. What do scientists do when they want to prove something to be scientifically valid? They hypothesize and experiment—and repeat as necessary. Challenging legacy beliefs is not for the faint of heart. True innovation, at its core, disrupts legacy beliefs. The CEO of McDonald's challenged why they serve hamburgers in their restaurants. Marriott tested why a more communal living (sharing common space with separate bedrooms) approach to occupancy in its hotels may be appealing to business travelers over individual rooms.

Learning and growth occur in the process. In other words, the journey becomes more insightful than the destination. Your failures are simply observations that can help lead you to a *better* "right answer," or in the case of business—increase your odds of future success. Zig Ziglar got it right when he said, "***Failure is an event, not a person. Yesterday ended last night. Today is a brand-new day … and it's yours.***" Ziglar's comment is pretty uplifting and empowering!

2) Test, adjust, try again.

Of course, I don't mean to imply that you should intentionally make mistakes or that failing is easy or painless. Most of the time, we fail even when trying to do things "right." If you're focused on trying anything new in your business, then you're taking a chance and, in effect, experimenting. And as you know, with the scientific method, sometimes experiments don't go as planned. Our initial hypothesis can be proven wrong, and we sometimes have to start again from square one. Armed with new insights, inquiry, and observations, we can iterate and pivot to refine and improve our idea and connect the dots—data leading us to a better right answer.

3) Dare to fail.[54]

As I've said before, Failure is sometimes the price of admission for any venture worth pursuing. If you want to be an entrepreneur, you can't be afraid of the potential outcomes, which may include Failure, false starts, or big mistakes. As we all learned in our Corporate Finance class in college, the higher the risk, the higher the potential return. The challenge is to remove the emotion from Failure and when it occurs, to learn and recover quickly from it. How many times do you think the researcher who developed the polio vaccine had to start over? What about the inventor of the television? If they had accepted Failure as the only option, imagine how different the history books and our lives would be.

The lesson here? Always be experimenting, pivoting, and still be learning, discovering, and putting the pieces together—like a scientist. Keep in mind; you just need to start.

---

x. Resilience: The Key to Coping with Failure

According to the U.S. Bureau of Labor Statistics, about 50% of all new businesses survive five years or more, and about one-third survive ten years or more. U.S. SBA cites 34% of all businesses started will close in the first two years of operation. So why would anyone in their right mind start a company?

No business owner starts a venture to fail. Entrepreneurs are "all in." Failure is not an option ... or so they think. But sometimes, Failure is inevitable. When it happens, it can be a chance to pause and reflect on what you can do differently next time and increase your odds of a successful second, third, or fourth venture.

Successful leaders understand Failure is part of the game. Here are several practical ways to use Failure to your advantage and to identify it as Professor John Danner, author of *Failure: The Other "F" Word*[55], calls it, "a strategic resource":

1) Channel your emotions into something positive.

You have two choices at this juncture: wallow around in self-pity or be proactive and start fleshing out your next big idea. Find a way to transfer that nervous energy into motivation and don't waste precious time and emotional capital. **Smart and savvy eentrepreneurs are adaptive, iterative, and reflective.**

2) Don't forget about your passion.

You're far less likely to succeed if you pursue a concept that you don't love. After all, you must sell yourself first on the product or service before you can get customers on board. Fun is underrated. If you had little or no connection to your original concept, then maybe it's time to explore something that creates a visceral response this time around. **Smart and savvy entrepreneurs are passionate, intellectually curious, and determined.**

3) Resilience and resolve: part of the "Entrepreneurial DNA."

Entrepreneurs have resilience in their DNA. Take it from Richard Branson, Founder of the Virgin Group, who said: "You don't learn to walk by following the rules. You learn by doing, and by falling over."

Resilience means staying in the game, even when it's most inconvenient. Sometimes you have to remove all emotion from the situation and look at it from an outsider's perspective. For example, you might consider where things didn't happen the way you anticipated they would—feedback from customers? Production costs too high for a likely sale price of the product? What commercialization de-risking needed to happen but didn't? Once you have this intelligence, you can turn around and create something bigger and better next time around. **Smart and savvy entrepreneurs see around the corner, connect disparate dots, and possess incredible emotional intelligence.**

Homework:

Ask your boss or your board, out of every ten things you try, how many do you have to get right to be judged successful? This will help set the boundaries of how innovative you can be. The higher the number, the lower Failure is an option. This can be a fruitful conversation with your boss or board on what it takes to move the needle in your products or business model and to calibrate expectations.

Remember, Failure is a natural part of life—and business. The sooner we "lean into failure," the better off each of us will be.

---

xi. Lean into Failure with These Tips

As humans, we are inclined to bury and forget our failures. That's because Failure hurts and recalling past mistakes in our personal or professional lives can conjure up some painful or unpleasant memories. Despite all that, each of us needs to lean into Failure (sometimes called "pivots" in the startup world) because when we acknowledge, appreciate, and engage with our mistakes (learnings) and "do-overs," we can become a better-rounded individual and businessperson.

Below are some practices that might empower you to view Failure and risk differently and take more control of your company's trajectory.

1) Make peace with failures from years past.

Write down each of your major past business failures and share them with a mentor or trusted advisor. Practice saying, "This experience taught me _____ and has prepared me to be _____." Being at home with failures that take up headspace can open many powerful doors. This exercise also allows you to break old patterns that might be holding you back, make real changes, and improve your future performance.

2) Acknowledge that failure is par for the course.

To fail at something doesn't mean that *you* have failed. It only means you were unable to perform in a particular area. Failure teaches us what didn't work and allows us to consider other options that might even serve you better than the initial plan. When you learn to use failures as a launching pad for your next action, it can be fun!

3) Process recent failures instead of compartmentalizing.

Create a regular practice to dialogue about the details of your failures as they happen. Connecting with a trusted mentor or business associate about what you learned, how it made you feel, what you might do the next time differently, etc., is conducive to mental health. We all need a safe environment to experiment and risk ourselves.

The byproduct of this habit is that you consciously release any emotional baggage around failures that are left unresolved. Once again, by clearing the air, you will be more equipped to experience future shortcomings in a more intentional and meaningful way.

Aside from all this acceptance of failure business—don't forget to **celebrate your successes.** Create rituals that honor your victories along the way. We tend to move on to the next big thing. Most importantly, acknowledging our failures takes courage and resolve. Be courageous because Failure is inevitable, but how you recover, grow, and change as a result of Failure is squarely in each of our hands.

---

xii. How to Weather Economic Ups and Downs

Highs and lows are part of life—and business is no exception. No enterprise is immune to the fickle and unpredictable nature of a competitive marketplace. The truth is all business climates are entrenched in cyclical patterns that business leaders must accept in exchange for the opportunity to pursue entrepreneurial dreams. When I worked at G.E. in the 80s and 90s, Jack Welch always believed that the time to double down was when others were retrenching in adverse economic conditions. It helped ensure your ability to win when things rebounded.

While the overall economy may pose some threat to small businesses, most owners may be more in control than they think. That's because even in down markets, people spend money and buy goods and services.

Better managed and leveraged businesses are the ones that come out ahead following weak market conditions—if they prepare for the ride.

There are several things you can do now to survive and ride the natural ebb and flow of the market:

1) Always Keep Marketing and Always Be Closing (ABC)

When times are bad, it's tempting to take a myopic view of your business and gut the marketing budget. But that's the *worst* thing you can do. Instead, consider focusing your marketing firepower funds on the most optimal channels like online, content marketing, and social media. You have to build relationships based on shared and mutual value.

2) Remain Innovative

When there's any inkling of tough times head, weak competitors will go into hibernation mode. This is prime time for creative business leaders to make their moves and gain market share. Get to know your clientele better to offer additional **value-added solutions** that best serve their needs.

3) Find smart Tax Advice and Maximize the Highs

Taxes may be the single most significant cost to a small business. A solid strategy developed by a tax professional can reduce your tax burden. That newfound cash flow can be used for marketing, expansion, or reinvestment in the business.

In good times, take the time to prepare for the long haul and focus on the broader strategy. By running your business, a minimum of 90 days ahead, you'll likely be proactive versus reactive to volatility. A general rule of thumb: All small businesses should maintain a cash reserve of six months of expenses at all times. A strong line of credit can also provide a cushion for unexpected opportunities or surprises.

No matter what the state of the market is, you should **always be straightforward**. You owe it to your employees to communicate the state of the company regularly. When engaged and informed, employees become understanding and helpful. When things are good, reward them. Then they'll be more apt to stand by you and work extra hard. Celebrate the small successes along the way. It breeds higher self-confidence and a little more swagger when you need it most.

Chapter 4: Conclusion

"When the going gets tough, the tough get going" is a famous saying as it reminds us that difficulties are typical, and they don't mean you should stop, but that it's time to kick it into high gear. Tough times are chances for growth, opportunity, and inspiration—just like Failure is part of the creative path. Life is hard, running a business is hard, but we will continue on, and do the hard things. As President John F. Kennedy said in his famous speech at Rice University, "we choose to go to the moon … and do the other things … not because they are easy, but because they are hard because that goal will serve to organize and measure the best of our energies and skills."

Surround yourself with people who make you better. This is the practical advice I give my three boys about girlfriends and potential wives, and it is the same advice I give business builders about finding suitable mentors, partners, and investors.

Resiliency personal, professional and business is more important now than ever before. In these straining and traumatic economic times. Business resiliency is essential to your venture's ability to create a "runway" for stabilization, sustainability, and long-term success.

Building and maintaining a business requires the most, the best, and all of your abilities, even some that you haven't developed yet. It requires your complete dedication, constant commitment, and continual improvement. You will experience highs and lows and have to adapt continuously, but with the right tools and mindset, you can succeed. You must intend to win, to overcome any hurdle.

Chapter 4: Questions for Consideration

i. Time to Recalibrate?

Are you in a dry spell? Has the market shifted? Looking for full-time contractors? It may be time to recalibrate. Reach out to your local small business center or development center and investigate a mentorship relationship. Calling on outside help can fast-track changes and provide a valuable outside perspective.

ii. Recession-Proof Your Business

"A man who stops advertising from saving money is like a man who stops a clock from saving time," Henry Ford once said. Remember this next time you want to cut your marketing budget. Similarly, you should never stop learning. What are you currently studying? Take any kind of class to help bolster or supplement a skill deficit you may have. Read up on companies that made it through hard times and see what you can glean from their experiences—even if it's just the inspiration to carry on.

iii. Why Veterans Make Good Business Builders

Without going overboard, what military-like characteristics can you apply to your business or entrepreneurial approach? Having the mental toughness and courage to see things through till the end is probably the most basic and valuable trait to embrace.

Find ways to exercise and incorporate a military mindset into your practice for self-improvement, both on the business and your personal life. Even sticking rigorously to a schedule with regular exercise will catalyze positive effects.

iv. Stuck? Here's How to Get Unstuck

If you have recently struggled with a plateau, how did you work your way out of it? Make a chart with these three sections: Reframe, Reconnect, Reflect, and Recharge. Write out your plan of attack for each phase and execute it!

v. Three Ways to Overcome Founder's Syndrome

If you're a startup founder who has successfully walked away—how did you overcome the tendencies associated with Founder's Syndrome? Have you ever considered being a mentor? Talking someone through how you dealt with this situation could be a valuable experience for both of you.

vi. The Understated Introvert Advantage

Are you an introvert or an extrovert? For additional reading on this topic, Susan Cain's *Quiet: The Power of Introverts in a World That Can't Stop Talking*[56] is absorbing and advises on communicating better no matter which category you fall into.

vii. Firing on all Cylinders: Ways to Push Forward

Need to power up before moving forward? Consider some new fuel for your tank, from a new routine, new fact-finding mission, even a break, mix something fresh into your schedule and work on gaining an alternative perspective. Have you considered a business retreat? Also, getting out of your daily routine can help shake things up mentally.

viii. Got Grit?

Who in your life is gritty? What can you learn from their behavior? The next time things get hard, and you consider giving up, recognize that this is a chance to develop your gritty-ness. Persevere, and when you come out on the other side, you will be wiser and just a little grittier.

ix. Hypothesize, Experiment, Learn, and Pivot

When was the last time you intentionally permitted yourself to fail? Instead of viewing it as a negative, try viewing it as an opportunity for growth and as a way to learn. Creativity and Failure go hand in hand, just ask Disney Chairman and CEO Bob Iger—"successful failures" are essential steps toward innovation.[57]

x. Resilience: Key to Coping with Failure

The more you talk about Failure and failing, the less scary and paralyzing it will become. Talk with your boss, your board, or the people you work with about what will happen when someone fails. Managing expectations and knowing worst-case scenarios will eliminate the fear of the unknown. If those around you have been prepped for some failures, and there are no consequences, then your creativity has a chance to go wild and try something new. Don't hold back.

xi. Lean into Failure with These Tips

After you've cleared the air and dealt with past failures, concentrate on how much you've grown with each Failure. Write down all the successes, new perspectives, or advancements in patience and endurance that are dealing with and overcoming Failure has brought about. Keep a jar of "wins," or any small victory, and consciously recall how they relate to past failures. Review at the end of the month, or quarter, and reflect on the journey. The more you think about Failure and what it can eventually lead to, the less power it will have to hold you back.

xii. How to Weather Economic Ups and Downs

Does your business have a cash reserve? Now more than ever having adequate cash reserves is a business imperative. There are many potholes you might experience financially and having a cash plan may be essential to managing potential liquidity issues. Soliciting professional tax advice may help your company save money, which can be put into an emergency safeguard for turbulent times. Get your finances sorted now, so you won't have to cut crucial elements like marketing later. Find a new tax advisor if necessary. Have you celebrated or rewarded your employees lately? Can you do it this week? They can easily be your biggest supporters in tough times if you treat them right; human capital is one of the wealthiest commodities a business can leverage. Take action today.

CHAPTER 5

FUNDING

You have an idea, a product, a service, and the drive. No matter if you're already up and running, or trying to get off the ground, there will come the point where your business needs money. Deciding on how to best fund your business venture is no easy task and requires much consideration across all fronts. Can you do it yourself? Bootstrap your way through? Or what about outside funding? Either way, you're going to have to make some hard choices and stick to them.

Funding is often a highly misunderstood aspect of building a successful and sustainable venture. The entrepreneurial mythology often placing more emphasis on investors and rounds of funding than finding actual customers for your product or services. Despite popular folklore, the vast majority of new ventures bootstrap and self-fund. They don't take outside investment from angels or venture capitalists.

The good news is, many others have gone before you, and there are blueprints and roadmaps for you to follow if you believe outside investment is in your best interest given how difficult it is to find suitable investors and how it changes the trajectory of the type of company you are building.

i. Crowdfunding: Is It for you?

I recently heard a sobering statistic today, 1:72 ventures applying for funding from the Tech Coast Angels (this is pre-COVID-19) was successful. UNH Center for Venture Research says, on average, 15% of early-stage companies that are brought to the attention of investors result in an investment.

As an alternative method to raising outside capital, I talked with industry expert Kathleen Minogue, Founder & CEO of Crowdfund Better[58], to put this misunderstood investment approach in perspective and to peel back the onion on investment strategies for early-stage ventures. When considering various economic stimulus approaches and funding mechanisms, it may be worthwhile to consider crowdfunding.

Definitions:

Crowdfunding is a large number of people sharing small amounts of their social, creative, and financial capital via the internet within a limited time window.

OR

Crowdfunding is an old-fashioned barn raising using new digital tools.

Karl: When does it make sense for micro-enterprises to use crowdfunding as a platform for access to funding?

Kathleen: It makes sense for micro-businesses to be thinking about crowdfunding from Day 1—long before they need funding. People often focus on the "funding" in crowdfunding. Still, you can also gather several non-financial benefits through the crowdfunding process that will help your business generate revenue in the future and make your business more resilient.

For example, crowdfunding can help you get proof of concept and market validation for your business idea while acquiring customers, testing pricing, and getting customer feedback.

Crowdfunding is also a way to market your business and acquire funding simultaneously. You can use the same marketing dollars you would have used to help people discover your company to raise capital via crowdfunding.

Karl: What are the three most important critical success factors in launching a successful campaign?

Kathleen:

1) **Story** —_A specific project with a compelling story and a clear call to action.
2) **Relationships/Communication Channels** — Crowdfunding's success depends on the width and depth of your networks. These networks can be those you have built personally or a network of engaged community members around your business.
    You can build a beautiful campaign page, but if no one sees it, it won't raise a penny. Identify which online and offline channels are best to communicate with potential backers.
3) **Consistency** — People are, busy so you will need to reach out multiple times to encourage them to take action. Have systems in place to support consistent communication with your network.

Karl: I was struck by the 2017 PWC Women Unbound Study[59] that found women are better at crowdfunding than men? Why is this so?

Kathleen: A study out of UC Berkeley and Northwestern University[60] found that language was one reason why women see greater success at crowdfunding than men. The researchers revealed that women tend to use more relational and less transactional language than men do when they crowdfund.

Women's crowdfunding stories are also more compelling because they use more inclusive language. They focus less on the money and more on connecting with others who have an affinity for what they do. As I mentioned earlier, the ability to tell your story in a way that makes people feel connected with your business is integral to crowdfunding success.

Karl: What are the most significant benefits of crowdfunding over more traditional private equity funding options for a young, early-stage venture?

Kathleen: When you raise money privately, the upside is that you also benefit from the perspective of a handful of experienced investors. Still, statistically, only a small number of companies are funded by these investors.

What if you could reach out to a much wider group of financial supporters to raise the capital you need? Instead of looking to one person to invest $10,000, you could try raising that same $10,000 from 100 people contributing $100 each.

In 2019, less than 3% of venture capital went to women, and less than 1% went to people of color. In crowdfunding, your potential backers represent the actual demographics of the market for goods and services. This opens the door to funding for a greater diversity of entrepreneurial ideas.

About Kathleen Minogue:

Kathleen Minogue is Founder and CEO of Crowdfund Better. This crowdfunding consultancy guides entrepreneurs, small businesses, and social enterprises on how to use crowdfunding strategically to unlock the financial and creative support of their networks and to empower individuals and communities with new capital-raising tools to fund projects not supported by traditional finance. She has coached highly successful donation, rewards, and investment campaigns and is mainly focused on bringing the crowdfunding opportunity to women, minorities, and rural entrepreneurs.

A thought leader in crowdfunding, Kathleen has been featured in *The Wall Street Journal* and *Forbes*, contributed to industry publications *Crowdfund Insider* and *Local Investing*, and has presented at venues including the Director's Guild of America, Association for Women's Business Centers National Conference, and Global Crowdfunding Convention. She has also contributed to international and local access to capital initiatives, including the *PwC Women Unbound* report, the *Milken Institute/SBA Partnership for Lending in Underserved Markets,* and *The Local Crowd 4SE Incubator* funded by the National Science Foundation. Kathleen sits on the board of With Love Market & Cafe, SPC, and is an advisor to the OmniWorks US Incubator.

---

ii. Lessons from the Campaign Trail–The Advocacy Imperative

Don't be alarmed I am not going to talk politics other than to make an analogy between campaigning and business building.

Looking back on the 2020 presidential election season, we saw how each candidate approached his campaign. Some are veterans, and others are relative newbies to the scene. The campaign showed it takes more than money to be a legitimate presidential candidate. Still, regardless of platform or political party, business builders Today can learn a lesson or two from the "business" of politics.

1) Rally Support

Whether on the debate stage or in the boardroom, you need to be at home by asking for support. Campaigns need money, grassroots support, and other resources to thrive. Similarly, business builders need capital and talent—entrepreneurial resource partners and help organizations, service providers, mentors, investors, and customers—in their corner to advance the organization. After all, it takes a community—an entrepreneurial one—to succeed, regardless of the context. Leaders that take we/us approach and not an I/me one is better positioned to accomplish their goals.

2) Hold Yourself Accountable

Politicians make promises on the stump. They know their reputation is at stake come reelection, so it's imperative to say what you mean and mean what you say. The same goes for business builders. When you market a product or service, customers count on you to stand behind the claim—your personal credibility is at stake. Companies that have generous warranty programs are more trusted than those that don't stand behind their quality. For example, all Away Carry-On cases come complete with a limited lifetime warranty[61] that covers any damage to the shell, wheels, handles, zippers, or anything else that functionally impairs the luggage. The electronic components are guaranteed for two years.

However, recently, I had a bad experience at an Embassy Suites by Hilton in Florida, and their "we'll *make it right promise*[62]" actually translates into, "*what is the least we can do to make you go away?*" Contrast Hilton's lack of empathy and bureaucratic customer experience and service recovery efforts with the incredible stories I am reading in *The Power of WOW*[63], and you would never buy anything from anyone other than Zappos.[64] In short, if you have a promise—you better live up to it in the moments of truth.

How can you earn trust in a time of a great discontinuity[65]? This is the million-dollar question for candidates and business leaders alike.

3) Stand Out—Be a Seth Godin "Purple Cow"

One of the keys to an influential political campaign is the candidate's ability to carve out a niche policy-wise. How are they different from the status quo, and what will that mean to the electorate? Business builders can take a similar approach in the marketplace by building and telling a brand story. By communicating how their business model is different and better, potential customers, partners, and investors can better understand how you will add value. Remember, what former Proctor & Gamble's CEO A.G. Lafley said regarding leveraging innovation for a winning business strategy: **"Winning is at the nexus of a company having a unique market position, leveraging a sustainable competitive advantage, and delivering superior value to its customers."**

Bottom Line: Today, business builders are competing for funding and resources, so finding ways to be remarkable, sticky, and memorable is paramount to success. While some politicians can buy their way to a debate stage by spending over $460 million, most business builders have to earn their way to success—one building block at a time.

---

iii. An Entrepreneurial Mandate—The Business Case for Indiana

The Indiana Chamber's Vision 2025[66] makes a sobering observation, "Despite economic momentum and new business creation in certain regions of the state, the overall Kauffman ranking for new entrepreneurs declined again—with Indiana's rank falling from 44th to 47th. This points to the ongoing importance of regional economic development and quality of place initiatives."

Unfortunately, business creation (the rate of new venture formation) has been on a national decline for many decades. Sadly, Kauffman stated, "In a given month, only three out of every 1,000 people start a business.[67] Moreover, the startup rate is lower for the young and underserved.[68]"

The Kauffman Foundation smartly observed, "Globally, entrepreneurship has become an economic priority, and the U.S. has fallen behind.[69]" I would add that Indiana, in particular, is missing opportunities to ensure its economic priorities align with the pillars required for a thriving entrepreneurial community. It takes a lot more than outside capital to build a successful startup. Talent, workspaces, and networks are prerequisites for success.

Three key things I think you should keep in mind as we focus squarely on the new venture formation rate:

1) When there is low unemployment (and especially when there is wage growth versus wage stagnation like we have had for a long time in the U.S. and Indiana in particular), entrepreneurship venture formation rate typically declines.

2) Millennials are not as interested in the entrepreneurial career path because of cultural attitudes, biases, and high student debt loads.
3) Underestimated founders are not able to fully participate in entrepreneurial endeavors at the same rate as their non-diverse counterparts because they acutely face barriers and obstacles—management, money, markets, and mentorship. This untapped entrepreneurial pipeline is a big opportunity for Indiana to differentiate itself from its peers.

While there isn't a one-size-fits-all solution, it will take more than regional economic development and quality of place initiatives to solve these many decade-old problems. There needs to be targeted, segmented strategies to leveling the playing field for all interested and motivated business builders based on their unique circumstances, barriers, and obstacles. We do a considerable disservice to entrepreneurs by classifying them generally into categories—lifestyle, scalable, growth, etc.—versus categorizing them by their unique story and needs.

Equally, it is disturbing, to say the least to me that one contributing writer to *Forbes* magazine concluded, "Now, the class is, even more, a factor in our concept of entrepreneurship.[70]" Entrepreneurship is the best anti-poverty program, and it should be a great equalizer for everyone to participate in economic prosperity. We can't aspire or settle for less nationally, regionally, or locally.

The Urban Institute defines "inclusive recoveries as those occurring when a place overcomes economic distress in a way that provides the opportunity for all residents—**especially historically excluded populations**—to benefit from and contribute to economic prosperity."

The greatest opportunities for new venture formation lie with our most marginalized segments – rural, minorities, women, formerly incarcerated, disabled and others who have fallen through societal cracks. Our next generation of successful entrepreneurs will reflect a different breed than the stereotypical and prototypical type of entrepreneur we have traditionally seen in America.

We can't ignore the untapped potential in our pipeline. By fully integrating and engaging all members of our community—especially those in historically excluded populations, we can tap into our talent pool. A 2018 report[71] found that more than 70% of startups still have no women on their board of directors, and 57% have no women in executive roles. It's a bit of a chicken-and-egg problem. Many entrepreneurial women business owners have shared with me that they don't need heroes or saviors, but opportunities, networks, mentors, and relevant experiences to boost their confidence and lift themselves and each other up. This is why entrepreneurial programs geared toward women fill such an important role in addressing the gap in entrepreneurial gender equity.

In short, our goal should be to curate and maintain an environment that creates the right opportunities for underestimated founders to participate and achieve their unique human and financial potential fully. If we do so, Indiana's startup ranking will rise, reflecting greater inclusive economic prosperity and higher levels of entrepreneurial energy and potential.

iv. What Makes a Great Pitch? Start Here

Ah ... the investor pitch. While it's not necessarily an indicator of future success, it can propel your business venture or idea forward. A great pitch can attract the right kind of attention and lead to potential partnerships and outside investment.

This is your time to shine. Everyone wants to craft a winning presentation that captivates their audience's attention—but how?

The following are some of the critical things to keep in mind as you prepare to "wow" your potential investors:

1) Know your story—and your numbers.

There is no one better than you to share your *why*. Watch the Simon Sinek TED Talk if you don't know your why. As Simon reminds us, people may get what you do but not *why* you do it. Your passion and the problem or pain you identified for creating the company may make a big difference in investor sentiment. Remember, studies have shown that the initial screening of the company by angel investors is about the deal, but ultimate investment (writing the check) is about you—the chemistry, the trustworthiness, your team, and your track record.

Part of your story includes your stats. There is nothing worse than a story that doesn't hang together with the numbers. You need to know the key drivers and sensitivities of what drives value and relate that to potential investors. You should know your economic drivers of value and be able to answer critical questions about your likely hockey stick projections and what drives them. Otherwise, your credibility will be in jeopardy. There is a reason only 15-18% of early-stage ventures seeking outside capital typically receive any early-stage investment.

2) Know what differentiates you—what's your secret sauce?

If you say you have no competitors or that you only need 0.5% of a giant or growing market, you and your pitch are done. You must have traditional or non-traditional competitors, and you must be able to narrow your customer segment in a way that builds investor confidence. Can you identify your potential customers by name or type? Do your financial projections identify the specific customer segments and types in the pro forma? If not, keep working on it because you are not ready. Do you or your team members have any domain expertise in the industry in which the business operates?

3) Know if you want a boss.

This is *the most* essential thing to think about. When you take outside, third-party investment, you are getting a boss, whether you like it or not. Think this through before taking someone else's money because it is a game-changer. Sometimes (and in fact, many times), it is better to find customers first. Your valuation and ownership are most vulnerable when you have not de-risked the venture when you have not validated your product, when you have no assets or brand equity, and when you don't have paying customers.

Here are some key things to keep in mind for the art of the pitch:

1) Practice your pitch out loud and record it.

It would be best if you did more than memorize or recite your thoughts in your head. This doesn't always translate to quality delivery. The best tactic is to practice out loud so you can pinpoint any mistakes or missing content and adjust accordingly. This is also a good idea so you can make sure the length is appropriate. Doing it in front of a mirror can help you assess your body language and make changes, too. Tell a story. Pause often. Listen. Don't interrupt the investor's questions or say you will answer them later. Be sure to answer the question you are being asked directly. If you don't know the answer, say so, and that you will get back to the investor.

To take this a step further, put your smartphone or tablet to work. You might dislike seeing or hearing yourself at first, but this tip can help you hone your pitch. Video can help you observe any nervous ticks and poor posture, both of which can detract from your message. So, don't be afraid to record several versions until you're confident you've got it dialed in. Time is on your side, so don't be scared to use it! Practice, iterate, and adjust your pitch with the guidance and knowledge of a business coach or mentor. Your flow and delivery need to be natural, and you need to be confident.

2) Rehearse in a similar situation.

Fear of the unknown can cause anxiety and make you feel less prepared on the day of the big event. If you have the luxury, practice beforehand in a similar setting or context. This will allow you to get a feel for how your voice carries and your relation to the audience spatially. When you are prepared to face your audience, you will appear more confident and more poised to succeed because you have accounted for significant variables. You don't want to walk into a situation blind. Remember, the pitch is the beginning of developing a relationship with potential investors. If you have a product demo, make sure it works. If your pitch depends on high-speed internet, make sure you have it. You don't get a second chance of making a great first impression.

3) Seek honest feedback.

Do you have a brutally honest friend or family member? That's the person you want to recruit to test-market your pitch. Ask them to evaluate you through a critical lens. What did they love? What did they hate? Did your message get through to them? What would they change? Were there any questions left unanswered? Do you know your product or service inside and out? Listen and then take their feedback to heart and prepare for any worst-case scenarios.

Remember, some companies have become serial pitch competition winners, but that doesn't mean they are building a thriving entrepreneurial company. It just means they are good at pitching. When you read a pitch deck of all the competitions they have won, you should begin to worry about whether they have lost their focus.

There are considerable pitch resources on the internet, including examples of high impact presentations, pitch clinic sites who work with you to fine-tune your message and story, and outside advisors who can coach, encourage, and support you in your efforts.

---

v. Lessons from Shark Tank

Shows like "Shark Tank" have made the concept and discussion of angel investing more commonplace, but we should not forget that Shark Tank is about show ratings. While the show premiered in the U.S. nearly a decade ago, there are several worthwhile lessons Shark Tank offers business builders.

1) Know your value.

You won't go far without knowing your benefit—and owning it. The sharks can sniff out when the entrepreneur doesn't have a solid base. As a result, they can see reduced valuations, passing on attractive investments and keen insights of a fatal flaw in the business model requiring a pivot because the business builder doesn't have a viable Plan B, or they often walk away empty-handed. The best business builders are contingency-minded.

Where do you stand in the proverbial food chain? In business, if you aren't on top, you'll be eaten by new disruptive thinkers or market-smart competitors. In other words, think like a shark. Small or large, your business depends on sound judgment and prudence. No matter the industry, you'll have a better chance of surviving if you set the terms of engagement, and don't let anyone take advantage of you.

2) Show up prepared.

Winning in business (and life) means putting in the time to do your homework—about customers, the market, your business model, the customer channels, and the value proposition. The business builders who leave the show with an attractive deal usually have a substantial and validated pain/problem/opportunity and the tenacity and resilience to make things happen. They also have mastered the art of tailoring their message to the right audience. As a result, they actively listen, anticipating the questions the sharks might pose and are prepared to respond thoughtfully and intelligently. Even if they aren't successful on the show, they can walk away knowing they did everything they could to make the best impression and have a better understanding of their business' financial picture.

3) Don't take things personally.

Business is business, and that means business builders need to learn how not to internalize criticism. One of the reasons the show had such high ratings (in the earlier seasons) is that it capitalized on the tension between the business builders and the sharks. These tensions are real in how business builders interact with angel investors every day. Put simply, "Shark Tank" has harnessed the power of suspense. As a professional, you have to learn to manage pressure and not let it get to you. You've heard the expression, "never let them see you sweat." The business builders who go home with a deal know how to separate their ego from their idea (they demonstrate humility, grit, and passion in their interactions with others). They are mindful of their communications and look at situations objectively. **Business owners who fold under pressure never come out winners.**

---

vi. Is Your Venture Really Investment Worthy?

Many entrepreneurs yearn for the day when an angel or venture capital (V.C.) firm is interested in helping them get to the next level. But without a strong track record coupled with the right contacts, it can be hard to identify the right opportunities.

While it is sexy to say your venture is venture-backed or angel-backed before you embark on V.C. or angel investment, you have to realize a couple of sobering realities:

- Only 0.6% of businesses ever raise V.C.
- 78% of all V.C. went to 3 states (N.Y., MA, CA) in 2019[72]
- <1% went to rural areas
- <2% went to women founders
- 1% went to African American and Latino Founders.

That said, entrepreneurs should keep the following points in mind if they wish to be more attractive to potential outside investment.

1) Determine your comfort level and check your attitude.

Are you more comfortable with the idea of bootstrapping, or open to the higher stakes potential that comes with angel and V.C. funding? This is an essential question because it can affect autonomy (or lack thereof). Some founders wish to keep the reins close so they can direct and execute their vision, even if it means more sacrifices. Others may look to build skills and a more robust network through such means as an incubator or accelerator program. Most founders try to raise money too soon in the venture's life and often give up more control and equity than is necessary. Find paying customers before taking someone else's money. Remember, once you take someone else's money, you have a boss.

Speaking of working with people, are you coachable, or do you come across as knowing it all? How willingly do you accept feedback? Investors want to see that you have the E.Q. to empower people and lead and inspire diverse teams. Many are using psychometric assessments and other tools to vet emotional intelligence more formally. Dissonance in the management team is one of the top three reasons new ventures fail.

2) Evaluate your team.

Investors will put your founders and core team under the microscope. That means considering the experience and past successes. For example, if a founder has proven he/she has what it takes to set their mind to do something (and achieve it), then investors will feel more confident about potential outcomes. Research studies show that at the time of first discussions with angels it is about the deal, but at the time of the decision about whether to do the deal, it is all about the founder and his/her team (domain expertise, chemistry, trustworthiness, etc.)

3) Think beyond the here and now.

Potential investors want to see a business model and evidence of planning that indicates you've given thought to how you'll get from Point A to B. That means robust financial projections, marketing plans, customer segmentation, and business intelligence, among other things. Also, they will expect to see a credible, not theoretical exit strategy.

In short, you have to have some critical pieces in place to ensure that your business is investor ready.

Capital fuels growth. Plain and simple. High-performance companies require constant access to a continuum of capital to ensure stable, long-term success. To capitalize on product introductions, geographic market expansions, strategic acquisitions, and new customer segments, you'll need financial partners capable of growing with you.

---

vii. How to Invest in Yourself on a Budget

Young or budding business builders often don't always have the funding to invest in expensive seminars or life coaches. However, they can tap into free or low-cost resources to develop personally and professionally. Here are three ways to invest in yourself on the cheap:

1) Read

This sounds simple, right? But according to Pew Research, "About a quarter of American adults (24%) say they haven't read a book in whole or in part in the past year, whether in print, electronic or audio form." I read about 3-4 books a month, a myriad of blogs, and at least 3-5 research papers. Charlie "Tremendous" Jones said, and I agree, "Leaders are readers." Jim E. Johnson has a terrific technique[73] for polishing off a book in a month or less. Be sure to visit the link in the endnotes and check it out. Everyone can be successful in reading a book if they follow his straightforward approach.

I love reading about entrepreneurship, innovation, self-help, and books on market trends and the stock market. A library card can genuinely be the portal to unlimited knowledge. And the great thing about learning is that no one can take it away from you. In other words, books can take you to places you've never been and inspire you to think and act differently. And these days, there are no excuses not to read continuously. Whether a physical, electronic, or audiobook, you can take a book with you virtually anywhere.

2) Network

People can be your most significant resource. Reach out and connect with people who you admire for a meeting—and truly listen to what they have to say. Thank them for their time and offer to help how you can. You might even find a mentor in the process. Attending a Global Leadership Summit or joining local networking or a mastermind group may just be the ticket to new insights and knowledge. Go on learning journeys or schedule breakfast or lunch meetings with exciting people.

What's something in your business that you're frustrated with that you know could be better? Look to resources in your community (and beyond) for help. Many small business centers have free monthly workshops geared to innovators, business builders, and corporate leaders. These skill-building, competency-based workshops might just be the edge you are looking for in your life and are excellent places to network.

3) Find your "happy place" by staying centered.

It's easy to feel frazzled as a business owner. Clients often wanted things yesterday, and you're juggling multiple obligations at once—while trying to pay the bills. Eating, right, exercising, and finding some time for joy daily is essential to keeping your cool. Maybe you can't take a whole day off, but can you take a 30-minute walk and regroup? Studies show that exercise has the power to make you healthier and wealthier, so it's sound business sense to exercise self-care. Carve out, "me time."

Part of staying centered means you know your limits and respect them. A grounded person knows when to say "no" and has the maturity to realize it's not personal. People will respect you more when they know they can count on you—and that starts with not biting off more than you can chew.

---

viii. Early Stage Investing Trends

A sobering but realistic article was shared with me called "The Early Stage Slump."[74] Today's reality—inflated early-stage valuations are/were unsustainable, and the early stage bubble did burst.

This article makes several important points about the investor's appetite for getting into a deal early. The article opines that investors are being more selective in their investments and moving upstream toward Series A type of investments and reminds me of three key points that should be kept in mind by entrepreneurs as they decide on their funding strategy for their business.

1) You must price your round appropriately.

Given investors have to plan to lose 60-80% of their investments, they need to structure for a 10-30x (the article says 20, but many strive for 30) to get the winners to cover the losers. Realistic pricing may make the difference between a successful, fully subscribed round, and a seed round that can't get off the ground (historically, about 1 in 7 early-stage deals looking for money get any). Entrepreneurs need to remember—valuation is not about what ownership percent you are willing to give up, but about a reasonable price with appropriate investor upside for the risks inherent in your business model.

2) Executing a robust, dynamic, and winning business model is essential.

A business model with multiple bites at the apple will distinguish itself from the one-trick ponies. Pivoting is a badge of honor, not a mark of shame. However, pivoting fast and cheap is the difference between a savvy team and likely business failure or false start. Execution is paramount and critical. A Harvard Business Review article[75] entitled, *What is a Business Model*, explains: "A good business model answers Peter Drucker's age-old questions, 'Who is the customer? And what does the customer value?' It also answers the fundamental questions every manager must ask: How do we make money in this business? What is the underlying economic logic that explains how we can deliver value to customers at an appropriate cost?"

3) A focus on finding and securing customers goes a long way to validating customer pain.

Paying customers can absolve lots of early-stage commercialization sins. Finding paying customers who buy into your solution as a means to solve their pain/problem is a big step forward in validating your business model. Answering the question—what does your customer value (and what are they willing to pay for)—is critical to success.

---

ix. Three Ways to Bootstrap Your Business

Bootstrapping is a fancy word for "self-funding" your venture. Self-funding can take many different flavors—credit cards, friends and family, customer billable projects, and the like. While a small percentage of all ventures can secure third party investment from angel investors, the average U.S. startup launched today requires upwards of $117,000 to start a company (Census Bureau estimates escalated into 2017 dollars). By being well-capitalized, it is less likely that these ventures will close.

The stresses of starting and growing a company are daunting—making payroll, purchasing materials, buying equipment, finding talent, and making sales calls to potential customers—it is no wonder why, so few people consider entrepreneurship a viable career option. While some startup costs are inevitable, there are ways to rein in expenses smartly.

1) Conduct fieldwork.

A well thought out strategy allows for flexibility, change, and a pivot if necessary. Planning means zeroing in on your goals, rather than only running with a concept you hope will succeed. It's an aim first, then a fire scenario. Be sure to do your due diligence. That means reaching out to your intended audience and getting feedback on the product before you (or an investor) make a considerable investment. You want to make sure there's a viable market before you put all your eggs in the proverbial basket. It's far too familiar for entrepreneurs to try to convince investors that their product will succeed when they haven't put in the time on the front end to discover and validate potential customer's pains and problems. When you do your research, you are doing two things—building your credibility and building your business case.

2) Save where and when you can.

Can you leverage the contingent workforce or partner with more established companies in supporting roles like marketing, accounting, and H.R.? When you hire an independent contractor, you don't incur the usual expenses related to employee benefits and other employee-related costs. Many talented individuals are willing to perform in the new "gig economy."

Can't afford to rent or purchase a brick and mortar for office space? Look into other options for a coworking arrangement. By doing so, you get the flexibility of a timeshare arrangement with the added benefit of an easily modified length of your membership agreement. Daily, these kinds of areas are bustling with motivated entrepreneurs and small business owners—eager to connect, engage, and bounce ideas off of like-minded entrepreneurs.

3) Have the "right" people on the bus.

If you plan to launch a venture with a co-founder, you must share the same vision. The beauty of having a compatible business partner is that you can divide up the workload while still maintaining control over the strategic direction. There's also a certain level of emotional support you won't find from family or friends. Remember, as Martin S. Feldstein opined in an article entitled, *Why the U.S. is Still Richer Than Every Other Large Country,* "Individuals in the U.S. demonstrate a desire to start businesses and grow them, as well as a willingness to take risks. There is less penalty in the U.S. culture for failing and starting again.[76]"

---

x. Are You Getting What You're Worth?

One of the most challenging tasks for any small business or entrepreneur is determining how to price their products and services. Often, startup ventures are unproven and feel to get a foothold into a new customer relationship, or out of desperation, that they have to "under-price" their products/services to win the customer.

Ash Maurya, the author of Running Lean[77], makes an incredibly important and insightful point when he says, "pricing drives behavior, what behaviors are you driving when you set your price?" Are you trying to be the K-mart of consulting, or are you trying to offer a high-end Nordstrom service experience at Walmart prices? If you give your value or worth away for little or nothing, you will be setting the ceiling and marketplace expectation for what your services are worth.

1) Set boundaries.

If you're in a service-based business, like a graphic designer or a management consultant, you know it can be hard at times to gain legitimacy in the marketplace. Unlike a tangible product, a service is not as easy for clients to fully grasp or appreciate. Because you can't see it, touch it, smell it or taste it, it's more intangible what your offering is. This is particularly frustrating because most wouldn't dine and leave without paying the bill. Why should you, as the service provider, be expected to give a lot of your expertise and value away for free? Setting boundaries in the various phases of a consulting engagement is paramount.

2) Have an "abundance mindset."

How then can you shift from a mindset of scarcity to one of abundance[78]? It starts with asking the right questions. You're probably asking yourself two questions when you set your prices. They are, "What are my clients willing to pay?" and, "What is my competition charging?" While it's true that these questions may influence the client's decision, you can't put too much weight on any single factor. If you do, there is a chance a cost-conscious client will take advantage of you, or worse, it leads to scope creep and unrealistic expectations—the proverbial client from hell, or even worse, a toxic relationship.

3) Know your market.

Pricing services should be based on deeply understanding the needs of the customer/client, the value you create by monetizing your knowledge, and as the master consulting guru, Peter Block advises in his seminal work Flawless Consulting, "on how to ask better questions, how to deal with demanding clients, and how to leverage your gifts/strengths in consulting engagements.[79]" Peter also covers authenticity in consulting engagements and walks you through precise methods of engaging with your clients. (This is a must-read for any consultant or anyone thinking of becoming a consultant selling your professional services). The book has been around for over three decades. I was first exposed to it in one of my graduate school classes in organizational development in the early 1990s.

The next time you are putting together a proposal, remember to capitalize and measure the value you create and not strictly measure your worth or impact by the hours you bill. Put yourself in the client's shoes and figure out what difference/impact you will make on advancing their agenda and outcomes and then price accordingly.

xi. One Form of Exit—Sell the Business

Startups who raise money must plan for their investor's liquidity event – the exit. Most investors have a time horizon between 3-5 years but more realistically, if they do see an exit it often can take 7-10 or more years.

Every investable startup must have a credible exit; however, most don't. By default, most startups usually provide the perfunctory strategies of selling to a strategic buyer, doing a roll-up, or executing an IPO. With only 159 IPOs in 2019 (less than half of the number of IPOs 20 years ago), it is an unlikely strategy for the 3 out of 1,000 people who start a business every month in the United States.

A credible exit means that the management team has thoughtfully considered how it will position itself for sale, the timeline for sale, and the likely buyers. The team has cultivated relationships and built its business model to be attractive to others in the industry, to potential financial buyers or has considered itself how it will "roll-up" the players in the industry to be a dominant powerhouse. This disciplined approach can't be left to chance, it must be designed and curated from the day you accept outside funding for your venture.

While selling a business can prove to be lucrative, there's a lot that enters into the equation. That's why sometimes it makes sense to seek out the assistance of a business broker. He or she acts as a de facto agent for businesses, helping set the asking price, find potential buyers, and market the company to the right audience.

But how exactly do you find the right broker to sell your business? The following are a few considerations to keep in mind as you do your due diligence.

1) Thoroughly vet the potential broker.

Does the potential broker have a network of contacts in and around your likely industry? The best business brokers are not just transactionally focused. They are focused on finding the right organization to take your business to the next level. A key indicator of their compatibility might be the specific industries they're familiar with and how many of their past and present listings fall within your particular industry.

Be wary of statements like the one made by Raytheon and United Technologies "of a merger of equals." There is no such thing, and any organization that believes there is will inevitably fail. With over 90% of acquisitions failing to achieve the pro forma synergies (new revenue opportunities and expense reductions), there is more downside than upside in keeping your culture intact after you sell. Be emotionally ready. Despite what you read and what you are promised, things (culture, rhythm, etc.) will not be the same, even if you are promised a merger of equals.

2) Evaluate their business and marketing practices.

It takes more than listing your business in a directory to sell your company. Right now, there are more than 74,000 businesses for sale on the website Businessesforsale.com alone. How can you expect to find a quality buyer when there's so much noise?

Instead, look for a broker who employs both inbound and outbound marketing strategies. Beyond an online presence, he or she may have access to an exclusive "go-to list" of targeted relationships—high net worth individuals, family office private equity groups to get reliable results. Thus, a multi-channel marketing strategy is essential to maximizing your exposure and your potential value.

Check references carefully to see how well they served their clients and how satisfied past clients are with the results the broker achieved. Check to see if the business broker has obtained additional expertise through certifications, professional development, or involvement and affiliation in professional associations that show learning agility, credibility, and adherence to high standards.

3) Round off your professional advice.

Tap into your professional network of trusted advisors. For example, you might attend industry events and ask your peers whether they know anyone in the market to buy a business. You might tap into the expertise and connections of your business attorney, CPA, or banker. These experts may also have insights into people or companies that might be potential acquirers.

Business brokers, backed by high levels of professionalism and experience, can give sellers an edge in the marketplace. The important thing is to understand your needs, do your homework ahead of time, and stay engaged throughout the process. Watch for the red flags or signs things are not going as planned.

Chapter 5: Conclusion

One of the biggest attractions of entrepreneurship for many is the freedom and ability to be your boss. It also comes with heavy responsibilities and a lot of pressure (/stress) to come up with funds. If you have a little ingenuity and are a go-getter, this can be no problem. If you need a significant amount of funding and have already tapped out all your resources and network, the time may come where you open your business up to outside capital. It becomes a question of accepting a boss (your new funder) or giving up your business altogether. Only you will know the right move to make—or if it's time to sell and move on to the next project.

Be prepared for a roller coaster ride of rejection and skepticism. To secure outside funding, you have to be prepared to hit potholes head on, and you have to prepare to experience a range of emotions throughout the process. Only a very small percentage of startups obtain outside funding, and those that do realize that initially the investors interest is about the deal (return, exit etc..) but to close investment and to get an investor to write a check it is ultimately about the relationship and the trust and bond formed throughout the process. Investors will assess you by asking themselves:

- Did you follow-through on your promises?
- Did you deliver on the business milestones in your plan?
- How you handled difficult conversations and situations?
- Are you "all in"? What skin in the game do you have to align your interests with those of your investors?

Chapter 5: Questions for Consideration

i. Crowdfunding: Is It for you?

Have you considered crowdfunding for your business? If so, are you ready to leverage your story, relationships/communication channels, and consistency to launch a successful campaign?

ii. Lessons from the Campaign Trail

Are you ready to rally support for your business, while also maintaining your integrity, holding yourself accountable, and standing out for the right reasons? Work on developing your brand story and identity, focusing on how you will bring market value to your customer. You may want to hold off stepping into the spotlight until these areas are finely tuned.

iii. An Entrepreneurial Mandate—The Advocacy Imperative

What is the Kauffman ranking for new entrepreneurs in your state? What steps are being taken to help stimulate the venture formation rate? Is there something holding you back from starting a business? Are there economic development initiatives in your state that could provide assistance?

iv. What Makes a Great Pitch? Start Here

Practicing a pitch, or even a speech, is an essential part of proper delivery. Unless you do it often already, speaking in front of a group of people can be extremely nerve-wracking. Don't fool yourself into thinking that practicing "in your head" is good enough—it isn't. Consider joining a local Toastmasters group or public speaking clinic to help practice and test out your presentation. At the very least, have a friend record you so that you can see how you come across and get their feedback.

v. Lessons from Shark Tank

Do you know your value and where you fit into the proverbial food chain? Showing up prepared and with thick skin will help you stick around longer in the game. Don't the hard truths get you down, work on adapting, thinking on your feet, and always have a Plan B.

vi. Is Your Venture Really Investment Worthy?

Are you looking for outside capital? Think about all the ways you can become more attractive to investors. At each step of the way, consider if having to answer to someone else for everything you do is worth it and, if so, work on having a clear exit strategy ready—just in case.

vii. How to Invest in Yourself on a Budget

If you regularly practice one or more of these habits, how has it changed your life? Reflect on the ways your life has improved and consider adopting another life-changing habit for even more breakthroughs.

viii. Early Stage Investing Trends

When deciding on your business funding strategy, keep in mind: management team matters. Track record, credibility, domain expertise, and founders with self-awareness and coach-ability will win the day with potential investors. Investing at this stage is all about the jockey. Serial entrepreneurs preferred. Remember, if you take outside money, you have a boss. Are you ready for that reality?

ix. Three Ways to Bootstrap Your Business

How can you curb or mitigate your startup costs? Have you considered looking into a local business development center? Set up an appointment and investigate what programs and offerings are available for startups. You might be surprised.

x. Are You Getting What You're Worth?

What skin in the game will you have? Are you transactionally oriented, or are you relationship driven? How you price your services will set the table for the type and quality of engagement you will have.

xi. One Form of Exit—Sell the Business

Have you reached a point where you're ready to sell? Seek out the assistance of a business broker and talk through your options. After this, you'll have a better idea of what to do next, and even if you're ready to let go.

CHAPTER 6

NETWORKING

You've probably heard the phrases, "your network is your net worth," and, "it's not what you know, it's who you know that matters." Even in a post-2020 pandemic world, these phrases have never been more exact. The people around you, or those you connect with online are essentially your lifeline. When you or your business needs something, who are you going to reach out to? Someone you know, or who one of your friends can put you into contact with. Social capital is just as, and maybe even more important than financial capital when it comes to running or building a business. To make things run smoothly, it is essential to have the right people in place and to have access to the right resources to support your business.

A quote by Malcolm X has been standing out to me recently, especially in the face of physical distancing measures: "When "I" is replaced with "we" even illness becomes wellness." Together, we are stronger and can tackle any obstacle. Don't ever stop building your network – digitally and relationally. The Internet is not a substitute for building deeper engagement with people who can be influential in your life.

i. Stronger Together: The Case for Entrepreneurial Networks

One of the terms used in the Accountable Care Act is Essential Health Benefits (EHB). Theoretically, EHBs were put in place to cover the care people need. This same concept can be applied to the Essential Business Builder Tools. One of the essential tools in building a business is not a thing, but people. Any city, large or small, has entrepreneurial communities. There is strength in numbers, as they say. If you haven't tapped into the power of these networks, it's better late than never.

My organization, The NIIC, established four essential entrepreneurial pillars (The EHBs of entrepreneurship), which are access to capital, talent, workspaces, and networks.

Here are three reasons to engage with fellow business builders:

1) Learn From Each Other: Compare Notes by Exchanging Industry Know-How

Do you have anyone holding you accountable at work? Co-workers can be too close to the situation, which is why you should look to people outside your organization. Fellow entrepreneurs and business builders may recognize mistakes early on and help you get back on course. Sometimes it takes someone who has no personal stake in the business to tell you the truth and enables you to avoid a total flop at the same time.

While it helps to hear or read books and material from industry leaders, sometimes the best knowledge is ascertained from your peers firsthand. These exchanges about the "tips of the trade" will help you forge deeper connections with these people. They will, in turn, reciprocate and seek you out, which can boost your confidence.

2) Find or Become a Mentor

In these circles of trust, people feel comfortable sharing their anxieties as well as hopes and dreams for the business. These conversations can develop into more formal relationships. Soon you might find that you're acting as a de facto mentor or have seen one to lean on yourself. Mentors are accountability partners who can challenge your thinking, expand your mindset, open doors and provide emotional support in the tough times of running your own business. It is often lonely at the top.

3) Make Connections: Learn New Transferable and Marketable Business Skills

There's a saying that people do business with people they know and like. Networking builds trust and confidence, making you a more attractive referral partner. Advertising may be one venue to grow your business in the short term, but face time can yield long term results.

You may be an expert in your domain but unfamiliar with other skills that can enhance your offering. Your community of B2B entrepreneurs can serve as a resource for professional development. For example, you might consider hosting a skill share summit where each person presents on an area of expertise so that everyone walks away with a takeaway they can apply to their business. Share your insights and knowledge through teaching, workshop facilitation, and one-on-one interactions with others. This is a great way to do the soft sell and link up with other entrepreneurs.

---

ii. Trade Shows Done Right

Every year, many business builders will gear up for spring trade shows. Each is a potential opportunity to market and gain customers and partners. But do you know how to approach it to maximize value and ROI from experience? Trade shows are a significant investment of time and money, so here are some tips to consider when preparing for one:

1) Start with the budget and make the display your own.

Make an overall budget calculation for the event, including costs from the organizer, handling of exhibits, travel/accommodation, costs for booth staff, insurance, marketing materials, and promotion. Aside from the booth space rental, these other hidden expenses can add up fast, so plan accordingly. Also, evaluate the market segment you will reach the show and ensure it aligns with your target market.

Keep in mind who you are trying to connect with when you consider using attention-grabbing graphics and a promotional giveaway of some kind to bring attention to your area. A giveaway, game, or an interactive tablet or monitor can get people to stay longer at your booth and engage more with you and your brand.

It probably goes without saying, but make sure your presentation reflects the image you want to portray. If something needs to be ironed or replaced, do so before the event. A sloppy tablecloth or cluttered booth does not project the right image. Your image also extends to you and your employees' appearance. Make sure everyone is on board with company-branded shirts and work to create a welcoming environment.

2) Think engagement.

Think beyond the go-to promotional literature of business cards that often get ignored or simply thrown away. Instead, I think utility. Branded business card holders, pens, mousepads, water bottles, or bags that can be used throughout the trade show are typically well-received.

One caveat: You don't want to give people so much stuff or information that they leave feeling overwhelmed. Instead, decide how you will measure success and design your booth around that goal.

3) Don't forget the follow-up.

Your efforts will be fruitless if you don't follow up in some fashion. If you collect emails or phone numbers at the event, you might send a follow-up email/text campaign with a promotional offer. At the very least, you should have some way to qualify leads and benefit from your time at the trade show. You also should crunch the numbers to determine if the trade show was worth your efforts. You might not experience an immediate ROI, but some initial calculations like cost-per-visitor reached and total trade show attendance can offer some insight.

---

iii. Tips for Meeting with Legislators

America was built on the backs of entrepreneurs, and today their role is still very much relevant and critical to the 21st-century economy. However, there are barriers to starting up and growing a business for certain underserved groups, including women, immigrants, and minorities.

To ensure entrepreneurship is a national priority, business builders and their support organizations must bring their concerns to policymakers. But where to start? Here's how to prepare for a meeting with your elected official.

1) Do Your Homework and Keep It Simple

First and foremost, in advance of the meeting, make time to conduct your research. Please get to know which specific policies they support, the critical issues on their dockets, and on which committees they serve.

From here, gather information on their pet causes or issues. Make a note of any obstacles you are facing because of red tape and research whether the legislator has had a history of working on such matters.

After you've done your due diligence, create a sheet with your top talking points. Touch on relevant legislation, issues in the news, and success stories. You might even bring in photos, testimonials, impact statements, or demonstrations of how you and your team are making an impact in their district. That means showing how you've been able to create jobs, access funding, and add value to the local economy.

2) Engage and find Champions

Make sure to listen as much as you talk. Be sincere and authentic. Take notes and address concerns. Inquire as to whether you should include a legislative staff member in your follow-up communications. He or she can be instrumental in helping your cause. Having legislative champions and sponsors are very important to advancing your legislative agenda.

3) Follow-Up

Have actionable next steps and requests ready ahead of the meeting. What might success look like in your corner of the world? For example, if you are struggling to achieve growth due to bureaucracy, be forthright. Don't be afraid to present the opportunity to help your business and the policymakers' constituents if that barrier is removed.

Rather than point fingers, your time might be best spent focused on educating the official on issues affecting small businesses/startups instead of taking a stance on a specific piece of legislation. This keeps the conversation productive because it's focused on the big picture of fostering a more robust entrepreneurial ecosystem in America—everyone wins!

---

iv. Cultivate and Invest in These Relationships: Self, Team, and Network

The new venture creation process often has business builders focused on the technical and systems aspects of building their organization—getting the product made, hiring staff, finding early customers, locating the business, and developing and producing marketing assets. However, in the process, they often overlook essential variables (people) and adaptive leadership (with emotional intelligence) traits that contribute to their success.

Here's some food for thought to work *on,* not just *in* your business. Take care to prioritize, giving attention to the following vital constituencies and activities that will result in a better version of yourself.

1) Invest in Yourself

Make sure that as you work to cultivate an exceptional customer experience, you are giving yourself enough attention. Be mindful of burnout—you can't pour from an empty cup. Find outlets for self-care and personal development, for example: Optimize.me[80] mastery series, attending yoga, joining a mastermind, participating in a Bible study, or something that inspires you and gives you energy.

2) Appreciate Your Tribe and Elevate Your Team

Most business builders are often square pegs in round holes. They do their own thing because of a desire for freedom, wanting to make a difference and set their own rules. However, in the pursuit of their business, they can often neglect their loved ones because they're so caught up in the hustle. Don't forget to stop and smell the roses! Prioritize not only your business tribe but your family tribe.

Behind every growing company are a hard-working team and outside partners, vendors, and trusted advisors. How do you inspire and recognize jobs well done? Don't forget that no matter how capable and motivated your people are, they are human and need time to recharge their batteries. Today, a work-life balance seems nearly impossible and almost mythical, so you must consciously strive for personal and professional satisfaction. Author Matthew Kelly[81] believes we don't want balance; we want satisfaction. How can you create the cultural conditions to facilitate an environment in which people feel comfortable catering to their needs, both physical and intellectual?

3) Nurture Your Network

Your network is anyone else who comes in contact with your business that could become a customer or could be a potential source of referrals. Most companies and organizations are challenged to think through what makes them special, different, and unique. To that end, communicating your value proposition[82] clearly and effectively can make it less costly to acquire a new customer, find "right fit" partnerships, or validate product-market fit—to create products and services customers want.

That said, your experience needs to be exciting enough that people want to spread the word. Think beyond the obvious and consider what types of experiences are most sought out and how you can infuse them into your brand experience.

Bottom Line: Your venture touches on all areas of your business and personal life. Don't forget to tend to these meaningful relationships! They are essential building blocks in building a business.

---

v. Three Ways to Network Your Way to Success

Does the mere thought of networking make you run in the other direction? Many small business owners are reluctant to networking for various reasons. For some, it's mostly in part because they've had a poor experience at an event. No one wants to feel like they are bombarded with sales pitches or feel like they're merely a transaction. Many business owners don't see attendance as a good ROI on their time because networking members are just trying to get leads from you or sell you something.

It's too bad that a few bad apples can ruin it for the bunch. There are professionals out there who have mastered the art of effective networking—both on and offline. Successful networking requires a combination of activities to increase the likely ROI on your time, and networking is broader than just going to a networking meeting every Tuesday morning.

Here's what you can learn from the best:

1) Come ready to serve.

Many small business owners come to events to find a solution to a need. That's not the most constructive approach, though. Instead, ask yourself how you can add value and share your insights. When you give advice, you position yourself as a subject-matter expert, and people are more likely to seek you out when they need your product or service.

2) Get cozy with the right kind of media.

Traditional advertising only goes so far. Earned media, as it's commonly called, can be invaluable. You can get on the local news outlets' radars by issuing regular press releases. If you can build trust and rapport, over time, you might find that you are the person the reporter calls when he/she needs a comment from an expert in your field.

Remember, no matter what medium—content is king. There's a lot you can do with social, print, and alternative media to further your cause. Push out useful and consistent content, i.e., thought leadership, that your target audience might find helpful or beneficial. Be sure to keep the self-promotion to a minimum.

3) Stay in touch with past customers.

Everyone is focused on acquiring new customers, but don't do this at the expense of turning off your past ones. They can be your biggest brand ambassadors. It is always upsetting to me to see how a bank will pay a new customer $200 to open a new checking account but offers me nothing even though I have been a customer for decades. What message is my bank sending me?

Of course, it should go without saying that you should always be engaging in the small business community in your area. Attend workshops, seminars, awards ceremonies, luncheons, meet-and-greets, and of course, local chamber of commerce events, to name a few.

---

vi. Tap into Your Network to Grow as an Entrepreneur

There is a strong focus on connectivity, especially how networking and community-building can come into play, as a pillar of entrepreneurship.

The one truth people seldom acknowledge is that entrepreneurship and personal/professional growth can be a lonely process. Yes, people are often quick to share success stories, but it's rare to hear about the flops, failures, or false starts. I think that's because entrepreneurs tend to be very passionate about their pursuits, and any inkling that things aren't going right is interpreted as failure. I also think communities judge failure harshly. Believe it or not, the community of practice suggests getting 2 out of 1,000 ideas right and executing on them is world-class. Our society is conditioned for celebrating successes but not embracing and leaning into failure. However, with failure, there is growth, maturation, and savviness!

So, then whom can a hungry entrepreneur talk to—not only when we're emerging—but also when we're kickin' butt? Or when we're in a rut or unsure about what to do in a situation? The answer is to get out of your comfort zone. To practice what I preach, I enrolled in a one-year Certified Innovation Mentor Program at the University of Notre Dame.

Here is some of the "sage" advice I received that may offer a few ways to push you past your limits:

1) Schedule meetings with your "band of heroes" regularly.

If you want to know who the real players are in the business world are, try scheduling an early-morning meeting with someone. Most high-powered people don't have much time to spare during the workday, so they have to start early. So, trade in your midday salad for 7 am eggs and coffee. One speaker who was the president of a health system shared that he relies on testing his assumptions and ideas against a colleague who is an author, motivational speaker, management guru, and futurist. Who is your go-to "band of heroes"? Be sure to use them as a check and balance to keep you grounded and real.

2) Don't look to one mentor but seek out diverse and contradictory points of view and perspectives.

Many people are inclined to seek the professional guidance of one individual, especially when they are starting. The reality is that one person's perspective simply isn't enough. You need a team of people and therefore a variety of opinions and life experiences. It is essential to know the difference between mentor, coach, and trusted advisor. Test your "go-to people" against the Trustworthiness definition, which is defined as **(Credibility * Reliability * Intimacy) divided by Self-Orientation.**

The higher the overall number, the higher the trustworthiness. Credibility = how believable the person is; reliability = how likely the person you are interacting with will do what they say they will do; intimacy = how healthy the mutual relationship is, and how invested we are in each other's outcomes divided by self-orientation—is the person in it for themselves, or you? (Think WIIFM: What's in It for Me?)

3) One of the speakers suggested there are three leadership behaviors we should emulate in our daily life to embody and lead.

They are known by the acronym TAC. The T is Time. How do you, as a leader, spend your time? This says a lot about what you, as a leader, value. The A is Attention. Who and what do you pay attention to as the leader? The C is Care. What do you, as the leader, care about? What do you have an energy about? Organizations will assess what the leader sustains and shows excitement for over a long period.

Whatever you do, keep in mind that your comfort zone is a nice place to hang out, but it's not the place for professional growth and maturation. If you're not progressing, then you're going backward. *And who wants to lose traction?* Intellectual curiosity is a prerequisite for leadership.

---

vii. Meeting Madness: Cut the Clutter (Or Another C Word of Your Choosing!)

When my kids were younger, I asked them what they thought I did for a living. My three boys were quick to respond. They said, "Dad, you are always in meetings, and you eat business lunches out a lot." They certainly simplified my professional life, but as we have all come to realize—meetings can be the enemy of productivity and can zap your energy. We have all attended meetings where we play with our phones, look out the window, or doodle on a page in place of taking notes. If you've ever experienced meeting fatigue, then you know what I mean.

The key is to eliminate "meeting clutter" and become more intentional in the use of your time and others (in fact, time is really about your energy). In turn, this can help ensure employees are more engaged, invigorated, and productive.

Here are my top three tips to consider when preparing or hosting your next business meeting

1) Prioritize who should be at the table and have one team facilitator.

Who are the key players? Who are the non-essential staff who might benefit from an email summary instead? Meetings can be a real "time suck" and drain on peoples' precious resources. Be mindful when crafting the invitation list—think of who can make an impact or move the needle.

Designate someone to monitor the time and make sure the attendees stay on point. Be sure this person can illuminate all sides of the argument, play devil's advocate, or stimulate a conversation about the potential more significant issues. This will keep the meetings moving forward and help maintain order.

2) Limit size and frequency and clarify agenda and action items beforehand.

A smaller group can boost engagement, focus, and allow for more in-depth discussion. Are you meeting for the sake of the meeting? Can a weekly meeting be pared down to a biweekly frequency? Or could you communicate the necessary information in an email or via a one-on-one conversation?

Every meeting should have a stated purpose, talking points, and a decision (is it informational? is it for decision making? etc.). Email the schedule in advance and encourage team members to come prepared with ideas or solutions. Build-in time for brainstorming and discussion. Know the deliverables. What decisions need to be made? We use a RAIL report to focus on our discussion. RAIL is the Running Action Item List. It is the big rocks we must move to make our strategic plan priorities a reality.

3) Consider a change in scenery or make everyone stand up.

Off-site meetings can make the experience less cumbersome and might just be a dot connector (where your team experiences something that changes how they do something back at the office or identifies a new practice to address an organizational problem).

Stand up meetings are much shorter and more concise. The meeting doesn't last as long. Every Monday, The NIIC's leaders have a rhythm meeting (to describe progress, address roadblocks, and cover major events/activities happening on the campus), and by making the meeting a "standing up" meeting, we cut the meeting time substantially.

As a business builder or entrepreneur, you should always calculate the ROI of almost everything you do. Look at the cost per hour around the table and figure it. Make sure you know if the return on investment is evident from the meeting you just had or are contemplating. Could it be better accomplished by a phone call or email? You might be disappointed or disturbed by the low return and the high investment.

By evaluating factors like frequency, focus, and quality of meetings, you can increase morale and productivity while boosting your company's bottom line.

---

viii. Seven Seconds Matter: Hacking the Formula for Good First Impressions

You only have seven seconds to make a great first impression. If connections are the lifeblood of any business, then networking is the currency. Therefore, you're out, and about meeting people, you better be sure you are presenting yourself in the proper light.

A wrong first impression makes for an uphill battle, according to a new study recently published in the journal *Social Cognition*. In five experiments that studied first impressions, researchers from the University of Chicago concluded that: "People require more evidence to perceive improvement than decline; it is easier to become a sinner than a saint, despite exhibiting equivalent evidence for change."

In other words, once you've internalized that someone is "bad," it takes a lot to change your mind. Researchers believe it takes more to decide that someone you previously thought to be a good person is bad.

Naturally, you might be second-guessing yourself now. Maybe you were late for a meeting or showed up in a wrinkled shirt. Whatever the case may be, don't sweat it. While you may not get a second chance to make a first impression, you can hack the formula for putting your best foot forward *every* time. Here's what researchers have to say about the science behind first impressions:

1) Practice eye contact and loosen up.

Those who have mastered these skills are perceived as more credible and earnest—as well as more confident and well adjusted.

If you want to appear more approachable, focus on your posture, and how you walk. Believe it or not, in one British study, researchers found that "looser gaits are associated with extroversion and adventurousness."

2) Smile and perfect your handshake.

Not only can it increase the positive effect toward a favorable interaction, but it also compensates for a negative one. Sometimes social situations are awkward, and things don't go as planned. A simple handshake can help to offset some of the damage. Think a mix of firm, confident, and friendly.

3) As far as dress, meet the person where they are.

When you dress similarly to the person you're meeting—whether casual, business casual or professional—you'll seem warmer and more likable. No one wants to feel like they've been one-upped.

---

ix. Women Seeking Mentors: Questions to Ask

Working with a mentor can serve as a leg up for any professional at any career level. The potential gain is significant, especially for female professionals. That's because a mentor's advice can help her better face gender-related challenges still prevalent in the modern workplace.

It comes down to helping maximize strengths and working to carve out a future you want. Mentors remind us of who we are and empower us to push forward on our paths. That's why a good mentor can make all the difference. He or she can help you get "out of your head" and rise to your fullest potential.

Karl R. LaPan

I asked Alison Martin-Books, Mentoring Expert, Founder, and CEO of Diverse Talent Strategies[83] and author of the book, "Learning to Lead Through Mentoring,"[84] how women should go about seeking a mentor, and she shared with me the three questions female professionals should ask themselves to help find the right mentor:

1) Why this person? Can they guide me toward my professional goals?

Alison: In considering approaching a potential mentor, it is essential first to find what your goals are. What is it you would like to accomplish personally and professionally? Is there a particular skill you are trying to develop? Armed with this information, assess who might be a good fit to serve as a mentor. Seek out someone who has accomplished what you would like to achieve or someone who excels at the skill you are developing.

When you feel you have identified someone who might be a good fit, reach out to that person to set up a call or invite them to coffee rather than first asking them to be your mentor, unless they are part of a formal mentoring program. Remember, this is a relationship, and like all relationships, mentoring relationships grow over time at a natural pace.

2) Am I able to work well with this person?

Alison: As you get to know your mentor, you should also determine if they are someone you can work well with and build a 'trusting' relationship. As with any relationship, try to get to know the person to understand if your personalities mesh well and if you have similar values. Having said that, it is also good to recognize the importance of being able to work with a wide variety of people, so approaching mentoring relationships with an open mind and being able to work with those with personalities that are different than yours is also critical. It is most important to determine what you can learn from this person and what you might be able to teach them.

3) Does this person have the qualities of a good mentor? Are they successful?

Alison: There are *six* competencies of a good mentor. Be sure to select a mentor who demonstrates these essential traits. They are:

1. Having the desire to help and support.
2. A commitment to continual learning; motivated to continue developing and growing.
3. Having confidence and an assured manner.
4. Ability to ask the right questions.
5. Active listener.
6. A willingness to provide constructive feedback.

Along with these traits, success is perhaps the most critical question to consider. If you are seeking guidance and wisdom from another, they should demonstrate success on the topic they are mentoring about to get the best results. While someone unsuccessful at achieving his or her goals certainly attains knowledge based on that attempt about what not to do, the right mentor has demonstrated success on the topic you are seeking. Do an honest assessment of the person giving you advice and take their opinion with a grain of salt if they do not have demonstrated success on the topic, they are sharing their opinion with you. While this might sound harsh, there are many imposters out there and listening to them might set you and your venture back.

---

x. Three Tips to Help You Master the Art of Networking

Seasoned business owners and up-and-coming ones alike need to make it a point to the network now and then. You never know when you could meet someone who could change the trajectory of your career and personal life, after all.

At a meeting the other day, an advisory board member shared that her goal from networking was to learn something, to experience aha moments, and to have meaningful takeaways. Other advisory group members shared their frustration with the selling, soliciting of donations, and the other less beneficial aspects of networking groups. Be strategic in how you invest your time and choose which networking groups you participate in wisely and strategically.

Here are three tips to help you master the art of networking and get the highest ROI on your time and energy:

1) Embrace the human side of networking. It's about meaningful connections—quality over quantity matters most.

Although networking can seem self-serving, keep in mind you are building a social network founded on mutual respect, genuine interest, and a clear understanding of reciprocity. In other words, everyone is there for the same reason. They are businesspeople with a lot of the same fears, strengths, weaknesses, and hopes you have. Once you see the human side of such interactions, you can start to relax and thus appear more approachable. Remember, only through personal discomfort (making yourself vulnerable) can there be meaningful personal change.

2) Refine your approach. It's about mutual investment in each other's outcomes— think WIIFM: What's in It for Me?

The first step is to think about your goals. What do you hope to take from the event? Then it's time to craft your story: who you are, what you offer, and how you can add value (think Osterwalder Value Proposition[85]). You might introduce a challenge, describe how you solved it, and explain what you learned. Don't forget to include a call to action. Do you want them to schedule a coffee date? Visit your website? Connect on LinkedIn? Be specific. Once you have a firm foundation, it's time for practice. Recite it several times, but do not memorize it—or else risk sounding robotic. You want to deliver your pitch from a place of sincerity and confidence.

3) Schedule a follow-up. It's about personal growth, discovery, and greater self-awareness—no pain, no gain!

It's all well and good to make a stellar impression, but that doesn't pay the bills. You should focus on the follow-up and your prioritized list of networking activities. Be clear about your intentions for a coffee or lunch meeting. For example, explain how you hope to discuss how you might be a resource for the individual or their company. Once you have secured a meeting, send a quick email thanking him or her in advance for their time. Finally, build further rapport online through social media outlets like LinkedIn and Facebook. While mentorship is an overused word today, there is significant demand for mentors and trusted advisors to help people grow and develop into the very "best version of themselves."

With a little practice and experience, you'll be developing relationships, outreaching, and expanding your network like its second nature.

---

xi. Growing Beyond a Solo-Entrepreneur

In a Kauffman Foundation Report[86] on proposed visa changes titled, **"International Entrepreneur Rule: The good, the bad, and the unknown,"** the author opined, "Many entrepreneurs use revenue as their investment capital, yet bootstrapping is not recognized in the proposed rule as a legitimate way to finance business growth." While this statement was made regarding ways for immigrant entrepreneurs to benefit from changes in visa rules, this statement is excellent advice for aspiring entrepreneurs and solopreneurs on how to fund and build their business ventures.

As entrepreneurs, it's easy to get caught up in the day-to-day demands of running a business. Inadequate planning, under-capitalization, and missed market opportunities characterize why so many solopreneurs never break the employment glass ceiling (employing someone other than themselves). The average size (number of employees) of a business is shrinking, and the number of solopreneurs and contingent workers is on the rise, according to the Intuit Future of Small Business Report.[87]

Consider these three tips:

1) Build a reserve fund for emergencies AND opportunities.

The rule of thumb is 3-12 months of operating expenses in the bank so you can weather the long sales cycle, the over-dependency on a few core customers for revenue, or to take advantage of an opportunity to grow, expand or scale your business. If you are bankable, having an open line of credit (through your home equity, etc.) may be a practical thing to do, so when a market opportunity materializes, you can quickly capitalize on it.

Note: Less than 8% of all the fastest growing companies in America used angel investment.

2) Iterate, iterate, and pivot in your business model.

In the same article cited above, the Kauffman Report observed, "Failure is a real part of startup culture and embraced by entrepreneurs, who realize that the first, second, or even third iteration of an idea may not work. But quick learning and constant refinement of a business model may mean that the fourth iteration is a big success." Seldom is your first idea your best idea. Discover, validate, iterate, and pivot. Learning is about continuous learning, skillful market execution, and refinement. Our most significant opportunities live in the uncontested market space between the blue and red ocean space (Remember the book, *Blue Ocean Strategy*.[88])

3) Put passion into it.

You have passion, or you wouldn't be pursuing your entrepreneurial dream. The best thing you can do is apply that same passion into business discipline and planning for the future.

While we all believe we are super-human on some levels and can do it all, focus and prioritization of our essential rocks (think Covey and Harnish) can be accomplished through a commitment to discipline and rhythm. So, with this in mind, commit yourself to:

- Put together a roadmap with triggers (events that drive decision-making);
- Define what success looks like and create an advisory board to hold you accountable; and
- Think a bit bigger and broader than your original business concepts. Be focused, deliberate, intentional, and smart on how you seize and capitalize on market opportunities.
- Balance all your stakeholder's expectations (family, employees, customers, investors, and community, etc.) Matthew Kelly speaks of personal and professional satisfaction versus work-life balance. Take the Off-Balance Assessment[89] to see how you are doing and to target areas of improvement.

As you head down this path, review your progress regularly. Occasionally, you might have to adjust your plans according to some business and life changes, including adding your first employee, diversifying your business offerings, moving into your first commercial or incubator office to legitimize your business (and to commit to growing) while balancing your personal life—having a child, buying a home, or paying back your student loans.

Surround yourself with smarter people. In a seminar I once attended, a speaker said, "A players hire A+ players." Are you following this advice? How have you planned and reimagined your future?

Chapter 6: Conclusion

It should come as no surprise that building a business is much harder if you do everything on your own. Entrepreneurs already wear many hats and must be self-sufficient in many ways, however, building up a network and team of connections, close confidants, and mentors can exponentially improve not only the success rate of your venture but the speed at which it develops. One person is just one person, after all, you wouldn't want to go to a general practitioner for brain surgery, now would you. Lean into your connections and glean their wisdom instead of killing time, trying to figure everything out yourself.

Networking doesn't have to be painful; you can structure it and plan it out so that you are efficiently utilizing your time and mental resources. As with anything, practice makes perfect, and there are ways to network smarter, not harder. Reach out to your local business development center, business incubator, entrepreneurial support organization or chamber of commerce and start where there is an extensive collection of like-minded individuals who can inspire, challenge and make you and your venture better!

Chapter 6: Questions for Consideration

i. Stronger Together: The Case for Entrepreneurial Networks

What insights or market knowledge can you share through teaching, workshop facilitation, or one-on-one interactions with others? Have you considered how you can use your business to know how to connect with others? Research organizations in your area and how you can start to connect to other business builders.

ii. Trade Shows Done Right

A successful trade show is just one-third of the equation. Ample preparation beforehand is imperative to strike the right tone with your booth and presentation, and adequate follow up with new contacts afterward is crucial. Be sure to practice before you go and ask a friend to review your material and content before you go to ensure everything makes sense. What are your specific and measurable goals from taking a booth? What gets measured, gets managed.

iii. Tips for Meeting with Legislators

Have you ever reached out to an elected official? What did you learn about the process? So much of the experience depends on you and their actions—be sure to thoroughly prepare and consider getting people on your side to help tip the scales.

iv. Cultivate and Invest in These Relationships: Self, Team, and Network

When was the last time you invested in yourself? Schedule personal time today, even if you don't have time today, make time this week and get it in your calendar. When was the last time you did something for your team or those closest to you who support you? Think of a small act of kindness you can execute this week and make it happen.

v. Three Ways to Network Your Way to Success

Try to contact at least one prior client a week. Yes, it can be uncomfortable, but according to Marketing Metrics, you have a 60-70% probability of selling to someone who has already done business with you versus a 5-20% probability of selling to a new prospect.[90] New networking opportunities are always excellent, but don't neglect the chance to nurture your existing client and contact relationships.

vi. Tap into Your Network to Grow as an Entrepreneur

What's one thing you can do this week to challenge yourself and advance your "community of practice knowledge"? Lean into it and do it! If you can stick with it for 21 consecutive days—it will become a new habit!

vii. Meeting Madness: Cut the Clutter (Or Another C Word of Your Choosing!)

Meetings can be productive, useful, and a great way to network. However—they can also be a giant time suck and kill your bottom line. Create a company meeting policy, as well as a network meeting policy. Set rules and guidelines for both you and your business. Always make sure an agenda and time limit are set so that things are accomplished. Having this policy in place will help you recognize, decline, and nix unnecessary meetings.

viii. Seven Seconds Matter: Hacking the Formula for Good First Impressions

Body language is huge when making a first impression, and it's a relatively easy thing to adjust. Watch videos of body language do's and don'ts to get a visual representation of what you should and shouldn't be doing. **Record yourself as you practice your introduction to see how you match up.** Whenever possible, find out the dress code before you arrive. Showing up in the right attire can make any meeting much more comfortable for both parties.

ix. Women Seeking Mentors: Questions to Ask

What qualities do you think are essential in a mentor? Have you ever had a mentor? Why or why not? Perhaps it's time to set aside your reservations and find one. Make a list of the professional accomplishments you are aiming for, and then find someone who has already accomplished those goals. Approach them and see if it would be a good mentoring relationship.

x. Three Tips to Help You Master the Art of Networking

Chances are, you have a drawer full of business cards you've collected throughout the years. After you've crafted your story (who you are, what you offer, and how you can add value), landed on a call to action, and practiced your approach several times, make your move. Try and schedule a few lunch or coffee meetings and be sure to do your homework before you arrive. Each time it will get easier. Have some standard discovery questions to get the conversation off to a strong start.

xi. Growing Beyond a Solo-Entrepreneur

"A players hire A+ players," is an excellent rule of thumb for entrepreneurs. To push yourself outside of your comfort zone and scale your business strategically, you need to have some heavy hitters on your side. Tap into successful brains who have already done what you are trying to do, and you will save yourself years as well as blood, sweat, and tears. The best organizations select talent, they don't hire talent. What are the non-negotiables when it comes to traits that you look for in acquiring talent?

NICHE MARKETING

CHAPTER 7

OPTIMIZING YOUR NICHE

A famous saying in business is some form of "niches are for riches," which goes hand in hand with the fact that if you're selling to everyone, you're selling to no one. You can't be everything to everyone, it's simply not possible—or logistically feasible. To find business success, you must know who your client is, what problem you are solving, and how to best get in front of them. If you don't know these simple things, you will waste time and money on fruitless mass appeal.

Sharpen your focus, have a clear picture of who your company is serving, and how to market to them, and your business will have a much better chance at cornering the market.

i. Case Study: Planet Fitness and Knowing Your Niche

At the beginning of every year, American gyms are packed. Some gym-goers are new to the pursuit of fitness altogether, while some are returning after a stint away during the holidays. Planet Fitness has carved out a niche pursuing the former. The New Hampshire–based gym franchise's business model relies on this critical demographic of newbies as its bread and butter.

"Forty percent of our members had never belonged to a gym before joining Planet Fitness," CEO Chris Rondeau told Forbes.[91] "We're going after that casual first-timer."

1) Know Your Niche

But how can you win charging $0.25 down and $10/month, you might be wondering. Oddly enough, of the members who get gym memberships, "about HALF never actually visit the gym once." This is the dirty little secret of why low-cost gyms make money—because their facilities were never built to accommodate the number of people who buy memberships. While almost 11% of all gym membership sales happen in January each year, enthusiasm wanes by the 17th of the month with attendance dropping even more dramatically by late March. Less than 20% of gym-goers use their gym membership consistently.

2) Solve a Paint Point

There's a market here, because amateurs can feel intimidated, or shall we say "gymtimidated" by typical fitness environments. Cohorts of ultra-fit people at the gym can deter some newbies from returning because they don't feel like they fit in, or people are judging them.

3) Target Your Market

Although in their marketing they imply they're "for everyone," that's not the case. They don't explicitly say "no meatheads," but it's implicit in their availability of equipment, rules, and marketing. You won't see bodybuilders deadlifting 300 pounds at Planet Fitness gyms because their facilities don't accommodate that type of activity. They discourage audible displays of brawn (like grunting) that you might experience at other gyms. According to their website, "we create an environment where you can relax, go at your own pace, and do your own thing without ever having to worry about being judged."[92]

In a sense, Planet Fitness aspires to be the opposite of competitors in their approach. They know who they are and what they're about—and that's precisely what makes them so successful. In this way, Planet Fitness can serve as a case study for businesses in any industry. While most organizations create a niche by figuring out who they DO want to help, Planet Fitness has built their business by deciding who they DON'T want to serve.

---

ii. Plant-Based Power: Lessons from Natural Foods Disrupters

By now, you've probably heard of the Beyond Burger and its competitor, the Impossible Burger. The latter is available nationwide at Burger King[93] and over 5,000 restaurants nationally. According to a CNN article[94] by Linda Drayer, "One of the Impossible Burger's ingredients is a genetically modified version of heme, an iron-containing molecule from soy plants, like the heme from animals—which is what gives it its uniquely meaty flavor."

As more Americans cut back on their red meat consumption and move toward more mindful eating, the purveyors of meat alternatives are capitalizing on this shift. I am not advocating for meat-alternative products, just merely restating the context for my observations.

What can food startups (and those in other industries) learn from the success of such brands?

Here are three takeaways:

1) "Storyliving" / narrative matters.

Finding a way to frame the genesis story, so it resonates with consumers, can be a golden opportunity. Beyond Meat founder Ethan Brown has been open about his experience growing up on a farm and, most recently, his skepticism of meat consumption as a necessity. His message is that plant-based patties don't have to be bland and such alternatives to meat can be healthier and better for animals and the environment. In this way, he's found an in-road into the hearts and minds of meat-eaters, animal rights activists, and investors alike. "Storyliving is modernized storytelling where a company enables consumers to experience their brand narrative."[95]

2) Healthy eating is top of mind.

There has been a sea change in recent years. Most Americans have a working knowledge of the basics of a balanced diet and activity. Moreover, that's translating to sales at the grocery store—at the expense of more traditional venues.

Consider the impact of the burgeoning natural foods movement. The health and wellness food market size are expected to grow to $280.97 billion during 2018-2022, according to Technavio. The rise of healthy meal kits like Purple Carrot, Green Chef, and Sun Basket, while restaurants are struggling[96], underscores American's collective mindset and purchasing shift.

3) Product development matters.

Innovation never sleeps, and these plant-based Goliaths are taking that to heart. Beyond meat has elected to invest its operating cash flow back into development, upping the ante on their commitment to marketing, production, distribution, and product development.

Also, Quorn Foods, producer of faux meat, is following suit, after experiencing an uptick in sales. The British company announced its plans to spend over $8.5 million on a research and development facility at its North Yorkshire headquarters, in an attempt to keep up with the demand in light of the rise of plant-based eating and increased competition in the marketplace. Quorn's Kevin Brennan told The Guardian his company is poised to keep up with rivals by developing its bleeding vegan burger while it aims to reach $1 billion in annual sales by 2027.[97]

iii. A Marketing Case Study: Earth Day 50 Years Later

World Earth Day is April 22. Each year, the world's largest environmental movement unites people from nearly 200 countries. According to the Earth Day organization[98], "Earth Day broadens the base of support for environmental programs, rekindles public commitment, and builds community activism around the world through a broad range of events and activities."

While I am not debating the efficacy of this movement or its political underpinnings, I am using this example as a good case study for the power of cause marketing. To understand its success, consider the backdrop of the late 1960s. When anti-war activist John McConnell proposed the day of recognition and action in 1969, Americans were just starting to embrace environmentalism for the first time. It's no coincidence that a 1971 "Keep America Beautiful" ad took off, which further advanced the ideas behind conservation into the public sphere.

The timing for this movement was fortuitous. With much of the country divided over the Vietnam War, Americans needed something to bring them together. Earth Day, a non-partisan cause, served that purpose. Republicans, Democrats, city dwellers, rural residents, and the rich and poor alike were drawn to the message. It worked. There was something for everybody.

Earth Day also proved to be convenient for environmental groups to advocate and align with—whether curbing emissions, cleaning up waterways, or promoting for less dependence on oil, organizations found that Earth Day fit their ethos—and they capitalized on it.

Organizations of all types can learn a lesson or two from the Earth Day movement:

1) **Earth Day resonated with people because it was broad but specific at the same time.**

The idea behind Earth Day is **inspirational and inclusive**, and that's why it has staying power. Earth Day is now a global event each year, and the organization believes that more than a billion people and organizations in 192 countries now take part in various activities.

This now-50-year campaign has stood the test of time because of the way it was created, packaged, and sold to its constituents.

2) **Evolve with the times.**

While clean water was and is essential, the original organizers likely did not imagine a time with electric cars.

3) **As the attitudes and needs of consumers change, so should brands.**

Earth Day has found a way to keep people engaged even as times and technology change.

---

iv. **A Call to Action on Rural Entrepreneurship**

This is not a myth. This is a call to action. Only 1 in 10 new businesses will likely start in a rural community.

While not lacking in entrepreneurial energy or potential, rural startups are lacking in proportion to their more urban counterparts. To foster business builders in less populated areas, rural communities need targeted and specialized resources to address the challenges and obstacles faced by today's demanding business builders—by focusing on the 4Ms—management, mentorship, markets, and money, rural communities can better grow, diversify, and thrive.

What can we do to surround better our rural entrepreneurs with the resources they need to grow? It starts by leaning into three myths and by conducting a comprehensive needs assessment and an in-depth gap analysis in your rural community to determine how to leverage your assets.

Myth 1: There aren't entrepreneurs in my community.

While we lack a strong pipeline of entrepreneurs and business builders in the United States due to a myriad of factors, we need to inspire future generations to see entrepreneurship as a career option. It is never too early to inspire future generations to start and own their business. Also, we should not ignore existing businesses with ideas that might be more likely to create startup businesses to address specific unmet needs outside their core markets.

The key is identifying, connecting, and promoting all types and stages of rural business builders via outreach, mentorship, education/training, and connection. Monthly meetups, mentoring, and seminars can unite business builders who might otherwise feel isolated. There's a sense of empowerment that can come from community building.

Myth 2: Only big cities are poised to build the infrastructure and connect the dots for business builders.

While every rural community may not have the critical mass for specific types of accelerators, incubators, and coworking spaces, rural communities can brand themselves as an entrepreneurial destination for business builders by offering services that address one or more of the 4Ms (management, mentorship, markets and money) I mentioned in the opening paragraph. As researcher Tim Wojan and his colleagues at the U.S. Department of Agriculture's Economic Research Service found, "there is a strong statistical association between the arts, innovation, and economic dynamism in rural areas. And this leads them to conclude that the arts are a direct force in agricultural innovation, not just an indirect factor that helps to attract and retain talent."

Beyond the demographics, it's not as much of an issue of size—it's all about being plugged into the business building community and identifying what they need, what they will value, and what will move their idea or innovation into action (formation of a new venture). From here, it's a matter of aligning with champions in your community to fill the gaps in entrepreneurial services or partnering and connecting with established service delivery organizations to deliver and support the services. After all, that's what the right entrepreneurial infrastructure does—provide the framework for an entrepreneurial base to take off and pool resources to address the most expensive part of entrepreneurship—technical assistance to the entrepreneurs.

Myth 3: Entrepreneurship isn't sexy enough or is perceived as too risky.

This attitude is understandable, as some rural areas stricken by the recession haven't fully recovered, and economic developers and politicians are looking for bigger job creation headlines than what a typical startup might deliver. Nearly 9 out of 10 business establishments are businesses that employ less than 20 people, but these local success stories don't often make big headlines in the press.

And startups, in general, face a steep incline when it comes to survival rates. However, rural ventures are statistically more resilient than their metro-based peers, despite less money (of the total VC dollars less than 2% go to rural entrepreneurs) and markets (access is often an issue due to less developed community infrastructure). As Professor Stephan Weiler[99] observed, "the resilience of rural startups is perhaps due to more cautious business practices in areas with few alternative employment options.

v. Launching a Venture? Some Potential Pitfalls

Many dream of starting a business—few do. And even those who do, don't necessarily get it right, initially. Here are a few of the most common missteps we see in general with new startups.

1) Failure to get plugged into the "right" method to commercialize your idea

The best way to gauge what might work (and what won't) is to get in front of prospects from day one. You'll learn more from surveying your target market face-to-face than putting in hours of market research. Get people interested in buying your widget now, before you invest too much time and effort, and risk getting it wrong. There's a reason minimum viable product is essential to the customer discovery and validation process. They are a proven means to curb failure outright. You can always improve on a good thing, but you may never recover from a total flop.

2) Pricing too low to get your product some exposure

It may be tempting to offer discounts or freebies to entice customers early on, but this can backfire when you need to raise the price later. Plus, it can cheapen your brand. As Seth Godin says, "the problem with the race to the bottom is that you might win."[100]

Many consumers associate price with quality or value, after all. Ask for what you're worth from the outset—and stick to your guns. Consumers just looking for a "good deal" aren't usually loyal anyway. The lean movement has taught us that pricing drives behavior, so what behavior do you want to drive?

3) Thinking you only need money to get your idea launched into a venture

Most entrepreneurs are seduced by the mythology of starting their business in their garage, a Starbuck's, or in the basement or spare room of their house. They forget to think about their new venture's credibility and the need to surround themselves with like-minded people. The latter can offer peer support, knowledge sharing, valuable connections, accountability, and the business shared services that allow the founding team to focus on working *on* the business versus *in* it. I have met a lot of entrepreneurs who think they just need money to get their venture off the ground. They fail to consider the importance of the "intangibles"—like having experts assist them in managing venture risks and uncertainties and accelerating the growth and development of their venture smarter and stronger than they might do on their own. This is where working with established entrepreneurial support leaders can make all the difference in the world.

---

vi. Tips for Nonprofit Business Builders

Who said innovation and entrepreneurship practices only apply to for-profit businesses? In my experience, some of the most creative and innovative people I know work and lead in the nonprofit sector. Someone once told me nonprofit is a tax status, not a business model. Nonprofits, while they sometimes operate differently "under the hood" than a traditional business, they can still benefit from the following success practices. Here are three things I believe nonprofit business builders need to keep at the forefront of their thinking:

1) Keep the mission-relevant and fresh, while always being transparent

A mission statement can serve any business, but for a nonprofit, it's especially critical, as it serves as a guiding principle of why the organization exists. It needs to be robust and concise at the same time, demonstrating the passion and call to action for your cause. From here, it's a matter of finding ways to consistently remind your staff, volunteers, clients, and stakeholders by ensuring strategic priorities and deliverables are connected and aligned. It is also essential to regularly "test" and "refresh" the mission to determine if any changes or enhancements need to be made. This is not mission drift but mission smart to do so.

Everyone needs to keep the mission in mind, and along these lines, donors and partners want to know how their money is being used. What are the outcomes, and how do you measure them? Social media, newsletters, annual reports, and speaking engagements are ways to share progress and needs at the same time. Above all, it's essential to cultivate a culture of transparency within your organization. To that end, some organizations choose to make public their 990s, financial statements, and other organizational documents (articles of incorporation, tax determination letter, or bylaws) on their website, in-person in their office, or on reporting sites like GuideStar.

2) Be gracious—don't discount emotional connection, but remember to flex your "no" muscle regularly

Volunteers are the lifeblood of all nonprofits, especially those with limited staff and resources. It is essential to show gratitude for your volunteers with recognition and perks as you would for an employee. For example, mentors with Big Brothers Big Sisters of Northeast Indiana have access to discounts at a variety of local food and entertainment destinations to make outings more affordable. Don't discount the need for volunteers to feel connected and have memorable experiences with your organization to stay engaged. Hospitality is an essential hallmark of effective engagement with one of your most valuable talent pools—volunteers.

On the other hand, nonprofits are often presented with ideas that sound great on the surface, but participation can mean a strain on limited resources or deviation from the organization's core competencies. At times, nonprofits are coerced or strongly guided to do things a community leader, board member, or funder push them toward even if it doesn't make sense to them. Nonprofit leaders must learn when to politely decline these invitations when the numbers or the approach doesn't add up. This is often very difficult because nonprofit organizations don't like to disappoint their stakeholders but saying yes can result in an unfunded mandate and cause undue stress in the organization.

3) Intentionally build your innovative capacity and capability

Many nonprofits are incredibly adept at pivoting their business model, finding new revenue sources, and consistently measuring their client impact. By focusing on their core purpose, nonprofits can often deliver exceptional services that meet or exceed their customer's needs. However, having a robust innovation pipeline is as important to the sustainability of a quality nonprofit organization as a good fund development plan.

Nonprofits need to embrace innovative practices to strengthen their business model, continuously improve their programs and services, and retain talented team members. Research has shown that employees who bring their creative gifts out at work are more likely to have higher organizational engagement than those that don't.

---

vii. Your Product Demo Sucks (And How to Fix It)

Selling people on your product often starts with a demo[101], no matter how formal or informal. The problem is, many business builders approach this opportunity the wrong way because they are too close to their product. That said, here are a few tips to deliver better product demos:

1) Less is more.

You might think your widget is the greatest thing since sliced bread, but no one wants to hear you drone on and on about the technical minutia. Instead of getting mired in every little detail, come prepared to answer questions you anticipate will arise. In other words, make it more of a conversation. Sometimes the best presentations are more "off the cuff" than formulaic and rehearsed. Be sure to talk about the features and benefits from the customer's or end user's perspective—this is design thinking empathy, putting yourself in the customer's shoes. Remember to clearly and succinctly describe the pain, problem, or opportunity your product, service, or solution satisfies.

2) Don't forget about customer discovery—a key component of the business model search and execution process.

You may have an hour at most to make your case. This means the bulk of your work should be done in advance. What matters most to the prospect? What are their pain points? You'll need to understand where they are coming from before launching into your spiel—and you need to address those concerns somehow. Use this chance to gain important customer intelligence and to forge a connection with your customer or end-user.

3) Tune in.

It's always a good idea to know your audience and check-in. Consider the collective energy, their backgrounds, their vocabulary/jargon, and how they talk about their product and the potential fit with yours. Communicate the way they communicate, and you're more likely to have a deeper connection and close the deal.

When in doubt, remember it's not about you. It's about them.

---

viii. Carving Out Your Niche: Re-defining Success on YOUR Terms

What does it take to carve out your own personal niche?

Authenticity. Gravitas. Personal mojo. Stick-to-itiveness. Vulnerability.

Entrepreneurship is not easy no matter how you slice it. But it can be a difficult and challenging thing when an aspiring woman is breaking into starting their own business.

Over the years, I can recall several women business owners who shared their frustration with how some male leaders in our community tried to dissuade them from leaving their jobs at larger local employers. They shared with me how they were told that their businesses would inevitably fail, and they should not even try. Comments were centered on things like their idea was not good enough, or they were not equipped to be an entrepreneur. So, against the odds, what where some of their techniques to address these early adversities and blaze their own trail?[102]

First: They had a strong belief in themselves.

Don't let anyone take away your personal power. Trust your gut—while at the same time—do not be afraid to go against the grain. These women possessed confidence and humility. They didn't take no for an answer. They focused on getting and satisfying customers. Often, their initial customers came from outside our community.

Second: They built their network—powering it with smart and focused resources and cultivating an "inner circle of influence" by establishing a brain trust.

The most successful business builders understand that it's okay not to know everything, and it's perfectly acceptable to lean on business partners for knowledge and support and to access resources that might give you a leg up in starting your venture. Many entrepreneurial women's groups foster a "we're in this together" mindset, with meetings to converse with like-minded individuals in a supportive and welcoming environment.

From there, focus on establishing a close-knit group of confidants. There is a lot of wisdom to be gained from the success, and failures, of your tribe. Maybe your company or business idea lacks focus, or you don't have a plan for scalability. A mentor can help you troubleshoot, support you in gaining insights and higher levels of self-awareness, and implement the necessary changes in you and in your business. He or she can also serve as a sounding board for decisions and an emotional support system for the choppy waters of starting a business or leaving your job. These are close advisors with rich and deep expertise whose only interest is in your success.

Third: They embraced positivity and focused on their energy level to produce early wins—not on their activities or to-do list.

You can't do it all well—at least without going crazy, no matter who or what gender you are. Time is a limited and precious resource. Hiring your first employee is both scary and necessary. It puts you on a path that only 12% of female businesses can accomplish. Savvy entrepreneurs know when to replenish and refresh their energy levels.

One female founder told me that our local women's entrepreneurial center "represented her B12 shot." As you might know, a deficiency in B12 vitamin can mean that if "you come up short on the vitamin, it can result in intense fatigue to wonky vision." So when you need a "boost" to be built up when you are facing rejection, experiencing loneliness, or feeling like you are not making faster progress, seek out a knowledgeable, trusted entrepreneurial support provider to inspire and co-create and engage mentors and trusted advisors to bring out the best in you. Female entrepreneurs can gain confidence from the encouragement and support network, with guidance through the entrepreneurial path step by step to make sure you are heading in the right direction. A mentor of mine once opined, "Don't live in the rear-view mirror. Live in the windshield."

---

ix. Three Lessons Entrepreneurs Can Learn from Food Trucks

Food trucks have been one of the fastest-growing food businesses for quite some time. No longer just a trend in L.A. or New York, food trucks have enjoyed a loyal following nationwide and in the Midwest for several reasons. I am not going to get into a political and esoteric debate on whether food trucks are suitable for a community or not—let's just agree that they are. It's no accident that food tourism and a food truck culture are permeating our society, given some surveys have shown 88% of millennials want to explore new types of food.

Here are three lessons you can take from these mobile food startups and apply them to your business. You may be wondering what food trucks can teach you. Well, this booming, bohemian industry is now over $2 billion[103] (for comparison purposes, it was 25% of this size in 2012), so the food truck industry can teach us a lot.

1) Think hyper-local.

The most successful operators know where to go and when to attract business. By analyzing trends, they are able to build and implement a marketing plan. Other business owners can follow suit. Even if your business isn't geographically defined, you can home in on your target demographic. What are their likes and dislikes? Where do they like to hang out? Who or what influences their thinking? Gleaning such business intelligence allows you to execute your marketing messages with laser-like precision. How can your company and its products/services create a new experience for your clients/customers?

2) Go where the action is on-demand, real-time.

Whether it's a 5k race, music festival, or another public event, food truck operators can be at the right place at the right time. The mobile nature of a food truck allows for operators to pivot in response to market or environmental forces as necessary. While your business may not be mobile, you can still enjoy similar success. How can you pare it down and hit up the hot spots? For example, if you own a clothing store, maybe you could bring a few top-selling items to a farmer's market or expo show?

3) Find your niche.

All the great food trucks have a unique selling value-proposition. It might be eye-catching art or a signature menu item. It could be the way orders are taken or executed. Infusing some "personality" and "life" into your brand experience can be vital in standing out in a competitive landscape. Your business can learn a lesson or two in this regard. Think beyond your branding when it comes to dazzling the customer. If you have a storefront, what sights, sounds, and smells will they encounter? How can you leave a lasting impression in the consumer's mind?

---

x. Marketing Failures and Lessons Learned

For every "win" out there in the marketplace in terms of innovation, there are likely at least nine other failures. It's just that we don't always hear about the flops. Indeed, history doesn't tend to favor mistakes. But sometimes the most important lessons come from failure. Here is a look at several flops over the last few years and the takeaways:

1) The Fail: Guerrilla Marketing Gone Wrong

The Cartoon Network went overboard with this promotion and instantly became a case study for guerrilla marketing gone wrong in 2007. The company was trying to promote the show Aqua Teen Hunger Force with LED circuit boards featuring the show's pixelated characters on public structures around the city of Boston. What they didn't account for was the anxiety they induced with a bizarre creature making an offensive gesture, along with complex electrical circuits laid out for no apparent reason. The campaign completely backfired, as some were concerned the boards were bombs and contacted the authorities. As a result, the parent company Turner had to pay $2 million to the Boston Police Department for the resulting investigation.

The Lesson: If you plan to do something unorthodox, it's always good to work with law enforcement from the outset. Keep them informed of what you're doing and get the permits and licenses that are necessary to execute something that might seem—at best—out of the ordinary, or—at worst—suspicious.

2) The Fail: Codename Fizzle

Critically acclaimed as a marketing disaster, Radio Shack's decision in 2009 to call itself "The Shack" failed faster than you could say "OMG." They flushed decades of loyalty down the toilet for the sake of adopting a cooler brand persona.

The Lesson: Some brands aren't meant to be "cool," and that's okay. Stick with what works with your target audience. There's a danger in trying to pander to a particular demographic at the risk of seeming out of touch with your base or even worse alienating your loyal customers.

3) The Fail: Controversial Hot Water

Coffee behemoth Starbucks went out on a limb in March 2015 when it launched a campaign encouraging customers to talk about race. Their stock plummeted, and consequently, Starbucks dropped the campaign in less than a week. In my opinion, Starbucks CEO's efforts to be a polarizing voice in the 2016 election was also detrimental to their brand.

The Lesson: It's often best to stay clear of controversial issues unless it's part of your brand DNA. If you serve coffee, serve coffee—and spare the social commentary. Starbucks ' CEO should spend his time focusing on sluggish store sales growth rather than pontificating on political and social turmoil in the United States. Frankly, I agree with Schultz's critics who remind him that his "role is to create shareholder value and profit; not to use Starbucks as a political tool."

Save yourself the trouble and be sure you know your metrics—the acquisition costs of new customers, the lifetime value of a customer, and customer churn rate. Then you can decide on who the *"right customers"* are and how to market to them.

According to the Harvard Business Review, depending on what industry you're in, "acquiring a new customer is anywhere from five to 25 times more expensive than retaining an existing one."[104] It has been further revealed that if you increase customer retention rates by just 5%, it can potentially increase profits by 25% to 95%.[105] Remember these stats next time you have an impulse to spend a fortune on experimental marketing to a new audience.

---

xi. Three Practical Lessons from Running a Lemonade Stand

Kids don't take life too seriously, and they also know how to bounce back from adversity quickly. If you've ever seen a lemonade stand enterprise, then you know exactly what I mean. Sometimes the kid behind the stand knows more about how to succeed in business than many adults who tend to over-think things. We all could learn a thing or two from these young entrepreneurs. Here are the three business lessons grown-ups can glean from kids' no-nonsense approach to business:

Lesson 1: It's okay to start small.

For many kids, setting up a simple lemonade stand and selling sugary drinks to their neighbors is their first entrepreneurial venture. Talk about modest! But the critical point is the fact they started in the first place.

The lesson here is simple—don't get overwhelmed by an aspirational goal. Focus on your current strengths and wins. Don't forget the everyday victories that often go overlooked. It's okay to start small and grow from there—do what you can, with what you have, right now.

Lesson 2: "No" is not the end of the world. According to J.B. Bernstein, "No is the beginning of a negotiation."[106]

Kids tend to handle setbacks and disappointments differently than adults—and that's usually to their benefit. Lemonade stands aren't always cash cows. Sometimes the weather is terrible or there's competition. While facing setbacks in the business world, look for opportunities to keep propelling forward, rather than fixating on a single deal that didn't go well. It's okay to reflect on what went wrong and correct course, but don't obsess—or else you'll do yourself and your business a disservice.

Lesson 3: Zero in on your "target" customer.

For many kids, their first customer will probably be mom, dad, or a sibling. Knowing who and who isn't your target customer is crucial. Finding your "desired" customer is often the result of rigorous and disciplined customer discovery and validation efforts. Often, this means experimentation and trial and error. Kids learn quickly who the real buyers of their services are, and they focus and target relentlessly on that demographic or customer segment.

Chapter 7: Conclusion

The most important part of knowing your niche is understanding who exactly your ideal customer is, and what pain points you are solving for them. Once you know who, and what, you can work on the how—highly specific targeted marketing. This will save you so much time and money in the long run. Don't worry about being popular with everyone, because if you try, you'll be interesting to no one. No one wants to water down milk—they want the real deal. Embrace your company's unique value add and build a tribe of loyal customers who believe in your brand.

Chapter 7: Questions for Consideration

i. Case Study: Planet Fitness and Knowing Your Niche

What can you learn from Planet Fitness' approach? Consider those you *do not* want to serve and keep them in mind while you market your business, almost as much as you keep in mind whom you *are* selling to.

ii. Plant-Based Power: Lessons from Natural Foods Disrupters

What do you think? Do meat alternatives have staying power? And does the opportunity shift reflect lessons or interactions for other disrupters in other industries? Does your brand have a narrative? What is it, and how can you leverage it in your marketing efforts?

iii. A Marketing Case Study: Earth Day 50 Years Later

Regardless of whether your brand is "green" or not, how can you find a way to draw people into a movement that inspires and is inclusive? Is it possible for your brand to be both broad and specific at the same time? If your marketing material is several years old, it could be time for a refresh and update, don't let your message become outdated.

iv. A Call to Action on Rural Entrepreneurship

What myths or beliefs are holding you back? Have you considered that they may be entirely self-actualizing? Write down and then research the most significant obstacles you are facing. With a little ingenuity and assistance from a local business center or incubators, you could almost surely get around each and every one.

v. Launching a Venture? Some Potential Pitfalls

What potential pitfalls have you fallen into? Perhaps there have been some hidden stumbling blocks not mentioned here, what did you do to cope? You wouldn't pull your tooth if you had a toothache, you'd go to a professional. Likewise, consider avoiding the pain and suffering, and tap into your community's most comprehensive resource for high-potential ideas, companies, and talented business builders. Why go it alone when you can have a robust and organic entrepreneurial ecosystem behind you?

vi. Tips for Nonprofit Business Builders

I often ask organizations; how many ideas are in their innovation pipeline and how long have they been there? And more importantly, what are you going to do about it? Innovation is critical to the long-term success and sustainability of the nonprofit sector. How is your nonprofit building and sustaining its innovative pipeline and evolving its culture around innovation? These same questions can also be asked of for-profit businesses—you're either growing or dying.

vii. Your Product Demo Sucks (And How to Fix It)

What were some of your surprises (both positive and negative) when you had the opportunity to demo your product? How could you have better prepared in order not to run into them? The importance of customer discovery and understanding your client cannot be emphasized enough.

Here are some tips on creating a buyer persona representing your ideal customer.[107]

viii. Carving Out Your Niche: Re-defining Success on YOUR Terms

When you need a boost, where do you go, or what do you do to replenish your energy? If you don't have access to a group of like-minded entrepreneurial individuals, look into the local business development centers and think of them as a wellspring of business savvy vitality.

ix. Three Lessons Entrepreneurs Can Learn from Food Trucks

Which of these strategies could you adopt and apply to your business? How can you think hyper-local or go where the demand is? This doesn't have to be taken literally either, get creative, and think about harnessing the power of technology to accomplish this, for example, setting up a geofencing for targeted ads.

x. Marketing Failures and Lessons Learned

Do you know the acquisition costs of new customers, the lifetime value of a customer, and the customer churn rate? Be sure you keep these metrics in mind, along with your ideal customer before you start any marketing campaigns.

xi. Three Practical Lessons from Running a Lemonade Stand

What other lessons have you learned from young entrepreneurs? How can you put them into practice in your business today? Think about starting small, and how to turn a no into a yes.

CHAPTER 8

COMPETITIVE ADVANTAGE

Having a proverbial leg up on the competition can make all the difference in the world, as being forgettable is the antithesis to success. For you to stick in your client's head and have a chance to make it as a viable company—you must be memorable, remarkable, provide a unique value add, or inspire them to act. To do this, you and your company must act with intentional purpose in everything you do. From honest communication and genuine connection to being helpful and always going above and beyond, if you build a solid base of committed fans from day one—you will have staying power for the long haul. The truth be told, competitive advantages have to be refined and reimagined over time to be durable and sustainable.

In 1999 in a Fortune article, The Oracle of Omaha, Warren Buffet was quoted as saying:

"The key to investing is ... determining the competitive advantage of any given company and, above all, the durability of that advantage. The products or services that have wide, sustainable moats around them are the ones that deliver rewards to investors."

i. The Truth About Competitive Advantage

The truth be told I have always been a student of management strategy. From my early introductions to Michael Porter's seminal work[108] in college to my admiration of Jim Collins in my favorite business book of all times—Good to Great[109], I think there is an industry obsession with the concept of competitive advantage. However, it is often misused and misapplied.

Audit any website or piece of marketing collateral in any industry, and you'll likely encounter something to the tune of "competitive advantage" mentioned or alluded to somewhere. *What does that even mean in 2020?*

This phrase has become trite because well-meaning business builders have co-opted the meaning to their detriment. Competitive advantage is *not* a list of your strengths. Furthermore, if your list is only comprised of strengths, it is not a "competitive" advantage. If you don't have a competitive advantage built on more than strengths, you can't effectively compete. You exist, and that's no way to be. Competitive advantages are rare, special, hard to imitate, and don't last a lifetime. Innovative organizations have to continually morph and grow with changes in the competitive landscape and market conditions. For example, a tax firm may claim the following:

- Good reputation in the community
- Experienced staff and responsive customer service
- Robust client list and loyalty

At first glance, you can see that this is not a list of unique competencies or advantages. Anyone in business needs to have those core competencies to stay in business. An earnest business builder may think these points are something to write home about. Still, in reality, these are strengths in a SWOT analysis but seldom arise to become competitive advantages.

This begs the question, what is the right way? Think of your competitive advantage as your organization's DNA—a collection of genes or traits that makes you one of a kind (special and rare) in your industry or geography. Your competitive advantage is what your company or your division does better than anyone else. It's what you *are*, not what you *do*.

Maybe your business is young, and you're still charting those waters. Or perhaps you've been around for decades and are too close to it to be objective. Either way, the easiest way to find or rediscover your competitive advantage is to remember what one of my undergraduate professors once said, "figure out what you do better than anyone else (distinctive competence) and pick competitors you can beat (competitive advantage) by doing what you do best." Competitive advantages are not a laundry list. Companies may only have one; that is why they are rare and fragile!

Now that you have figured it out, how do you put it into practice? When you have it defined and internalized, it will help you and your team know:

1) Which opportunities to pursue and which to decline (what should you stop doing is often more important than what you choose to do—know the difference between an opportunity versus a distraction);
2) Where to allocate resources and where to cut back (this includes when to outsource (cheaper) and when to keep it in the house (more expensive)); and
3) How to improve on what you already do well. The most innovative companies have an acute understanding of how to shape, evolve, and continuously refine and invest in their competitive advantage, and it shows.

---

ii. Thinking Big: How to Penetrate a National Market

Many home-grown success stories started small, with a local or regional account base. Take Sweetwater Sound (https://www.sweetwater.com/about/team/), for example—founder Chuck Surack[110] set up shop out of a bus. Sweetwater's website[111] captures this incredible success story: "Back in 1979, Chuck Surack had a 4-track recording studio in the back of his V.W. bus. He'd record bands in local clubs, then take the tapes back to his home to mix and master them. Like every musician and studio owner, Chuck was always looking for new and better gear."

Decades later, and despite significant changes in the marketplace and technology, he has not veered from that goal, and it has served him well. Today, his company is considered a leading retailer of musical and professional audio equipment on a global level with unparalleled customer support and raving fans everywhere.

How can your business scale to become a player in the national marketplace? The following steps are essential:

1) Select "best of breed" suppliers

Competing nationally and globally requires next-level partners, processes, and tools. Unless you're willing to place a monster of an order, beware that national suppliers may not be interested in doing business. Talk about a chicken-and-egg problem!

That's why, as an emerging firm, your procurement strategy should focus on strength in numbers. Join forces with other local companies before submitting your order. This is a way for national suppliers to take you seriously and help build a relationship that could take your venture to the next level. You might also distinguish yourself by sharing with the national supplier your venture's roadmap, and how you plan to grow and build into a significant enterprise so they can see the potential. This approach might cause them to buy into your plans and support your business accordingly.

2) Leverage data into strategic decision-making

Businesses of all sizes and stripes stand to benefit from data mining. For example, if you own a kennel, can you track local trends related to travel? Are there weeks during the year where people with pets go out of town (spring break, summer vacation, holiday) and therefore, might need your services? What weeks tend to be slow? With this data in your arsenal, you can target prospects and customers to drum up business during those quiet times.

I am also fascinated by the demand-driven pricing of airlines. Delta does this exceptionally well selling some tickets at a really low rate and then selling additional seats at a higher rate followed by more seats at an even higher rate. Also, why is it prices go down on Tuesday but might go up on Friday when more people might be planning their trip?

3) Curb labor costs

Full-time talent comes with a price, and related expenses tend to add up fast. Lean on independent contractors whenever possible, especially for ad hoc projects or temporary increases in demand. By going this route, you can stretch your dollar and transfer the full burden of labor-related costs to your outside provider—payroll taxes, unemployment insurance, workers' compensation, pensions, sick days, health insurance, and vacation time all add up.

As an entrepreneur looking to scale, a flexible workforce on the labor front means you can invest resources in other areas that might deliver more of an ROI.

Many view national brands as giants because they have the resources at their disposal to take more risks. However, startups have something in their back pocket that more prominent firms don't—the ability to innovate. A younger company is often nimbler and therefore, can change processes and course faster than a larger and more established corporation. Simply put, startups are hungrier. It should go without saying but always *play to your strengths.*

An excellent article in the Harvard Business Review entitled *Why Entrepreneurs Don't Scale*[112] makes the leadership difference in scaling crystal clear: "entrepreneurs who grow into leaders almost always scale because they are open to learning. They want to be molded by new experiences and to improve their leadership selves. In fact, leaders who scale do so regardless of background, skill, and talent. Rather, they scale because they take deliberate steps to confront their shortcomings and become the leaders their organizations need them to be. Instead of floundering, they learn to fly."

Bottom Line: The national stage is only so big. However, to get bigger, as a nascent company, you have to think big and execute small.

---

iii. "Would You Like Fries with That?" What Business Builders Can Learn From These Chain Successes

Despite what you think of the quality of their food, the customer experience you enjoy, or the business model challenges they face, U.S. based quick-service restaurant (QSR) chains are increasingly vying for market share. The top three are competing neck and neck with each other, according to the most recent data available. Per the report, McDonald's, Starbucks, and Chick-fil-A took the top three spots in that order.[113]

So, what's the secret sauce? Here are three reasons why I believe these chains are such powerhouses:

1) McDonald's

McDonald's has mastered the art of consistency and brand recognition. It doesn't matter if you're visiting a McDonald's in Ohio or Hong Kong—you're going to have a similar experience wherever you are. This highlights founder Ray Kroc's vision for McDonald's from the very beginning and part of the reason why Micky D's is still relevant today.

The consistency is rooted in a systematic approach. McDonald's training program, Hamburger University, has taught future franchisees how to run a store the way Kroc laid out over five decades ago. This methodology informs the entire experience, from ordering to enjoying the food.

Finally, McDonald's has been at the forefront of innovation in the industry. They were among the first QSRs to add a drive-thru to their stores. Moreover, over the years, they've test-marketed dozens of new products and innovations. The willingness to take risks has played a significant role in fending off stagnation over the years.

2) Starbucks

Starbucks has managed to offer much more than a cup of coffee and snacks. They've worked hard to become a "third place" or an alternative venue (from work or home) for socializing. Not coincidentally, the company operates with a strong sense of attention to detail, meaning, like McDonald's, it offers a consistent customer experience globally. That applies to the drinks and the atmosphere. Although there's room for some interpretation store to store, the general Starbucks interior design concept is fairly consistent no matter the locale.

On top of all that, Starbucks has been recognized for its social reasonability practices. For example, they employ ethical, sourcing practices and work with coffee farmers to empower them with education and training. Most recently, the coffee giant announced it would eliminate all plastic straws globally by 2020, a move that has captured the attention of people committed to sustainability practices.

3) Chick-fil-A

On the surface, closing on Sundays might not seem like a decision with far-reaching effects. However, I believe this move is inherent to its success. Chick-fil-A has profited from creating a concept of scarcity and reinforced their core purpose and values. By closing on Sunday, the restaurant chain creates more of a demand on the other days of the week. Therefore, the Chick-fil-A experience becomes more of a novelty than QSRs that remain open seven days a week.

The corporate culture is no doubt informed by its intentional approach to operations. Since 1973, Chick-fil-A has given more than $35 million in college scholarships to employees. They help out employees in other ways, too. With a guaranteed day off (Sunday), the company promotes a healthy work-life balance. Leadership knows that happy employees are productive ones, only adding to the bottom line.

iv. Discounting 101: Good or Bad for Business?

Macy's marks-up products to mark them down. That good deal at a final clearance of 75% of MSRP? It was never sold anywhere close to MSRP—it probably started at 67% off. Kohl's gives you Kohl's cash, and then you feel obligated to spend it, so Kohl's increases its product prices during the redemption period when you go to use the cash—but you still feel like you got a good deal. The bottom line is: pricing drives behavior, so what behaviors are you trying to drive?

Customers want a product that fits their wants and needs. Of course, the price is a significant factor in determining if the widget is attractive. It's classic economics—price is the exchange rate on the value that you've created. That means if the price is commensurate with value, both your customer, and your company walk away happy from the transaction. It's a win-win.

But what if sales are lagging? Do you need to unload inventory? Or maybe you're new to the market and want to generate brand recognition? Regardless of the situation, you might be wondering if offering a discount is a good idea. On the surface, discounts may be enticing to you, the seller, because they appear to provide the value that the customer is seeking for a price lower than your value metric indicates. Keep in mind value is relative, and your price sets the initial expectation of your product or service's perceived value.

Let's dive into the psychology behind discounts. The appeal of a discount is based on the first number we see to influence our decision about a subsequent price. Discounts use the original price as the basis of comparison so that the second price offered is evaluated with this context in mind.

Here's an example:

Say you're a photographer, and you offer a package at $900 that would typically cost $1000. Great deal, right? Though at first discounts might get more people in the door, messing with price/value proposition has consequences. That's because you're either promising your customers less value, or you're lowering the value of your product in their eyes. Delusional thinking would have you believe that you will make up the lower price with volume.

Your potential customer's perceived value of your product or service determines his or her willingness to pay. Too frequent discounts erode this perceived value and needlessly lower a customer's willingness to pay.

The good news is there are viable alternatives to discounting. You can achieve a win-win strategy for both your company and your customers without cannibalizing your revenue. Here are three proven techniques. While these aren't suitable for all industries or businesses, they are worth considering as case studies:

1) Create a freemium or low-cost tier.

This structure allows you to target many different sections of the market without having to compromise on profit margins. This model works because when your product's core value scales at a lower price, you can cater to more cost-conscious customers without cheapening the overall consumer experience. Netflix's pricing model is an excellent example of this.

2) Enhance value.

Instead of fixating on price, add value. You could throw in a free product, service, or asset that adds value to a full-price sale at no extra cost. For example, a cosmetics company might include a sample of a top-selling product with the order. This is a win-win because the customer gets a bonus, and the company can cross-promote products and potentially drive sales. Consider these online elements *of value framework*[114] that can help you sort through how best to do it since the value is often hard to define and measure.

3) Add a sense of urgency.

By creating online buzz, and feeding "the hype machine," Kanye's Yeezy footwear collaboration with Adidas was able to supercharge the traditional supply-and-demand model for lucrative results.[115] Available for a limited time, the Yeezy Boost 350 V2 sold out in under a minute. By creating urgency as a result of scarcity of a limited edition or release, combined with excitement and anticipation, you can charge full or a premium price for your in-demand product or service. There is an inherent draw in exclusivity, and people will often act faster if they feel like they might miss out on a deal or opportunity.

A closing note: If you lean too heavily on discounts to drive conversions, you may have broader underlying issues. Your product needs to fulfill the needs and problems of your target market. To determine if your product is "sticky," survey your customers and ask how they would feel if they could no longer use your product or solution. Their answer may surprise you.

---

v. Don't Get Burnt: Three Lessons from the Fyre Festival

When the "dueling documentaries" chronicling the Fyre Festival disaster of 2017 premiered on Netflix and Hulu, the internet almost had a meltdown.

The festival (positioned as an "immersive music festival") was the brainchild of entrepreneur-turned-fraudster Billy McFarland. He assembled a team of the best and brightest in their respective fields and sold them a false bill of goods in the process. Hundreds of festivalgoers, models, musicians, etc. were promised an experience that seemed too good to be true—and it was. His real motivation was to promote The Frye media app.

The documentaries follow all the drama and tension between the players, leaving you scratching your head. How did one man manage to fraud hundreds of people while not seeming to flinch? As the films seem to suggest, McFarland is either insane or a genius. While the festival was a colossal failure by all accounts and a significant fraud, there may be a few lessons you can glean from this ruse:

1) **Status sells.**

One thing the Fyre Festival tapped into was the power of influencer marketing. They engaged such personalities like Kendall Jenner, Bella Hadid, and Ja-Rule to help spread the word and set the tone that this event was exclusive. (It was, by definition, with tickets ranging in price from about $1,000 to $12,000.)

These celebrities weren't paid, but many received perks like complimentary airfare, festival tickets, and accommodations in exchange for taking to social media to promote what was billed as the event of the year. Did this strategy work? The proof was in the conversion. Jenner's post alone produced a crazy amount of impressions on Instagram, immediately surging ticket sales.

However, in the end, this growth was not sustainable. Why? The event team was scrambling to organize an event that should never have taken place in the first place at that location—the island lacked essential resources and basic amenities.

The same goes for bands, who knew the island (Great Exuma, in the Bahamas) was not set up for such infrastructure. It was slated to take place on *abandoned* resort development. Many would-be concertgoers, unhappy with the lack of response from customer service, canceled their tickets as they began to catch on that all was not as it seemed. Still, business builders can learn a lesson here in that aligning with the right people can build trust and credibility for your brand. Assuming, of course that your brand is built on ethical and core values in the first place.

2) **Social media campaigns can net real results.**

The hundreds of people who did show up for the would-be festival were met with miserable living conditions. Think disaster relief tents and piles of mattresses left out in the rain. The fare, which was sold as gourmet and top shelf, was a cold cheese slice on bread served in a Styrofoam box. Medical care and security were non-existent. The list of appalling shortcomings goes on and on.

As you might imagine, these influencers (over 400 of them) did what they do best and took to social media. They shared the bad and the ugly of the hours marooned on the island. Their fans followed along as the situation went from bad to worse. If there was any hope for a Fyre Festival 2.0, the negative publicity and complete fraud utterly destroyed it.

It is imperative to strive for and deliver an exceptional customer experience in addition to fulfilling what you promise. In the event, something does go awry, get in front of it to keep it from spinning out of control.

3) Own your mistakes.

McFarland, confident beyond measure, never apologized for the travesty that was Fyre Festival. He burned many bridges and could not deliver on anything. There were several moments in the documentaries, which seemed to suggest he could have dismantled the whole plan and come clean with the people he took advantage of. However, being seduced by power and fame as he was, he pressed on—at the expense of so many and the cost of his freedom. He was sentenced to six years in federal prison for fraud.

---

vi. Success on Tap: What Business Builders Can Learn from Craft Breweries

"Beer is proof that God loves us and wants us to be happy."

Ben Franklin (supposedly) said this. I can't help but wonder what he'd think of our modern craft beer scene and its most loyal beer enthusiasts. In case you haven't noticed, the craft beer scene has exploded in recent years. That said, I think business builders of all types can learn a lesson or two from its success and growth.

1) Embrace your rivals—1+1 might just get you 3.

If you look at the craft brew community, there's an element of camaraderie and loyalty. Proprietors hang out with their "competition" and even exchange advice. It's not uncommon for brewers to form unofficial alliances to grow the craft beer/brewery scene in their region and beyond. There seems to be an attitude of "when one microbrewery succeeds, they all succeed." Consider, for example the Northern Indiana Beer Trail[116] as an example of local industry players coming together.

2) Engage the "right expertise," build the culture, and value your team.

As breweries or microbreweries are small by nature, their qualified and experienced staff (brewmaster, marketing/packaging, predictive data analytics, and the customer experience) are the lifeblood of their operations. And it's not just lip service. New Belgium Brewing seems to have set the gold standard for employee perks. According to *Business Insider*, "For instance, employees receive a branded fat-tire cruiser bike—a tradition started in 1999 as a nod to the brewery's flagship beer[117]—at year one, a one-week trip to Belgium at year five, a $1,000 travel voucher at year 15, and a four-week paid sabbatical at years 10, 20, and 30."[118] —*How cool is this culture?*

3) Never rest on your laurels—always be innovating the product, experience, brand, and the business model.

Beer is a dynamic and evolving product, meaning one ingredient or change in the process can completely alter the taste of a batch. Brewers know that the first batch is just a starting point—there's always room for improvement. They aren't afraid to solicit their customers for input and are open to experimentation so they can refine a recipe or scale a recipe as you just can't take a home recipe and expect it to be a commercial success. Businesses in any industry can follow suit.

Getting started is sometimes the hardest part.

---

vii. Relish the Competition or Fear Them?

Are you afraid of the competition, or do they make you better? Fear is not a productive emotion in business, or life (… well, for the most part). Did you know your competition could be an asset? Yes, as Forbes[119] argues, it's good for business! Let me discuss the competition on three levels: an entrepreneur or business builder looking to launch a new product or solution, an established company looking to regain traction in one or more of its business segments, and individuals inside a company looking to excel over colleagues.

1) For the new upstart venture, I always get concerned with business builders and entrepreneurs who say their product is so novel; they don't have any competition. Assuming you have no competition is not necessarily a good thing and is a red flag. Thinking you have the luxury of time, money, and resources to build a market from scratch is bunk. Find some competitors if you don't believe you have any.

2) In existing organizations and especially in strategic planning processes, there is an intense preoccupation with the competitors. The best advice I have received is, ignore them, but learn from them. Watch their missteps, false promises, execution failures, and be smarter, faster, and different. Management Strategist and Guru Dr. Michael Porter remind us that strategy is not about being better (in fact, being the best isn't a strategy)— but being different. He goes on to say, "Competitive strategy is about being different. It means deliberately choosing a different set of activities to deliver a unique mix of value."[120] This requires us to be astute resource allocators, place calculated bets, make tough trade-offs, and ensure a smart fit and proper alignment with your venture's core competencies.

3) Friendly rivalry within a company can be harnessed for good and utilized as a driving force for advancement. Individual one-upmanship, within reason, can inspire greatness and the urge to be the absolute best. It doesn't have to be individuals either; it can be whole departments. Disney and Pixar famously nurtured a culture of collaborative competition that kept each department, separate but together and constantly vying to secure more wins.[121]

We'd all benefit from pondering the following when evaluating the competitive landscape just by asking:

- **How can we be better at what we do?** This is operational effectiveness.
- **How can we be different/do something different—that no one else is doing?** This is at the heart of a healthy and enduring strategy.
- **How can we spark creativity together?** Incentivizing employees or encouraging friendly competition can galvanize outside the box thinking and unique solutions—even if this means collaboration with the game.

Once you have come to terms with your strategic approach, you can spend the majority of your time focused on executing your plan and aligning your resources to deliver the value that attracts and retains customers for life.

The lesson here? Don't be afraid of the competition. Embrace it with open arms but choose to be different and focus on unique value-creating activities that reflect your brand, your core purpose, and ignore the noise!

viii. The Midwest Advantage

So often, we associate innovation and entrepreneurship with Silicon Valley or Cambridge startups. While both coasts get a lot of press for having dynamic and engaging ecosystems, there's so much more to the entrepreneurial story. But as we know, good Midwesterners just don't brag enough about themselves like what we see in other geographies around the globe.

The middle-America entrepreneurial movement is energized. There are real and clear advantages to building companies outside the traditional entrepreneurial hotspots. Here are three reasons why the heartland is hot, when it comes to starting or scaling a business and why places like The NIIC attract global attention and have a world-class reputation:

1) Smart Right-Fit Talent

The Midwest is home to Tier One research universities with strong commercialization centers, which in turn develop talented engineers, scientists, technologists, finance professionals, and even entrepreneurs. And they are staying here. Organizations like the Questa Education Foundation locally incentivize Indiana students to pursue work in the state following graduation and lessen their school debt, making it more likely they can be entrepreneurial. A little-known fact is that the amount of credit card debt a graduating college student has, and the amount of school debt, have caused millennials to output the lowest new venture formation rate of any age group. Our workforce tends to be scrappy and motivated. Our work ethic is unrivaled.

2) Collaborative Spirit

Due in part to how leaders and people do business in the Midwest, the level of access you have to other entrepreneurs, larger supply chain companies, and political leaders is remarkable. Also, there tends to be a mentality of paying it forward that has helped businesses of all sizes grow and thrive. Business leaders tend to be less guarded here when it comes to sharing knowledge and experience—and that's a boon for the entrepreneurial community. Finding and engaging mentors, trusted advisors, and people invested in your success is a hallmark of the Midwest reputation.

3) Affordability and Proximity

Not everyone can afford to live in San Francisco. The Midwest is an attractive alternative to expensive apartments, hour-long commutes, and the general stressors that come with big city life. Fort Wayne, in particular, gets high marks for housing affordability. Homeownership for a middle-class family is in reach here, in contrast to coastal areas. Plus, from a business standpoint, costs like real estate and taxes tend to be lower in the Midwest. Indiana is known to have a pro-business climate. There's a reason Salesforce was attracted to Indianapolis. It leased about 250,000 square feet in Indianapolis' tallest building and is continuously expanding its workforce. Also, Indiana is at the crossroads of the United States. You can get to nearly 90% of the U.S. population in a day's drive, making us a magnet for the transportation and logistics industry, as Amazon and many others have found out.

---

ix. Three Lessons from Popular Super Bowl Ads

Sports fans and pop culture enthusiasts alike gear up every year for Super Bowl Sunday. Whether you genuinely love the on-field action or just tune in for the commercials, I think we can all agree that the Super Bowl offers entertainment value. Athletic performance and highly anticipated ads produce a winning combination. However, sometimes—they don't. Check out this list of famous Super Bowl flops.[122] Some of the flops included some important brand names: Ram trucks, Volkswagen, GoDaddy, and Groupon. Check out the end note to see how these ads received the wrong kind of attention.

What can business builders with more modest marketing budgets do to replicate this success on a smaller level, say, on social media? (The average cost of a thirty-second Super Bowl commercial hit $5.25 million in 2019.[123]) The following are a few lessons you can glean from the most memorable ads over the years to apply to your future marketing campaign.

1) Humor resonates.

Levity can be a marketer's secret weapon. Think about Wendy's, Doritos, Coca-Cola, and Career Builder commercials over the years. While more massive messages can stand out and have their place in reaching millennial audiences, many older viewers don't want to feel like they are being lectured or pandered to. Keep it light, and you'll have them talking for days.

2) Sizzle still sells.

How can you position your brand or product as cutting edge or something to be coveted? Look to the luxury auto industry for inspiration. They have a knack for making high-end vehicles synonymous with celebrity status or prestige, i.e., the sizzle factor.

How can your brand follow suit? Remember, as Seth Godin says, "be sticky, memorable, and remarkable."

3) Keep it short and sweet.

We live in an Age of Distraction, which means our collective attention spans are shorter than ever. Did you know a goldfish has an average attention span of nine seconds, and humans have an even shorter average attention span of eight seconds[124]?

If it's not bite-sized, it's not going to get through to younger audiences. So, don't bury the lead in a long and drawn-out ad. The most memorable Super Bowl ads are usually between thirty seconds to a minute. You'd be surprised how much you can say in such a short amount of time, especially when you have strong visuals to accompany.

x. Do's of Product Innovation

When most people think of innovation, products immediately come to mind. Think about driverless cars, iPads (360 million sold and counting since launching in 2010), or a new type of soda or sparkling water.

A product is only as good as its design. Many products start with a great idea or solution. But, by the time they launch, they fall short—not because of good intentions—but because they lack excellent product design, or they fail because the customer's needs are not well understood, or perhaps, the product targets the wrong market or is introduced at the incorrect price point.

Here are a few tried and true dos to help you avoid this fate and introduce a great product to the market.

DO.

1) Keep it simple. User-centered design is critical!

The possibilities in product design are truly endless. But often, what separates good design from mediocre is more about what is left out rather than what is included. The best products on the market are clean, intuitive, and solve a real-world—and validated—consumer problem.

While it may be tempting to implement every cool feature in the development process, it is more advantageous to keep only those features that genuinely improve your product. Recently, I purchased a Neat scanner to save time in preparing expense reports and to store documentation online. The product took hours to get it to work because it wasn't intuitive, and it lacked clear directions on how to enable the software. Even after use, it did a poor job of reading receipts—wrong date, not picking up the tip, and poor image quality. Despite the great marketing, the product is hugely lacking.

Keep your audience and their wants and needs in mind every step of the design process. It's easy to get trapped in our bubble and see product features as natural or even necessary. But ultimately you are ignoring a very important audience—the end user. What better way to get in tune with your market by doing a targeted test through a beta launch or involving them early through focus groups and human-centered interaction design efforts? You'll get a much better idea of how your audience is using your product and avoid having to invest in significant redesigns after the fact, which can cost you unnecessary time and money.

2) Collaborate and deliver WOW!

The most successful startups have proven that the best ideas come from working together in a team (letting just one person design your product limits you to one set of preferences and a singular point of view) or using rapid software delivery methods like agile and scrum. Don't fall into that trap of believing you can be Steve Jobs—while he was often a focus group of one, and he was a genius; most of the rest of us are not that good. Great design does factor in simplicity, a wow factor, and unmet consumer/customer needs.

I am a big Disney fan. I downloaded the My Disney Experience on my smartphone to enhance our trip and experience during my last visit. The app had the wrong number of days of our Park Hopper pass, often had incorrect tracking of our available Fast Passes, and didn't synchronize our dining reservations or Fast Passes across all of our family members using the app. This was meant to be a wow experience, but ... it wasn't. Every business needs to figure out how to be a "purple cow"[125]—both remarkable and memorable. The same is true of product innovations.

3) Do stay true to your company's core competencies.

As I mentioned above, not every feature under the sun will serve your end user. Stay true to the goals of what your product will do to address a need. Innovate in areas where you have expertise, insights, and capabilities. Core competencies are rare, unique, and hard to imitate. These "hard to build" and "hard to extend" skills distinguish your business in the marketplace. Product innovation should leverage institutional learning across the organization and provide the basis for competitive advantage in product innovation.

---

xi. Don'ts of Product Innovation

In the previous section, I shared some insights into best practices on product innovation. Therefore, it seems appropriate to visit the flipside. Don't let these "don'ts" sabotage or highjack your product innovation process:

DON'T

1) Operate in silos.

Innovation doesn't belong to a single department, function, or position. It's all around us. Think in terms of "Big I" innovation and "Little I" innovation. There are different kinds of innovations. And when they all come together toward a focused mission, great things happen.

Having the right people around you will make all the difference in the world. Great people beget great products. While it's tempting to settle for the talent you already have, selecting the right talent is well worth the extra effort. Settling results in subpar performance. Worst yet, putting someone into a role they will struggle with is a lose/lose. Don't settle—be picky, and you'll come out ahead. Gallup EP-10, StrengthsFinder, and psychometric assessments like Predictive Index can help you maximize each person's potential on your team.

2) Believe you will always get it right the first time.

You can avoid the high failure rate of innovation by experimentation and iteration. Talk early on with potential customers, avoid a one-size-fits-all solution, go beyond the price point, and finally, pick the winning pricing strategy—being conscious of communicating said innovation's value. Remember, pricing drives behavior. What type of behavior do you want to drive with the pricing strategy you implement?

3) Assume consumers will buy in right away.

"Build it, and they will come" is not a good philosophy on which to hinge your efforts in product innovation. Take, for example, Google's approach to the development of Google Glass. The tech giant built the product assuming consumers would buy it. As a result, the product flopped. However, had Google developed Glass for the professional and B2B segment, the outcome might have met a different fate. Take a look at this *Bloomberg Businessweek* cover story[126] to see the high price Alphabet was willing to pay for "moonshot" innovations. Alphabet calls its innovation efforts "Other Bets" in its annual report and racked up over $6B of losses in three years.

For many entrepreneurs, production design and launch are intense and personal. It's easy to get so passionate about the idea that you believe everyone will want to line up. Confidence is good—until it gets in the way, causing you to be blind to what's obvious to others.

Remember:

- Customers buy solutions, not products. You have to address the pain, problem, or job to be done.
- There is more to the innovation story than just product innovation. Think process, customer experience, brand, and channel among others.
- It takes more than one iteration or experiment to get your product "right." Your first idea is seldom your best idea.

Chapter 8: Conclusion

When trying to zero in on your competitive advantage, market research is your best friend. Fail fast, and often, until you hit the mark. Knowing and delivering what customers want in a hassle-free manner will win you a more loyal fanbase and greater success. A well thought out ad campaign in combination with a high-quality value add will help spur sales. Throw in a little healthy competition, and you have all the right ingredients for a productive and viable business venture. No matter what stage of the process you're at, it's essential to have outside perspectives—collaboration is critical.

Chapter 8: Questions for Consideration

i. The Truth About Competitive Advantage

What is *your* competitive advantage? There's no time like the present to re-focus, re-shape, and execute to create a sustainable and enduring competitive advantage! So, lift under the organizational hood, and find out what makes your company rare and special—and most importantly—different and unique.

ii. Thinking Big: How to Penetrate a National Market

Have you made any next-level partners? What's stopping you? Who can you reach out to? What insights can you gain from market data mining, and how can you leverage that knowledge to give your brand an edge? Are there any jobs you can outsource instead of hire in house? Virtual assistants can be very helpful and save you a host of extra time and fees in the process.

iii. "Would You Like Fries with That?" What Business Builders Can Learn from These Chain Successes

If you frequent one or more of the restaurants discussed in this section, what do you most enjoy about the experience? What can business builders learn from their success? Is there anything that you can apply or adapt to your business model.

iv. Discounting 101: Good or Bad for Business?

Let's just agree—discounts are not good in the long run. Can you create a freemium, add value, or create urgency? Or maybe you can cut out the middleman, buy wholesale, and pass the price savings on to your customer without losing your profit margin. There are many creative ways to avoid discounting and devaluing your product or service in the eye of the consumer. As Seth Godin always says, there are no winners in the race to the bottom. Don't undervalue yourself.

v. Don't Get Burnt: Three Lessons from the Fyre Festival

What can you take away from McFarland's epic miscalculation? Where and when did he go wrong? It is easy to spot his massive blunders, but hindsight and well researched documentaries are very helpful. It is imperative that you are able to heed the warnings before you go underwater. Social media and status can be seductive, erect a safety net to make sure you don't get pulled out to sea.

vi. Success on Tap: What Business Builders Can Learn from Craft Breweries

If you didn't view your competition as the "enemy" but as an opportunity to grow together, what more could you accomplish? How can you work with your community or others in your field to advance faster, and more creatively? Everything is a test in life; it's one big experiment. Don't be afraid to try many things and get failing out of the way faster—you just might learn something along the way.

vii. Relish the Competition or Fear Them?

How can you embrace competition? Think of it as a tool to inspire greatness and a chance to improve. How can you leverage unique value-creating activities that reflect your brand and core purpose? Make and execute a plan to attract customers for life.

viii. The Midwest Advantage

Have you assessed the pros and cons of which location would best be suited to nurture a startup? More and more companies are moving to remote work and satellite offices, eliminating the need to stay in a large, expensive city. If your cost of living was lower, what else could you accomplish, do, or invest back into your fledgling business? As crowded metropolises see mass exits after the global pandemic, maybe it's time to consider a more strategically advantageous home base.

ix. Three Lessons from Popular Super Bowl Ads

Can you take something popular and turn it to your advantage? Can you add a dash of humor? Great! Keep it super short, yet super catchy, and you're bound to get some traction—as long as you nail the visuals too but be careful not to alienate or offend your audience.

x. Do's of Product Innovation

Remember New Coke or Pepsi A.M.—for the "breakfast cola drinker"? Maybe you do, but these flash in the pans were only around for a brief time. They were "solutions" to nonexistent problems; no one was asking for them. In the end, both companies went back to the original, simplified version of their product. Be sure you get to know your customer, all their wants and needs, and remember, simple is best.[127] What pain/problem are you addressing in the marketplace? Have you completed customer discovery and validation field work to confirm the pain/problem?

xi. Don'ts of Product Innovation

Do you know if your product is viable for the respective market? Save yourself from unnecessary frustration by knowing the answer before going live, and don't fixate on price too early on in your market discovery and validation efforts. It's always good to "check yourself before you wreck yourself," meaning don't let yourself get too caught up in your head in the process. Check-in with others to make sure you aren't missing something big, have the right people on your team, and never assume anything without something to back it up. Self-assess your idea against the three don't. What pitfalls or obstacles might you anticipate?

BUSINESS INCUBATOR ICON

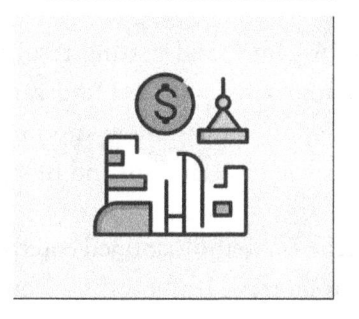

CHAPTER 9

SUSTAINABILITY

As with many things in life, building and maintaining a business venture is a marathon, not a sprint. It requires stamina, multi-dimensional thinking, and a wide array of skills—in short, it involves thinking and designing the business model with sustainability at the forefront of the thought process. According to the Small Business Administration, roughly half of small businesses will not survive past the five-year mark, with only one out of three reaching ten years.[128]

Aside from extreme commitment and courage, much like the philosophy of Stoicism, you will have to conquer many internal, as well as external battles. To increase your company's chances of survival, there are many things you can do. Keep reading to learn how you can take steps to safeguard the feasibility of your brand, model your business practices, engage with your organization, and invest in yourself and others. A key to a successful venture is to build it with sustainability practices from day 1. Cash flow liquidity is a key indicator of venture viability. Remember, the IDEO visual of the strength of an innovation is the degree of intersection of desirability, feasibility and viability.

i. Stay on Top of Your A-Game

You're bringing your "A-game" and getting results. Your customers are enamored with your innovative products and services. You're retaining the best and brightest, and your cash flow and profits are consistent and reliably stable. In short, you have rhythm and momentum.

But don't get complacent—a well-disciplined enterprise today isn't enough to keep you at the top tomorrow. If you want to continue to enjoy growth, you need to capitalize on your opportunities and relentlessly focus on execution.

Here are the three areas to self-assess:

1) Invest in your people.

Are you investing in the professional development of your best people? How do you keep them at the top of their game? Growing your talent pool is essential to capitalizing on strategic opportunities. In this healthy economic cycle, I hear more and more from businesses that they have had to turn away business because they can't find the human capital and talent, they need to fulfill the orders!

2) Push innovation.

When was the last time your company added value with a new product or service? Businesses that develop and market offerings that customers appreciate have a competitive advantage over the companies that just go with the status quo. If you need some inspiration, check out *Fast Company's* 50 Most Innovative Companies of the World.[129] Innovation is integral to an organization's long-term success but often is not a core competency of companies today

3) Reimagine your business model.

Stagnation doesn't happen overnight, but it can catch up with you over time. An adage is relevant here: If you're not growing, you're losing. Leadership calls for looking at novel ways to boost performance. Business model engineering—aligning and altering your business mix or launching new products or services can be an essential consideration in better managing your profitability and growth. Every strategy has a financial footprint. What is the financial footprint of your business strategy? What pivots or business model changes do you have to make to get better operational results?

So, if you want your business to come out on top—and remain there—you need to be proactive and intentional. Make sure innovation is a priority, tune in to financials, keep your employees happy and engaged, and be ready to pivot when necessary.

ii. The Importance of Delegating

Best known for co-founding both Kiva and ProFounder, Jessica Jackley[130] has helped entrepreneurs around the world gain access to funding through micro-loans. According to Jackley, the ability to prioritize and delegate directly impacted her success as an entrepreneur.

"As all entrepreneurs know, you live and die by your ability to prioritize. You must focus on the most important, mission-critical tasks each day and night, and then share, delegate, delay, or skip the rest."[131]

You've no doubt heard the phrase "work smarter, not harder." That adage applies to how you might delegate tasks in your business or professional life. While it can be hard to relinquish control of some functions in your business for various reasons, there comes a time when you have to offload so you can stay focused on growth or jeopardize your success and achievement of your goals. You can't do it all.

While the specifics while vary according to the organization, there are a few general areas in which most business builders could benefit from shifting activities to other parties:

1) Start with your digital assets.

In its annual survey, Adobe found that people, on average, spend more than five hours per day checking their email. That's more than half a typical workday. Yowza! Find better and smarter ways to manage the demands on your time and energy and better filter your inbox management.

Social media management can also demand a great deal of time, especially when there are multiple channels to monitor. If you're at the executive level and handling reputation management, you might rethink your priorities. An outsourced firm or part-time contractor can help do the heavy lifting on the day-to-day tasks with ease.

2) Check-in with employees on how to improve workflow.

Are you the source of delays in workflow? Ask your employees and encourage them to be candid. Do they experience lags in productivity because you're preoccupied with the minutiae? Are they waiting on you for the green light on projects more often than not? Those delays are usually because you don't have the time, the bandwidth, or the desire to do those things—another sign you need to transition such responsibilities.

3) Look for inconsistencies in your rhythm and energy.

Finally, take stock of things you're pushing off until the very end of the day. What are the tasks you're scrambling to complete when you'd instead call it a day? Those are precisely the things you need to consider offloading for everyone's sake.

As you're going through your day, make yourself aware of the tasks that are time sucks or sources of anguish. Talk to your team and see how you might be able to focus on the tasks you enjoy and fit into your schedule. That's the recipe for a happy and productive workday.

iii. Rethinking Busyness

"It is not enough to be industrious; so are the ants. What are you industrious about?"

— Henry David Thoreau to H.G.O. Blake; November 16, 1857

In other words, what are you busy about in your life? Busy seems like a badge of honor these days. Everyone is "busy" with some pursuit of pursuits. But what does this even mean anymore? Often, reducing clutter in our life, prioritizing what's important, and getting organized will make it to the top of our new year, new us lists—yet 80% will give up on their resolutions by the second week in February.[132] What can we do, at any point of the year, to make these new habits stick?

A business associate once shared with me his mantra, *"Never come home with an empty tank."* How often are we depleted, low on energy, and just managing to get through our day? People obsess about and almost worship "busyness" because they seem to equate it with productivity or a badge of honor. However, I am reminded by what my first boss taught me, "Results, *not* effort, get rewarded." It can quickly become a contest of who's more oversubscribed. For example, you might answer 80 emails in a day, attend 5 meetings, or share about some other way you measure busyness. But the truth is, such tasks don't always translate to meaningful results, or more importantly, a purposeful, fulfilled and connected life. They can become mindless and leave us unfulfilled, demotivated, and disengaged if we don't check our energy level regularly.

The next time you feel "too busy" to accept a compelling invitation, I challenge you to:

1) Take a step back.

What is currently filling the time you'd need to do X or Y? How does it rate in the grand scheme of things? We *can* find the time. And we *can* make time. If something is a priority, we often can find a way to make it happen. But when we get caught up in the moment, it's easy to forget what *is* important. We create a false sense of urgency around things that are not pressing, and what's near and dear to our heart can fall to the wayside.

2) Think for a moment about the life you are living.

What's missing, or what would you care to do more of if you thought differently? With this in mind, you'll have to carve out or make to a priority to find that time. While we might not be able to quit our jobs to write the next Great American Novel, there's one universal truth—there's always a time we let slip through the cracks. If you can take back those lost minutes and hours, you might be surprised how life can be more gratifying. You might be surprised by the time you can find to spend with someone. Often, at the end of life, we don't have regrets about the things we said yes too, but we often have regrets about the things we said no to. We often think in terms of next time—but next time might never come.

3) Check your tank.

Are you running on empty? Have you pushed yourself to the brink of exhaustion? Be honest with yourself. No one is superhuman, and the risk of burnout is real. Taking time for yourself can be crucial for your health and the long-term success of your business. When was the last time you "treated" yourself to a bit of downtime, an activity to feed your creativity, or even just some personal time? If you can't remember when it is long past due for you to refill your brain bank with something other than work.

---

iv. Don't Leave Change Management to Chance

It's said that the only constant in life is change. The business world is not immune from this truth. There's even a whole field dedicated to helping companies navigate times of transition, and it's called change management.

Change in any context requires a mindset rooted in curiosity and fearlessness, not fear. How do you foster this feeling in the workplace when uncertainty prevails? The following are practical way

1) Speak the same language.

Words matter and can be an unintended source of confusion internally. Start by creating a company-wide glossary or style guide with commonly used terms or phrases. Cut the clutter and limit the use of jargon for the sake of jargon. Get everyone on board, regardless of level or seniority, using the same lexicon.

The truth is if different departments use inconsistent language to describe the same thing, the higher the chance of misunderstandings and mistakes. That chaos could come across externally and weaken your brand and credibility.

2) Prioritize visibility.

It's a phrase heard in offices everywhere: Where are we with X project, and who's responsible for the next steps? The human element of project management (PM) can be the weakest link. That's why software solutions can provide a big-picture view so that everyone is plugged into status updates in real-time.

A comprehensive view, along with a unified strategy, helps break down silos and better prioritize projects. Real-time insights can encourage efficiency and reduce the amount of unproductive time on the job. With such tools, there's no need to wonder about project status or manually update spreadsheets.

3) Increase transparency.

A lack of transparency and communication can wreak havoc on an organization in the form of the rumor mill, coffee pot conversations, and undue anxiety. Transparency across the ranks and meaningful communication is critical.

Messaging should be consistent, personalized, and delivered to address different learning styles. For example, in some organizations, a weekly or monthly employee newsletter, social media posts, and Slack are some solutions companies have implemented.

Beyond the execution, you should seek feedback from employees about whether or not the communication is resonating with them. Consider employing surveys, polls, or using the Happy or Not[133] system to measure employee satisfaction in the workplace and easily accessible tools to capture their opinions.

Anyone living in the twenty-first century must accept the simple fact that the world is continually changing, especially when it comes to technology and the way things are done. You must be open to the future of work and how it will continue to evolve, especially in a post-pandemic world.

The digital age and knowledge work have created a paradigm in which constant innovation, collaboration, and improvement are necessary for organizations to remain competitive.

---

v. Staying Grounded: Beware of Carpetbaggers and False Prophets

What does science say might separate effective founders and business builders from mediocre ones? The answer may surprise you: a healthy dose of pessimism.

While it might not be the first trait that comes to mind (or at all) when you think of entrepreneurial greatness, the data provides a compelling argument as it relates to monetary success. According to one study published in the European Economic Review, founders with above-average optimism earned 30% less than their pessimistic peers.[134]

While I am not advocating for a glass-is-half-empty mindset per se, I do believe business builders and aspiring entrepreneurs would benefit from checking entrepreneurial mythology at the front door and "face the brutal realities" (as Good to Great[135] author Jim Collins reminds us in his book which should be re-read yearly since it is one of the best for business builders). Collins tells us, "Every good-to-great company embraced what we came to call 'The Stockdale Paradox': you must maintain unwavering faith that you can and will prevail in the end, regardless of the difficulties, and at the same time, have the discipline to confront the most brutal facts of your current reality, whatever they might be."

This is the paradox of entrepreneurship—entrepreneurship has long survived on the basis of mythology and storytelling passing through the generations. We all want to see Steve Jobs in ourselves, but the reality is he is part of the 2.5% club. Only 2.5% of the population has the rare and exceptional talent to build and grow an extensive business on their own. The rest of us need to account for the entrepreneurial skills we don't have.

Here's how you can confront your brutal realities:

1) Iterate, iterate, iterate, and pivot when necessary.

Enthusiasm and overconfidence can be a recipe for disaster without a clear road map. Ground your business model in reality (and data, evidence, and facts), rather than emotion. You don't want to launch and then discover afterward that there's no market for your product or service. Talk to potential customers early and often. Pivots are over-rated. The goal is not to have a lot of them. The goal is to learn from them and to get smarter in the execution of the core building blocks of your business model. Investors are not overly excited for you to learn over and over again from your mistakes, and false starts on their dime.

It is essential to be simultaneously humble, self-aware, and confident. Be grateful when things go wrong—and they invariably will. Instead of dwelling on missed opportunity or shortcoming, ask yourself what you can learn from a false start, a pivot, or a train wreck. You and your company will be better off for it. Resilience and recovery are critical dimensions of a fully capable business builder.

2) Face reality—dead on and without filters and blinders.

Problems are inevitable in a startup. You need to look at the operation objectively and determine what is not working. After all, you cannot resolve any issues without first identifying them. This calls for asking the hard and uncomfortable questions at times. Don't be afraid to invoke skepticism in the name of coming to the right solution. Be wary of carpet baggers and entrepreneurial false prophets. There is a lot of noise and reality tv buzz in entrepreneurship today. When people only give or tell you good news, you should begin to worry (think of Andrew Grove's "only the paranoid survive"[136] and apply the concept of a strategic inflection point to your relationships with others.)

It's going to be tough, so roll up your sleeves and get going. Hard work and long hours are part and parcel in starting or growing a business. Be prepared to invest a considerable amount of resources and make sacrifices along the way. Few legitimate entrepreneurs work 9-5 and take the weekend off. Business builders need to surround themselves with talent and people who reduce their loneliness, anxiety, and isolation.

3) Start small but think big. (Don't get seduced by Shark Tank thinking.)

When starting out, it doesn't have to be a case of "go big or go home." You will yield far more results if you break down a goal into critical milestones that will help you realize it. Then as your company expands, adjust your KPIs appropriately but size your vision for the greatness you wish to achieve. Surround yourself with people who make you better and who challenge your assumptions. Don't undersize your vision but be realistic that it is unlikely to occur as fast as you project in the financial model.

vi. Growing Pains: Three Missteps to Avoid

Where are you in the business life cycle? Expanding—whether that's via an additional location, increasing operating volume with new or existing customers, or adding to a product line—can be a way to take your enterprise to the next level. However, the risk is real, and therefore it's essential to be prepared for any roadblocks or growth challenges. Just like driving a fast car, business builders need to pay attention to the traffic signs to avoid some of the common mistakes made when considering expansion, and know-how to sidestep them:

1) Underestimating project expansion costs/timeline

It would be better if you had a clear idea about costs before you venture into any deals and get blindsided by bills you can't pay (growing broke syndrome). To avoid excessive debt or leverage, it's prudent to enter into the project with some contingency (padding). Best case scenario, you'll have some money left over—and your plans will not get derailed due to lack of funds.

2) Tackling too much too soon with unrealistic expectations

If you're not careful, expanding too more quickly can eat into margins and profitability. Please don't assume that opening a second location (restaurants make this mistake a lot) or launching another product will immediately yield double revenues or profits. You'll need to factor in variables like seasonal trends, customer needs, and the competitive landscape. There are times when waiting to pull the trigger can work to your advantage.

3) Failure to conduct market research with irrational exuberance

You may think you have a great idea, but the market might not be ready or willing to buy into it. Market research, customer discovery, and customer validation, even at the most basic level, can provide invaluable insight. The trusty marketing mix (infamous 4 Ps[137]) of marketing can be a great navigation tool to guide your decision, at least in the beginning. For example, if you're considering launching a new product, your research should substantiate that hunch. Similarly, if you're looking to open another storefront, business intelligence and incremental profitability need to justify that. In other words, you can't make a move solely based on intuition. Also, don't just chase "shiny new objects" for the sake of chasing new things!

---

vii. Habits of Highly Effective Business Builders

You've likely heard about Stephen R. Covey's "7 Habits…"[138] but I'd like to offer my own abbreviated version, the business builder edition.

First, I have a confession to make. Given how watered down the word entrepreneur has become and some of its stereotypical variants (intrapreneur, solopreneur, sole proprietor, business owner, etc.), Going forward, I will alter the language and speak also about business builders. This more inclusive and expansive word choice allows us to consider a broader cadre of entrepreneurial doers from government, education, non-profits, and the business world. Simply put, business builders do *great* things.

Here are three effective practices I believe the most effective business builders embrace:

1) Seeing Around Corners

Not everyone has what it takes to dream big. In fact, some are more comfortable staying in their lane. I find that business builders tend to have the biggest imaginations, and they use them to their advantage. The most effective ones aren't afraid to ask, "what if?" and do what they can to explore and achieve outcomes. They are rarely static and aren't afraid to push boundaries. They focus on satisfying the enthusiasts and visionaries (early adopters) on Moore's curve.[139] They are adaptive, reflective, self-aware, contingent thinkers adjusting real-time to environmental factors and conditions. They face reality and are not diluted or distracted by outside noise and hype. They are often contrarians and out of step with the mainstream sentiment.

2) Rhythm, Speed, and Intellectual Curiosity

Even when schedules can be erratic, the most high-powered entrepreneurs carve out time for self-care—exercise, meditation, social wellbeing, proper nutrition, etc. They make quality and consistent sleep a priority to stay happy and healthy. Similarly, they are often early risers because they know that an early start means they can put their energy and efforts into productive use. They are disciplined, intentional, and driven in what they do each day.

An empty tank is the kiss of death in the business of innovation and entrepreneurship. Because they remain insatiable, it is hard for the most effective entrepreneurs to feel depleted regarding new ideas. In fact, they usually have a running list of possible concepts to explore. While some people tend to stop working when they run out of creative juices, highly productive business builders always have methods or techniques in place to keep going (think Energizer Bunny) because they know their first idea is seldom their best idea.

3) Intentional Focus Inside a Selected Sphere

Successful entrepreneurs know that boundaries are healthy and necessary. They worry less about pleasing others and more about moving in the direction of their dreams and aspirations. Their self-imposed limits are how they stay focused on the prize. They may give back by sitting on boards or committees, but they do so with great intentionality and discretion. They look at their personal ROI, batting average, and keep score. They are deliberate on how they invest their time and know the difference between activity and results.

That being said, they are cautious with the people they surround themselves with. Behind every successful business builder is a tribe of people encouraging and supporting them. Not everyone is qualified to give advice. Be strategic and intentional in whom you confide in and lean on for support. Moreover, some people won't "get" what it means to blaze your own trail—and that's okay. You have to be mindful of who you let in. They purposefully surround themselves with positive, connected, energetic people who make them better, "plus them up" (in Disney speak), and challenge them to be better. Business builders are civic leaders, philanthropists, mentors, and angel investors in the broader community.

---

viii. Avoiding "Low Battery" Entrepreneurial Burnout: Practical Tip

By now the expression "you can't pour from an empty cup" is almost ubiquitous, and for a good reason. The saying applies to the general population, but entrepreneurs especially need to take note. Think about it—your iPhone might not be the only thing on low battery. You might be getting a "low battery warning" and pop-up notifications as well.

A study by Dr. Freeman at the University of California San Francisco found that *49% of those who start company say they have struggled with some form of mental illness in the past.*[140] Wellness is not just a buzz word du jour but an essential component of a healthier lifestyle for entrepreneurs and their families. Sir Richard Branson, opined in his blog, "Mindfulness is one way that many entrepreneurs choose to combat the toll wrought by round-the-clock emails, long working hours and other aspects of our accelerated business culture."[141]

But what is Mindfulness? Psychology Today says, "Mindfulness is a state of active, open attention on the present. It means living in the moment and awakening to your current experience, rather than dwelling on the past or anticipating the future."

The truth is, though, if you want to be at your best, you have to be willing to put in the time and effort. That means taking important steps to build and maintain balance alongside working on your business. Here are some of the basics of building healthier habits:

1) Carve out time for regular exercise and plan your meals.

Diet and exercise are critical; it almost goes without saying. Let's start with the movement. Proper rhythm has to do with consistency, so frequency matters more than time duration in the activity. Don't set yourself up for failure by overcommitting. Instead, ease into it. I need work in this area. Maybe start with a few days a week (walking, jogging, or running), then go from there. What's most important is that you find something you like. Engage an accountability buddy if you're worried about follow-through.

Remember, you can't outrun your mouth. You can exercise all you want, but if you're not eating right, it won't do much good—food is fuel, and it needs to be quality. Are you putting junk into your body? Your productivity will suffer over time. A steady diet of sugary, fatty, and greasy food will only make you crave more of it, thus putting you in a cycle of weight gain and lethargy. And that's no fun! Planning your meals is an easy way to stay on track, cutting down on portion sizes, and eliminating or reducing some of the ingredients. I am famous for asking for 1/3 of the dressing on my salad. Even better would be not having salad dressing at all, but I can't do that yet! Also, cut down on those impulse decisions and stock healthier snacks like fruits and nuts.

Want to stay on track? Use technology—apps like MyFitnessPal, iHealth, Health, and many others can help you log your activity, diet, and exercise and plug into a community of support. My Sleep number bed uses Sleep IQ technology and tells me what my optimal sleep schedule is and how to maximize the benefits of sleep.

2) Unplug and reset.

Our minds weren't meant for constant stimulation and noise. Take some time to unplug from technology and get outside. Don't forget about the importance of face-to-face interaction. No screen can ever replace that! Make it a point to schedule regular communications (surround yourself with people who make you better) and participate in other activities that give you a release like yoga or meditation.

3) Sleep quality is number one.

Try to maintain a consistent sleep schedule—do your best to go to sleep and get up at the same time every day. Avoid working and eating in your bed. If you work in your bed, your mind might associate it with stress, which can affect the quality of your sleep. It's proven that when we're well-rested, we have a sharper mind and healthier body, while sleep deficiencies can lead to chronic diseases and increased health risks. Sleep Cycle is an excellent app for measuring your sleep quality and activity levels.

---

ix. Surviving—and Even Thriving—After Five Years

No doubt you have heard the statistics that approximately 50% of businesses fail after the first five years.[142] Entrepreneurship is not for the weak. However, what separates those who survive and even thrive from those who close shop? Surely there are some commonalities. Here are some factors experts believe can make you resilient, or at least increase your chance of success:

1) Relevance and Market Smarts

Your concept must have value, or it will go belly up. Does the idea/business have staying power? Why? Markets change, and so does the demand for goods. A prime example is Blockbuster Stores. With the advent of changing technology, they just didn't keep their product offering relevant. Specifically, they did not execute on the transition from renting media to streaming services, and they eventually shuttered most of their stores. Today, there is only one (in Bend, Oregon) out of the over 9,000 that were open in the 1990s.[143]

Don't get left behind, and keep in mind the basics of Marketing 101: conducting a SWOT and PEST analysis. R&D, marketing, and sales activities are expensive. Every extra bit of market knowledge reduces the number of resources expended. A clear understanding of the competitive landscape and intimate knowledge and insights into environmental scanning—**P**olitical, **E**conomic, **S**ocio-cultural, and **T**echnological trends are essential to capitalize on business insights and potential market opportunities.

2) Lean in with Grit

Most startups have blind spots they might not even be aware of yet. You must lean into your opportunities and face the brutal realities of your industry and marketplace. It is not enough to only play defensively (defending your ground against unpredictable yet potentially destructible factors like market changes, lawsuits, talent loss, and more). You must also manage uncertainties (product, financial, management, technological, execution, and market). Do you spend more time on the offensive or defensive?

You will inevitably encounter setbacks, doubts, etc., but you must persevere and overcome them. Many businesses fail just because the founders gave up when times were tough.

3) Seek Out Trusted Advisors

You do not have to go it alone. Most successful people have a support system of some kind behind them. Need some direction or moral support? Reach out and talk to a business mentor, advisor, or business development center. There are people out there ready to help you grow and adapt to the mindset required to own and operate a business successfully.

---

x. From Side Hustle to Full-Time Entrepreneur: Is This Really What You Want?

It's estimated that nearly 40% of Americans have at least one side hustle. Whether out of economic necessity (losing a job), market opportunity, monetizing your talents, or intellectual stimulation, some people pursue these ventures intending to make their side gig into their future business ventures—but only if it can be sustainable, profitable, and challenging enough.

The difference between a side gig and an entrepreneurial venture is the motivation of the business builder. Did you start the business because you wanted to pay off a bill, send a kid to college, or take an extra annual vacation, or did you start the business because you had a burning desire to change and transform people's lives, you saw a solution to a problem, or you wanted to make a difference in the world by offering something to the world that is better, faster, cheaper, smarter, or simpler than anything else out there?

Unfortunately, it's not always smooth sailing, even when you make calculated decisions over time. That said if you decide to be brave and go this route, be prepared for some speed bumps and challenges along the way.

1) Getting Funding

Is your business capital heavy or capital efficient? How will you keep the proverbial lights on if you don't have customers right out of the gate? What's more, lenders may be leery about taking a chance on a young startup, especially if you don't have a track record or collateral to back it. Or worse, you may be desperate and decide to bootstrap the business with a high-interest credit card.

Side gigs are unlikely to garner angel investor funding or traditional bank financing, so you should make sure the business is capital efficient and that you have saved adequate cash to weather the ups and downs when you launch a side gig—especially if you are looking to transition it to an entrepreneurial venture.

2) Self-Care and Wellness

We don't talk enough about self-care and wellness as it relates to entrepreneurship. The entrepreneurial demands and lifestyle considerations can weigh on people for a host of reasons which further underline the need for candor. Starting or scaling a business can be isolating. You might find your own friends and family make critical or negative comments. You might begin to question your decision. It can feel lonely and bring about feelings of anxiety and depression. You are it—the chief everything officer. This can be fatiguing and overwhelming, a real juggling act to keep everything straight.

We all need help coping today with the anxiety, frustrations, and false starts we face as entrepreneurial business builders. The first step is admitting it, and the important next step is finding the right resources to help you lean into it, and to find ways to cope and deal with what is bothering you.

3) Finding the "Right" Mentors

You may feel confident in your abilities, but keep in mind that mentors can be invaluable. No matter how knowledgeable you are about your craft, you'll have blind spots. Recruiting, for example, is something many solopreneurs struggle with when deciding to grow their venture beyond themselves.

You'll probably need someone to provide guidance on mission-critical matters, such as financial planning, including investment and funding; business development; marketing strategies; human resources; general management, strategic planning, partnership agreements, and networking.

Side hustles are a great way to supplement your income, but often, these ventures are immune from the scope and scale of challenges full-time entrepreneurs face so make a conscious decision on whether you are really doing a side hustle, or if you want to build something to grow into a full-time venture. Look before you leap.

xi. Growth Mode: Navigating Choppy Waters

As a business owner, you must find the sweet spots for funding, facilities, cash flow, pricing, labor workforce, etc. That last—labor workforce—can make or break a business venture. It's your job to make sure you have the right people—and the right number of people—to keep your operation as efficient and sustainable as possible—especially during the venture's formative development years.

Nearly 80% of all U.S. small business establishments employ no one other than the owner, so-called "solopreneurs." Going beyond the owner/founder—growth mode—is a big deal. Now let's say your business is in growth mode, and you feel it might be time to hire additional staff to execute on your potential customer and market opportunities properly. *How can you really be sure the time is right to bring in extra staff, hire independent contractors, or partner with other companies to fill in the gaps and get to the next level?*

Remember growth isn't always a good thing.

New overtime rules by the U.S. Department of Labor may impact whether you want to hire in-house or work with a more flexible workforce of freelancers and independent contractors. Additionally, in-house-employee-related benefits (health care, retirement, and taxation) can take a big bite out of the budget. Consider these tell-tale signs:

1) Increasing sales and revenue

The sales of your "core" products or services have been growing over time, and you identify the sales performance improvements as a positive *trend*—not a short-term blip. Be sure to know the difference between purchase orders and expressions of interest. You can't go to the bank and deposit expressions of interest.

As a result of improved sales, revenue is at or above the target, and all signs point to a continued trend, and the revenue is converting to cash, giving you the self-funding, you need to make strategic investments, including hiring permanent team members.

2) Existing opportunity

You've done the research, and you see a clear opportunity for growth and expansion in your niche or related industries. Based on that, you decide that now's the time to get in on the ground floor. But current employees aren't available to take on additional responsibilities, or *you don't have employees at all*. If you are unsure if the growth is sustainable, outsource until you see strong evidence of the demand you expected.

3) Expanding staff

Your employee's existing job skills and knowledge meet the company's current level of productivity. But in order to grow, you'll need to acquire staff with a new and different set of skills and knowledge. You might consider a worker training program, local recruiters, staffing companies, or university internship programs as potential resources for qualified people.

While there are no hard and fast rules, if the market potential is opportunistic or short-term in nature, you may consider outsourcing either to independent contractors or a third party. If there is strong evidence of proven market demand that materializes over time, it just might be time to add an employee. However, if you decide to take the plunge and hire/outsource the talent, you need to determine what you'll do to get the most out of your investment. Here are some tips that will help make the plunge more successful:

1) Set "tangible" milestones and identify skill gaps.

Set some measurable performance milestones for determining what money you will invest when you invest it, and what you want to see in sales to continue to invest—set triggers for when to pull the plug if the money is chasing a premature market opportunity.

Do some company visioning to see what you think you will need in job positions and competencies to meet future demands for your company's products and services? Identify skill gaps and target training and development to address organizational deficiencies.

2) Recruit and select talent.

Always be in *continuous* talent recruitment and selection mode. The best organizations are continually looking to expand and upgrade their employee talent pipeline. "Right fit" talent is hard to come by, so always have your "antenna up" for potential new hires.

2) Be coachable.

Seek growth coaching assistance from knowledgeable experts who can help you avoid potential pitfalls from potential over-optimism in your orders and sales forecasts. Select seasoned and smart individuals who can offer insider advice on the day-to-day company culture and business building efforts.

Note: Mentors should be well-respected individuals who have expertise and insights into the business development opportunities and challenges you are facing in growing your business. Their role is to give you unfiltered feedback and express their honest and candid opinions.

As we observed earlier, poorly managed growth is not a good thing. There are many classic examples of *"growing* broke"—this includes companies that were on an accelerated path to profitability who derailed because they didn't have an early warning radar system to self-correct before they imploded. By being attentive to the tips above, your company may be able to navigate the choppy waters of growth *and* be profitable at the same time! Remember, your resources often lag your opportunities, and your business' success might just depend on it.

xii. Know When to Fold 'Em

We've all been there. We've continued to pursue a fledgling project just because we've put in a significant amount of time, money, or other resources into it, only to watch it start to unravel before our eyes. It would be foolish to walk away with so much invested, right?

If you can relate, you've probably subscribed to the sunk-cost fallacy at some point. This is the bias that anything you've already invested in deserves more significant investment—even if it was questionable in the first place, and also if the investment is unlikely to become fruitful. This attitude can result in a downward spiral of losing money from bad deals or projects we refuse to abandon, even if the writing is on the wall.

But how do we avoid falling into this trap in the first place? The following are a few helpful ways to recognize this bias before it's too late:

1) Fail forward faster and smarter.

Failures don't have to define people. A quick failure, in fact, can be a blessing in disguise, but it saves us from dumping more resources into something that's not viable. Reframe what failure is. Finding out that something isn't right or it's the wrong time for your idea to work is not failure; it is adaptive learning.

2) Know your value and separate your ego from business decisions.

What is your value proposition? How are you different from your competition? If you don't have a defined USP (Unique Selling Proposition), you'll have a hard time sustaining a credible and successful business model.

People notice and careless than you think. Are you making decisions based on what other people think, or what you know in your heart is the right thing to do? At the end of the day, your business will benefit from sound decision making, not emotionally charged ones. Making decisions sooner might just give you more peace of mind and less heartache in the long run.

3) Don't go it alone.

Have a brain trust and an inner circle of advisors. Involve multiple stakeholders in the decision-making process, so that you reap the benefit of diverse perspectives and ideas to ensure your decisions are well-informed and well-researched. Surround yourself with smart people.

When we learn to remove our bias from business decisions, we can indeed move forward faster and smarter. Sometimes ideas don't work out—and that's okay. Not every idea should see the light of day.

As Kenny Rogers famously said, "You've got to know when to hold 'em, know when to fold 'em, know when to walk away, and know when to run."

Chapter 9: Conclusion

As with many things in life, awareness is key—especially for the sustainability of any business venture. You have to keep an eye on market trends and demands, your own capabilities, and even your own personal wellbeing. If you're not around to run the business, who will? Do you have a proper support system in place, and enough employees who know what to do? You can't do everything; you must delegate and lean on your network of experienced mentors and guides.

You're only as good as the team you have in place, so make sure it's a good one with transparent and clear channels of communication. If you want to be in it for the long haul, don't be afraid to face the hard truths—they are opportunities for adaptability and growth.

Sustainability is especially important today when the unanticipated consequences of the pandemic undermine business models, elongate sales cycles and erode margins. Don't dilute your thinking by assuming profitability or break-even will just happen. You have to plan for it, structure for it, and design for it in your business model.

Chapter 9: Questions for Consideration

i. Stay on Top of Your A-Game

In business, you're either growing, or you're dying[144]—how can you take this to heart? The reason you can't afford to hire someone is that you're not hiring. How can you grow if you can't take on more business because you don't have enough help? Scaling your business correctly is integral for long term success. If you aren't pushing innovation, switching things up, or investing in your people—work on a plan to do so today.

ii. The Importance of Delegating

Make a "stop doing" list instead of a to-do list, like Jim Collins, author of Good to Great suggests.[145] Highly successful people like Warren Buffett delegate a large portion of their tasks in order to utilize the most valuable commodity of all—time. Save your focus for the important stuff and let others handle the day to day minutiae that can sap your energy and keep you from doing the *real* work.

iii. Rethinking Busyness

What's holding you back from a more purposeful and intentional life? Don't let busyness take over your life, or, like Arianna Huffington, your sleep. After overworking herself to the point of exhaustion and passing out, she realized she needed to make a change. It wasn't until she brought more balance into her life, and quit working round-the-clock, that she and the Huffington Post indeed became successful.[146] How can you take better care of yourself? Make a list of ways you can supplement your work life with personal life and put activities other than work into your calendar.

iv. Don't Leave Change Management to Chance

How can your company become more transparent? Promote open streams of dialogue and make sure everyone is on the same page linguistically. Embrace technology and be open to change. When was the last time you sent out a company newsletter? Keep everyone up-to-date and in the loop at all times.

v. Staying Grounded: Beware of Carpetbaggers and False Prophets

It is far too easy to live in a bubble or echo chamber of your own beliefs. We can even curate our social media feeds only to reiterate views we already agree with. Are you aware of all the hard or uncomfortable truths surrounding your business venture? Break out of your bubble and find people and test customers who will give it to you straight and not hold back. This will save you time and money in the long run. Don't be afraid to branch out, strangers and people who don't know you as well are more likely not to mince words.

vi. Growing Pains: Three Missteps to Avoid

You can never plan too much—and you don't have to go it alone. Having an experienced and trusted advisor dramatically increases your likelihood of success and improves your company's overall approach to managing key enterprise risks. Who, or what organization, can you tap into as a sounding board to support your analysis and testing of your company's infrastructure to determine your legacy beliefs, market assumptions, validation of new consumers, and identification of opportunities to optimize the launch of new, credible products and services to capture market share?

vii. Habits of Highly Effective Business Builders

Are you afraid to ask, "what if"? When was the last time you did? How can you push yourself to think differently? As Oscar Wilde quipped, "Everything popular is wrong." Try to eschew the trends and go against the grain, new perspectives and new ideas pave the way to significant breakthroughs. The people you choose to surround yourself with could hinder or help your process—take an inventory of those closest to you and make sure they are adding not subtracting to your energy and momentum.

viii. Avoiding "Low Battery" Entrepreneurial Burnout: Practical Tips

How many hours of sleep did you get last night? Was it good sleep? When was the last time you exercised? Have you been getting the recommended servings of fruits and veggies? Gone several hours with no electronics, or reconnected with a friend? If the answer to any of these is less than stellar, get out your calendar or notepad, and get to work. What can you do to fit these things into your schedule? How can you commit? Get an app, an accountability buddy, or promise yourself a big reward if you can stick to your new routine for a month.

ix. Surviving—and Even Thriving—After Five Years

Start with conducting a SWOT and PEST analysis—this will save you time and money in the long run. Understanding the competitive landscape is essential to capitalize on business insights and potential market opportunities. Need help? Find some. Don't shy away or quit when you hit a wall, or things get tough. If you want to make it the long haul, you'll have to overcome lots of bumps along the way.

x. From Side Hustle to Full-Time Entrepreneur: Is This Really What You Want?

Have you thought about funding? Is your venture attractive to many, or just a private hobby? Depending on how generally applicable or innovative it is will depend on the startup capital you're likely to receive. Are you prepared to face hardships both in your business and in personal relationships? Have a plan in place as to what or who you will turn to when the going gets tough. Be open to outside assistance. Before you commit, ask yourself if you can commit to it 110% and be happy doing so, if not, perhaps it's best left as a side hustle.

xi. Growth Mode: Navigating Choppy Waters

Are you ready to grow ... the *right* way? What trends have you noticed in your business, and how sure are you they are likely to continue? Have you conducted thorough market research? If and when you're ready, develop a plan with achievable milestones. Keep in mind what kind of company you are trying to build and bring people on board with the corresponding skills and vision to help make it a reality. Consider having more than one mentor in multiple fields.

xii. Know When to Fold 'Em

When should you throw in the towel? Can you trust yourself to have an unbiased opinion and to view the market viability of your venture objectively? The best thing you can do, aside from being unafraid to fail (and quickly), is to have experienced sounding boards around you who won't feed your ego. Do you have people you can trust? How do you know? Make sure the people advising you have a good track record and know what they're talking about.

CHAPTER 10

MINDSET

In a world full of uncertainties and unknowns, many people look for structure and constants in life to serve as ballast. Startups and entrepreneurs, on the other hand, must be willing to throw safety nets to the wind and operate under conditions of extreme uncertainty with no one to answer to but themselves. This requires great resolve and determination among a host of other mental and personal character traits to persevere. Often, in the beginning, business builders won't even know where or when their next paycheck will arrive, and things like health care and retirement funds are a long way off. It takes a certain kind of person to be at peace with such precariousness.

Yet, for many, the freedom, flexibility, and job security of self-employment provide greater rewards that far outweigh any risks. For someone to believe and commit to this line of thought, they have to have an entrepreneur mindset—to imagine a better future, to see around the corners, and to adapt to a changing set of business conditions.

Mindset is a tricky thing – how to experience and recover from failure, anticipate opportunities over problems, have a passion for excellence, and act with a bias for solutions over just merely identifying problems.

Entrepreneurs are doers. Winston Churchill offered some encouraging words by saying, Success is the ability to go from one failure to another with no loss of enthusiasm."

i. Understanding the Entrepreneur Mindset

"I could never do that."

"I don't have the discipline or the drive."

"I don't like to take risks."

"I don't know how people do it."

These are common reactions I hear from individuals discovering whether they have entrepreneurial DNA. I think these comments get to the heart of the matter—it's not for everyone—and that's okay.

One of the most significant differences between traditional W-2 employees and business builders isn't the amount of money they make, their business hours or flexibility (although it's true they can all vary), the most significant distinction is often unseen—their "disruptive and restless" business builder mindset. Consider three crucial mindset distinctions.

1) Ownership of problems and opportunities

As the saying goes, "the buck stops here" with founders. Employees sometimes don't necessarily take ownership of issues or feel invested in the result of their work. Often, they're siloed and responsible for one task or series of functions without the ability to influence the overall outcome. But entrepreneurs/business builders know that they're accountable for every result in their organization. They often scrutinize every decision because they know it can have a substantial impact down the road.

2) Goal-orientation and action bias

People are intrinsically motivated by different things. Entrepreneurs/business builders tend to be goal-oriented (they are focused on a pain/problem/opportunity), with a big picture approach. Employees, on the other hand, often have a process orientation. They can fixate on merely completing a task within a broader organizational context. They don't always feel a connection with their job and the company's mission or purpose. Less than 7 out of 10 people go to work each day actively engaged or committed to what they are doing.[147]

3) Risk management and landmine avoidance

Employees tend to shy away from risk and for a good reason. To them, taking risks does not always equate to rewards or any upside. There is often a fear of shaking up the status quo too much and being out of step with the leader or the organization's culture. Business builders, on the other hand, empower themselves to manage, assess, and mitigate risks while knowing that sometimes, failures or false starts are the admission price of learning.

---

ii. Lean into Curiosity

We all could stand to benefit from thinking more like a child. Curiosity doesn't have to be relegated to youth—it's an essential ingredient for effective leadership, robust company culture, successful team-building, and mental health. Here's how you can model this behavior at work and home:

1) Challenge the status quo.

If you've ever spent time with a small child, you know they ask "why" ad nauseum. This is how they learn to navigate the world. Adults in problem-solving situations can employ the same attitude. For example, why are specific policies and procedures in place? Challenging the status quo is sometimes necessary to move out of stagnancy and stay relevant. Questions can be posed to reframe your thinking, such as "how might we" or "who wrote the rule" will help you begin to challenge the conventional thought process.

2) Perpetually embrace learning opportunities.

Kids are usually more open to trying something new because they don't let their ego get in the way. Adults can follow suit by going out of their comfort zone. Whether it's enrolling in a masterclass online, reading a book on a topic outside of one's domain, or even learning a new language, such pursuits can make us better-rounded leaders and citizens of the world. This year, I am doing a deeper dive into optimize.me[148] and their mastery program to hone my skills and to support my intent to be a better version of myself.

3) Dare to create for the sake of creating.

Children are naturally inclined to build and take apart, then build again. Robotics challenges around the country are teaching kids the importance of problem-solving in a group setting.[149] Champions of these programs say exposing young people—young girls in particular—to STEM-related careers is critical as we need engineers and data scientists to build and maintain the machines of the future. However, leveraging problem-solving capabilities is only part of the equation, business builders must also see around corners, imagine what is possible, and see opportunities where others might just see problems or obstacles.

If you need a primer on how to create without fear, watch a group of kids in action. They don't have a plan other than focusing on the task at hand. This is a good lesson for adults who may feel stifled by expectations to create something flawless upon the first attempt.

Think more like a child, and you may discover your life will become a little richer. For further reading on this topic, here's how to identify your "curiosity type."[150] I will confess upfront my type is Type 1— "the fascinated," making me intellectually curious and a handful for my parents growing up!

---

iii. Goal Setting

Is this the year you're crushing all your goals? Great! However, if you are like many people, you start well-intentioned and then at some point, you derail or have a false start on forming new habits and keeping many of your commitments as the year progresses. If you have struggled with making a behavioral change, or are frustrated with your goal achievement performance/personal motivation in making the necessary behavioral changes, consider these mindset adjustments to help get you back on track:

1) Start by having a few personal things squared away.

Could your current habits be helping or hindering your progress? For one, you have to know what success looks like. What does the "ideal" look like in terms of health, productivity, finances, social life—wherever your priorities lie? Your goals must be in concert with these values; otherwise, you may be chasing the wrong pursuits—and end up even more frustrated.

2) Dream big but start small.

As the saying goes, "if your goals don't scare you, they're not big enough." The loftier the goal, the more you demand of yourself. So, let's say you'd like to boost profits by 25% this year or hire five additional staff. Experts would suggest doubling or even tripling the number when goal setting. The point here is to stretch yourself, so you don't get complacent. What's the worst-case scenario that can happen? Even if you don't hit the mark, you'll likely still end up further along than you are today.

Related to that philosophy, set visible KPI's (Key Performance Indicators) for your business or team. At the start of every month (or quarter), sit down with your colleagues, a mentor, or even go it alone to write down clear goals for whatever metrics matter most to you and your business (think revenue growth, new product introductions, hiring and selecting staff, or buying synergistic companies). Once you have clear goals in place—be diligent.

3) Don't forget about the human element in goal setting—we're humans, not machines.

We need adequate rest, exercise, healthy food, social interaction, etc. We can't run on empty 24/7. Something has to give eventually. You might consider allocating for planned or unexpected time out of the office when plotting out your goals. After all, research tells us that people who take vacations are more productive at work.[151] Paying attention to your wheel of life (by taking this interactive online assessment[152]) or downloading this worksheet[153] with powerful reflection questions might help achieve balance and rhythm in your life.

The more intentional you are in your planning, the more manageable goals are to achieve. But that doesn't mean it's going to be a straight trajectory. A goal tracker app[154] coupled with an advisor, mentor, or coach can help you chart your course and stick to it. Reach out to your local business development center where they can match you with subject-matter experts, serial entrepreneurs, life coaches, and service providers. The more people, technology, and momentum you have going, the easier it will be.

---

iv. The Stoic Leader

You've likely heard of someone practicing stoicism; for example, "They exhibited admirable stoicism in dealing with the loss of their job." This word is shared as a term of fortitude and endurance in Today's vernacular, but there are many nuances to its meaning in the historical context. Stoicism is a school of philosophy that hails from ancient Greece and Rome in the early parts of the 3rd century BC. Although not a widely popular or well-known philosophy in the United States today, it has made a comeback in recent years.

A quick overview reveals that stoicism "focuses on mindfulness, resilience, creativity, and more"—all of which are believed to yield a happy and full life.[155]

Not long ago, I was introduced to the concept of stoicism from a colleague and friend. As a result, I purchased The Daily Stoic[156] and began to learn and apply principles and practices embraced by top performers, presidents, and other great minds to find greater centeredness, joy, and meaning in my life. I have tried to incorporate some of the values and philosophies into my routine to become more mindful, aware, creative, and in control of my day-to-day professional and personal life. Take, for instance, Today's entry dealing with anger—an extreme emotion, and as such, it is toxic fuel and "never worth the costs that come along with it."[157]

The "thought leaders" of the time (Seneca, among others) embraced "a philosophy of life that maximizes positive emotions, reduces negative emotions, and helps individuals to hone their virtues of character."[158] The glass is always half full to the stoic.

What does this mean in the context of the business world, you ask? In general, stoics have mastered turning obstacles, or even failure, into opportunity. Here are specific nuggets you can take away from this philosophy and apply to your business, regardless of industry:

1) Be unapologetically you.

Imitation may be the highest form of flattery, but it's not good for business. It's important to have role models, yet admiration with imitation can be dangerous. In the quest to produce a better product or offer a more enticing service, you can end up with a second-rate one if you're not careful. On the contrary, stoicism means owning your quirks and even leaning into them to come out ahead.

2) Don't discount the power of intention and gratitude.

A stoic starts each day with goals and a plan to achieve them. It's been proven that writing daily goals helps cement them in the brain and increases the likelihood of achievement. A grateful mindset also compounds success. Harvard psychologist Shawn Achor's[159] research indicates that workers who employ a gratitude practice at the start of their day have better outcomes than those who do not.

3) Accept what you cannot change and tackle adversity head-on.

We have to control ourselves first if we want to change the outcome of events. Self-control gives us agency even when circumstances challenge us. Stoics turn obstacles into opportunities. Per the Pareto Principle, "life is 20% what happens to you and 80% how you respond."[160]

Stoicism can make you stronger in the face of challenges. Flipping obstacles upside down help you see your struggle from a different point of view. Also, remembering how small you are in the scheme of things keeps your ego manageable and in check.

As you begin to intentionally and meaningfully tackle your goals, I'll leave you with this closing thought from Stoic and Emperor of Rome Marcus Aurelius: "The things you think about will determine the quality of your mind."

---

v. Why Embracing a "Startup Mentality" Is Good for Business

Startups (and their fearless band of business builders) are often synonymous with their scrappy can-do attitude, creativity, and sense of innovation. They execute to bring an idea to life through a mission-driven culture. One of the most prolific writers and professors on entrepreneurship, Steve Blank, defined a startup as "a temporary organization designed to look for a business model that is repeatable and scalable."[161] Eric Reis went even further and evolved his definition of a startup company to be more inclusive by opining, "A startup is a human institution designed to create a new product or service under conditions of extreme uncertainty." Under this definition, a startup is not limited by years in business, the maturity of products, depth of management, or other arbitrary discounting measures typically used to define startups.

Imagine if every company thought about this paradigm shift through the lens of a startup. Today, unlike in the 1950s, the average longevity of a large publicly traded corporation is 20 years versus sixty. Within the past year at the time of writing, 172 CEOs were replaced in large corporations.[162] The most essential observation being the gap/need of these large companies of "adapting to changing technologies or finding new leadership based on current economic conditions."[163]

Startup thinking is beneficial for everyone, and even when you outgrow the "startup" phase, there's something to be said for maintaining these values to enjoy continued growth. Here's a look at how the most effective organizations grow past the startup stage while remaining grounded.

1) The founder/leader makes a point to stay engaged on some level, and adaptive, entrepreneurial leadership is valued and rewarded.

The founder must ensure the original vision is communicated and articulated through periods of change. This message informs the reason the mission is meaningful, brings cohesion to all teams, and allows people to prioritize during times of uncertainty.

Entrepreneurship gets its share of press, but adaptiveness is lesser known. Connecting and rearranging the dots, intellectual curiosity, determination, Tenacity, and seeing around corners is at the core of adaptive, entrepreneurial leadership. CEOs need to build the capacity for this in their organization so that employees find game-changing and transformative projects challenging and meaningful, which leads to higher engagement. Their passion and determination are contagious. As they grow professionally, so does the organization.

2) The company must be open to change.

Companies that rise from bootstrapped startup status to the likes of the eBays and Airbnb's of the world have one thing in common: they embrace a culture of healthy skepticism and curiosity. Such an environment can be a means to reinvent, repurpose, or challenge the status quo. The result? Better products, cheaper and more efficient services, and novel solutions to old problems. In other words, it's good for business.

3) The company must grow and scale strategically.

It can be easy to "move fast and break things" (as was the tech startup mantra), and with reckless abandon. However, companies that sustain long-term growth are selective, deliberate, intentional, and targeted in growth, whether that be new customer segments, new employees, partners, investors, and vendors.

Hiring for cultural fit should be embraced just as much as technical expertise. Emotional intelligence cannot be discounted. Treat any interview as an opportunity to see if their personality, goals, and vision align with your company's trajectory and whether the individual embraces the startup mindset.

---

vi. The Morally Courageous Leader

There are over 2.4 billion Google hits on the topic of leadership, but only 202 million (less than 10%) of those Google web hits speak about moral courage.

How do you show up when there's a lot on the line? How do you react under criticism or intense pressure at work? When your team finds itself in a bind, what kind of leader are you? Do you "take one for the team" or cower under pressure? It's my deep-seated belief that the measure of a person can only be genuinely determined when a lot is on the line.

Consider the discourse happening politically when party members call out a person's record of voting "no" on spending money on amenities that everyone *supposedly* wants or needs; or holding suppliers accountable for their promises or governance dysfunction in the non-profit sector where every vote taken by a board is unanimous; or abstaining from a critical vote because it would be harmful to have a recorded no vote, or not saying in public what you think in private; or being dubbed an outlier for not going along with the crowd on a critical community decision, priority, or vote.

In other words, these situations present opportunities to display moral courage or moral cowardice. The former requires leaders to be unafraid to do what is right, regardless of the consequences. As the saying goes, "integrity is doing the right thing, even when no one is watching." Moral courage "means having the courage to do what's right at the risk of personal harm."[164]

Here are some additional characteristics of moral leadership:

1) It is the most difficult to develop.

Even the U.S. Army recognizes that not all types of courage are equal or easy to develop. "The moral aspect of leadership—personally understanding, embracing, and inculcating ethical conduct in others is far more difficult to develop in leaders and can be far more time consuming," Distinguished Military Professor of Leadership Joseph J. Thomas wrote in a research paper on the topic.[165] "Despite decades of highly publicized moral/ethical failures on the part of its military members, the DoD has not achieved a satisfactory method for addressing the moral development of servicemen and women."

Whether in military or civilian life, moral courage as a habit requires a great deal of self-policing in one's everyday life. Allowing yourself to lower your standards and make excuses can be a slippery slope. Compromising your integrity gets more comfortable and easier, and before long, you've lost touch with your moral fiber. Fall off the wagon for too long, and you find yourself less courageous in your thoughts, words, and deeds.

2) It requires acceptance/assessment of failures and a willingness to go against the grain.

Moral courage also calls for taking stock of not just what we have done, but also our failures. Sometimes, choosing no action at all, especially in the face of difficulties, sends a powerful message in and of itself. Conversely, it should be mentioned that choosing to work in a certain way can pose inevitable consequences that can be detrimental to one's career. That's because some vocal pundits have power and influence. However, it might reaffirm your sense of self and inspire others if you were willing to say "yes" and "no" with selflessness, confidence, and moral courage despite the peer consequences and not backing down from confrontation and constructive dissent. The focus should be taking action to promote the best interests of the organization and the people you serve.

3) It is an active choice that needs to be reinforced frequently.

In short, encouraging yourself to make the right choice under fire begins with making a promise to yourself that your moral principles are not for sale. While "remarkable and upbeat" are admirable, integrity is a decision, not an afterthought. By disagreeing with the majority opinion does not mean you are rigid and have preconceived positions, it just might mean you have a moral compass. Moral courage displayed by a leader is essential for internal alignment, personal congruence, and trust (/strong followership). It also produces public confidence in your organization and shows your commitment and integrity are not for sale at any cost. Real personal and organizational growth can only be achieved when you take a stand (regardless of whether it's a popular position or not, and you are vulnerable and transparent in your interactions with others.

vii. Want a More Entrepreneurial Organization? Start Here

Whether working in the public or private sector, the key to enjoying a sustainable and satisfying working life lies in following the positive examples set by healthy business builders and entrepreneurs.

Let's look at three ways in which innovators show up in the workplace and how your company might follow suit:

1) Resilience, Civility, and Constructive Discourse

A baby learning to walk doesn't give up after falling down a few times. They keep trying until eventually, they're upright. Entrepreneurs are a special breed in that setbacks can make them more motivated to figure things out. The same goes for motivated business builders. They see initial failures or false starts as a necessary by-product of innovating or attempting to change. Instead of feeling dejected, they see botched attempts as opportunities to learn, grow, and improve. The lesson here? Cultivate a spirit of determination in your workplace and a mindset that encourages problem-solving in the name of innovation. At an event I attended, keynote speaker Dr. Ron Lewis noted that resilience is one of the critical characteristics of GRIT (*Guts*—the courage to make the step, *Resilience*—stick-to-itiveness, *Intensity*—not losing focus, and *Tenacity*—fighting for the right things).

When you remove your ego from the equation, it's easier to embrace potential failure and its benefits, as well as build a loyal and productive team. As the nature of work becomes more collaborative, the ability to demonstrate respect and consideration toward others and draw out their potential will never go away. It's amazing what teams can accomplish when the leadership doesn't care who gets the credit or what mistakes are made along the way. No one from the top down should be afraid of failure, and when it is viewed as part of the learning curve, everyone will feel freer to be creative and push boundaries. An organization's ability to confront its realities and have transparent, intentional, and encouraging conversations demands leaders who exhibit moral courage.

2) Ambition—AKA Passion or Purpose

This one goes beyond personal gain; it means being motivated by bolstering one's community and society. When the objectives of work exceed the desire for more money, status, and social stature—that work is likely to be more rewarding, which in turn increases employee retention. Think about some of the most successful brands and their corporate DNA. While they certainly profit from capitalism and consumerism, they also champion a philosophy known as conscious capitalism.[166]

3) Execution

Entrepreneurs ask, "what if?" and "how might we?" To that end, they often rely on both their head and their heart to make decisions. They approach their craft by combining knowledge and data with experience and intuition. Having the gift to translate ideas into reality based on real-world education and practical experience is extremely attractive in a rapidly evolving, complex, and uncertain world.

In short, it's no secret that the future and nature of employment raises more questions than answers. The most attractive companies know how to cultivate behaviors that address, rather than dance around those uncertainties. Entrepreneurs offer many lessons for surviving and thriving in the modern world of work. The question then becomes: will companies take note and embrace entrepreneurial thinking *and* action?

---

viii. The Minimalist Organization

An increasing number of people and organizations are coming to terms with the idea that *more* of anything does not necessarily lead to greater satisfaction. You see, this manifested in countless journal articles, TED talks, blogs, documentaries, and self-help books. Enter minimalism. What can you, as a business builder, take away from this mindset?

1) Embrace quality, not quantity.

No, you don't have to sell all your worldly possessions and live in a tiny house. Minimalist living is concerned with minimizing distractions to maximize more critical pursuits. In other words, it can be said that minimalism prompts us to re-evaluate our priorities. How can we live more intentionally and even do more, *with* or *on* less?

2) Think small.

Often, leaders subscribe to the notion that bigger is always better. As such, they look to expand product offerings, scale and ratchet up the workforce in hopes of turning a more substantial profit and becoming a household name. While they may be worthy pursuits, the flip side of "more" is seldom considered.

For example, more exposure means your brand is under increased scrutiny. You also might have to contend with more competition and attempts to steal your trade secret or institutional knowledge. Further, many customers require more support, but rising costs don't always equate to more robust profits.

3) Streamline innovation and ongoing evolution.

Sometimes companies outgrow products or customers. That's why it's necessary to always and often ask *why:* "Why are we doing this project or following X procedure, and what do we hope to get out of it?"

Ultimately by getting down (or back) to the basics, organizations can become nimbler and more efficient. This, in turn, enables them to innovate in a timely fashion according to market trends and achieve the objectives they had set in the first place.

Steve Jobs, while a controversial figure, built a reputation for his "zen" approach to product design and operations. The Apple ethos became a case study for not only Silicon Valley, but for entrepreneurs, designers, and executives everywhere. Often, he was a focus group of one!

The minimalist approach is not an event but a constant pursuit. Therefore, it is prudent for leaders to routinely look for distractions in their culture or systems that can be minimized for the sake of investing in areas where growth provides value to you and your customers.

Naturally, minimalism in practice will look different in every organization. But in general, a minimalist approach allows organizations to use the new-found time and money to improve—and make the most of—what they already have. Ultimately, minimalism creates space for the freedom we need to grow. So, in this sense, minimalism can mean more, not less.

---

ix. A Grateful Mindset

Psychology Today put is quite simply: "Gratitude is a prerequisite for true happiness."[167] It has been further expressed that, "Gratefulness—and especially expression of it to others—is associated with increased energy, optimism, and empathy."[168]

Each of us could stand to focus more on what we have than what's lacking. Paying it forward and sharing it with others can make a huge difference in our lives. Who doesn't need more energy and optimism in this crazy, complicated world we live in today?

Here are three qualities of a grateful mindset:

1) The Right Attitude

So much of success hinges on temperament. A grateful attitude matters and can reap positive rewards in both business and personal relationships. In a way, gratitude begets well-being and happiness, leading to a more prosperous and significant life. Taking time to slow down and acknowledge the good things in your life can help you seek out more wins, and help you feel more positive about the future.

2) Intentional Effort

But there's more to it than just positive thinking. Gratitude requires action, too. If you manage people or engage in professional or personal relationships with others (suppliers, strategic partners, mentors, friends, etc.), you have opportunities nearly every day to express these sentiments. It's a win-win, as they say. That's because employees who feel appreciated tend to be more productive. Additionally, appreciation, which begets positive morale, is a boon to overall retention. Studies have shown over and over the power of praise and gratitude[169] in creating emotional connections with your organization.

Consider the interpersonal advantages as well. Building these relationships can help employees trust their supervisors more and feel more compelled to give open and honest feedback, which in turn can bolster engagement with your organization.

But don't stop here.

3) Recognition

Referral partners and customers, you acknowledge are more likely to continue sharing business with you. When people feel they are valued, they have a favorable impression (and hopefully, an emotional connection) of your company and are more likely to do business again. It could be a simple handwritten note or gift card. Whatever you do, add a personal touch.

I'll leave you with this thought: Showing gratitude to those around you not only feels great, but it can produce results. You may even find that having a positive attitude increases your productivity, boosts mood and helps your bottom line. Studies show that grateful people tend to live longer than their less grateful peers.

So, start each day with a clean slate and be thankful for the opportunity to begin anew. Be sure to stop a few times during the day to slow down and reflect on the good things in your life. It's easy to get bogged down by life's stressors, but we needn't forget the joys.

---

x. Work Smarter Not Harder: Three Classic Mindsets to Avoid

Small businesses are notoriously resource-constrained, overcommitted, and often suffer from larger than life ambitions with poor strategic execution. While agile, small businesses often face growing pains that larger organizations may take for granted. Following are a few ways in which small business owners may be sabotaging their success:

1) Continually putting out fires (—the classic working "in" versus working "on" your business mentality).

Do you feel like your job title should be firefighter chief, instead of the chief executive officer? This ongoing state of affairs can stem from a lack of action planning or the absence of a strategic roadmap to guide your thinking, choices, and decisions.

If you're falling into this trap time and time again, it's probably a good time to conduct environmental and situational analysis using tools like SWOT and PEST to bridge the gap between performance expectations and where the organization is Today. Leveraging interested parties and stakeholders to analyze where you stand in critical areas might provide an early warning sign that a pivot is necessary. You also might benefit from bringing in a third-party expert to facilitate and guide the discussion and assist in faster implementation.

2) Working in silos (—the classic "not my job" syndrome).

When employees are informed about how their job relates to others in the company, it can create an environment where people and teams work in silos and not in concert with one another. This lack of coordination can mean tasks are duplicated, left unaddressed altogether, and may result in sub-optimized organizational performance.

This is why a strategic roadmap is critical because it spells out accountabilities and which resources will contribute to the company's success. When employees understand the work, they do help other employees execute, it fosters camaraderie and incentivizes people to communicate and solve problems when things aren't going as planned or surprises are experienced along the way.

3) Unproductive meetings (—the classic "activity" versus "results" mindset).

Just say no.

The decline of 90% of the meetings you are invited to attend. Our ISO auditor has repeatedly reiterated that you should only go to meetings if there are decisions to be made and actions to be taken. If not, don't ever go again because the meeting is unnecessary. As many favorite management books posit: if it can be communicated via an email or through an alternative non-face-to-face channel—don't call a meeting. That's because too often meetings become time sucks; informal discussions are drawn out, and there's no clear decision made.

If you must call a meeting, everyone there should know why they are there from the outset and leave with a clear sense of what they need to do. A focused plan with key objectives and decisions to be made should be provided in advance, and meeting minutes distributed shortly after. This can maximize productivity if issues are framed, decisions are provided, and action planning is enabled.

You also might consider limiting the time duration of meetings or require everyone to stand up for the meeting. Better yet, calculate the *cost* of the meeting (this should lead to limiting participation to be more productive). Multiple short meetings often can be much more productive than a single long meeting. Focused meetings may also cut down on the silo mentality because it gives them a chance to break out of their bubble regularly.

---

xi. Are You Sabotaging Your Success?

Are you getting in your way? This applies to people in all areas and facets of the business. Maybe you've had a good idea but didn't have the drive to pursue it. Or perhaps you've had a concept percolating in your mind for some time that won't go away. If this at all resonates with you, there's a good chance that your inner monologue may be partially to blame.

In working with business builders, we often encounter these three saboteurs, you know ... the voices in your head that try to hold you back.

Mindset #1: "I don't have the money to start."

While yes, ideas, businesses, or projects may require more money than you have in the bank right now. But this is all the more reason to start now with an investment in time. Low-risk opportunities, like side gigs or consulting, are easy ways to enter the marketplace without a lot of "skin in the game." Small opportunities done right can open the door to higher stakes and allow you to build up confidence and the savings to invest. The Kauffman Foundation has reported that the average investment required for a startup. Today it is around $30,000.[170]

Mindset #2: "I'm not smart enough."

Successful people are the product of a community of successful people who believed in them. If you doubt your intelligence, know that you are never alone in your business building journey. Your job then becomes to assemble the people, knowledge, and capital required to get the job done.

In short, intelligence is not a prerequisite for success in entrepreneurship. A degree, certification, or even high IQ won't make you any worthier to pursue your dream. Don't give in to your doubt. High EQ and working side by side with trusted and experts with a track record can make all the difference. Surrounding yourself with the right people provides credibility, community, and connections. These assets are all designed to do two things—accelerate growth and reduce likely false starts.

Mindset #3: "All the good ideas have been taken."

As long as there are problems, the world will need solutions. That said, if you have an idea that improves or enhances something that already exists, that's an opportunity. It's called incremental innovation. It's innovation in action. You don't have to reinvent the wheel—you just need to add value somehow. Some of the best ideas take an existing product or service from good to even better. Did you know that less than 10% of all innovation is breakthrough, radical, or disruptive, and the rest is incremental?

Chapter 10: Conclusion

Along the same lines as "life is 20% what happens, and 80% how we respond," Thomas Edison reminds us that "genius is 1% inspiration and 99% perspiration." Don't ever sell yourself short. If you are committed and conscious as to how you spend your time actively choosing what and how you focus and dedicated to following a plan of attack—you can do great things.

Mindset is hard work, and it takes continual awareness to keep yourself on track. Having a system of support helps, as well as tackling head on anything holding you back—you must clear the mental cobwebs to achieve laser concentration. Your mental strength is like a muscle, it needs exercise to improve.[171] Don't run *from* your problems, face them head on, and take the opportunity to grow.

Chapter 10: Questions for Consideration

i. Understanding the Entrepreneur Mindset

Do you have a disruptive and restless outlook on life and business? Are you hardwired to take action, accept the risk, and deal with the consequences? If your answer to these questions is yes, and you feel an overwhelming desire to take your career firmly in hand down a path of your choosing, chances are you already are an entrepreneur. What obstacles or objections did you have to (or plan to) overcome to take control of your professional life?

ii. Lean into Curiosity

When was the last time you challenged your beliefs, or the conventional way of doing something? Just because society does typically anything, doesn't mean you shouldn't consider if there is a better or alternate way. Don't let fear or expectations hold you back. What project(s) would you take on if you weren't afraid to fail? Out of every ten things you try, how many do you have to get right to be judged successful? Remember, all experiences and failures have learning and growth potential.

iii. Goal Setting

Norman Vincent Peale once said, "Shoot for the moon. Even if you miss, you'll land among the stars."[172] Big goals are important, but just like a moon landing, it requires acute attention to detail, a solid base, step by step processes, and often, an entire team on your side. The process of aiming so high can have unintended positive side effects and discoveries along the way. To jump-start your inspiration for thinking differently and challenging what's possible, check out Loonshots by Safi Bahcall.[173]

iv. The Stoic Leader

Are you in control of your thoughts and emotions? Or do you find yourself swept away by spur of the moment reactions to people and events as they happen? Stoicism can help you hold on to a center baseline as storms rage around you. If you're looking for a more grounded approach to life and business, delve deeper into the Stoic philosophy. As the quote most often attributed to Viktor Frankl reminds us, "Between stimulus and response, there is a space. In that space is our power to choose our response. In our response lies our growth and our freedom."[174]

v. Why Embracing a "Startup Mentality" Is Good for Business

Is your company or business adaptive to current trends, or entrenched in old ways? How can you become more agile? Are the leaders and executives resistant to change, or do they embrace new ways of evolving? Do you have a plan for growth, along with guidelines for ideal employees? An "improvise, adapt, overcome" mentality (see Chapter 4) is also beneficial for scaling strategically.

vi. The Morally Courageous Leader

When have you been courageous (and what was it that allowed you to be), or when have you thought about being courageous and were unable to act in accordance with your personal values? Have you ever had to take a stand that was unpopular with others who were close to you? How can you be more vulnerable and transparent in your interactions, while still sticking to your values?

vii. Want a More Entrepreneurial Organization? Start Here

Has your company embraced entrepreneurial thinking *and* action? Why or why not? How can ideas be translated into reality based on real-world education and practical experience? Can everyone work with a purpose without fear of making a mistake? Think of ways to promote and enact this kind of culture and community in your business.

viii. The Minimalist Organization

It is almost a given that there are areas that could be scaled back or down, both in your personal and professional life—it just takes commitment and execution. Have you considered all the potential flip sides to "more"? Make sure all your costs are correctly in line with your profits, even if that means scaling back. Can you answer *why* you are doing every project, following X procedure, and what you hope to get out of it? If not, take the time to figure this out for every situation, you may find some things can be culled. Getting rid of excessive projects can save you time and money that can be reinvested into more promising ventures. Remember, less is more.

ix. A Grateful Mindset

What are you grateful for? How can you embody an attitude of gratitude? Consider getting a gratitude journal, or any kind of notebook will do, and challenge yourself to write down five things you are grateful for every day for thirty days. Note what changes occur and work hard to bring your gratitude into the workplace, sharing and inspiring your employees with how much you value and appreciate them. Check out Shawn Achor's 6 exercises for happiness on the CBC News website.[175]

x. Work Smarter Not Harder: Three Classic Mindsets to Avoid

If you are continually taking care of urgent problems and issues, it's time to pivot. To get ahead, focus on ways to enhance performance, increase organizational focus on key strategic drivers, and deliver strategic boosts to simplify the process of strategic growth. Are your teams working in silos? Learn to recognize the warning signs before it's too late.[176]

Meeting peer pressure can quickly overtake us, stay vigilant. Just because many are so used to having meetings, it has become almost second nature. Resolve yourself to take a firm stand *against* meetings, and work on a standard script for how you will transition unnecessary meetings into phone calls or emails. Having a practiced policy will help you reject at the moment instead of getting swept along.

xi. Are You Sabotaging Your Success?

Which of the following three mindsets are holding you back?

1. I don' have the money to start.
2. I am not smart enough.
3. All the good ideas have been taken.

Is there something else that you feel is standing in your way? Remember, the most significant obstacles we will ever overcome are the walls we build for ourselves. If you're worried about money, start a side hustle, rearrange your budget, apply for a loan, and tighten your belt—where there's a will, there's away. Think the market is already saturated? Go to the grocery and look at how many kinds of juice there are. There is always room for a unique perspective.[177]

CREATIVE IDEA

CHAPTER 11

INSPIRATION

Inspiration can come from anywhere, in any form. We must be on the lookout and ready to make use of it when it arrives. If we are unprepared, the opportunity to make use of it can easily pass us by on our entrepreneurial journey. From instilling and nurturing inspiration in others, to actively seeking it for ourselves—we should be proactive about finding and utilizing creativity, not just waiting for it to arrive. Keep the goals, values, passions, and ethos of both you and your business close at hand and top of mind so that you can continually work toward achieving benchmarks along the way. Be sure also to think about who inspires you, where your best ideas come from, and at what time of day you are operating at your personal best. Find ways to keep your creative juices flowing by leaning into your curiosity and idea experimentation.

i. A Pipeline of Female Founders

Think about it—40% of all businesses today are founded by women.[178]

While overall new venture formation rates in the United States have been declining for many decades, we need to encourage more women to start their businesses. Now is the perfect time to inspire young minds to explore this meaningful and transformative career path.

Here are three ways to spot and encourage young, female entrepreneurship:

1) Help her to discern her passion and a path forward.

For example, does she love graphic design? Maybe she has an affinity for caring for animals. Both domains could provide a foundation for a business. How might we connect her passion to a startup venture? Along with shadowing a business builder, the uses of psychometric or talent assessments like Predictive Index and BP-10 can help clarify and confirm an aspirational entrepreneurial journey.

2) Have the money talk.

It's never too early to teach financial literacy. If she has some income from a part-time job like babysitting or mowing lawns, she can learn the basics of accounting. For example, half of her income goes into the bank for expenses, and the rest is considered "profit" for paying herself or reinvesting in the business. All kids need to understand that entrepreneurship requires money management—and there's no better way to learn than by doing. Bootstrapping and learning about customers before investors can help set the venture and the founder up for long-term success.

3) Don't "helicopter her"—show, don't tell.

As much as parents want to shield their kids from unpleasant experiences, that won't serve them in the long run. Failure is a natural part of life, and that's important to accept. On the flip side, in grappling with obstacles, she'll come out stronger with determination, grit, perseverance, and problem-solving skills. Along with the financial stress of college loans, young adults wanting to avoid failure is one of the reasons many young people don't even try entrepreneurship. Entrepreneurs are resilient and bounce back from adversity. Let your daughter lean into it and see firsthand how to succeed, dig out of a hole, and thrive.

If possible, introduce her to female business builders, and let her hear their stories firsthand. Such women probably had role models they learned from themselves when they were younger. In other words, show her what success can look like. Vibrant and inclusive entrepreneurial communities are available to serve as a support system launchpad pad for entrepreneurial success.

Speaking of success, the future looks even brighter for women-owned businesses, according to the latest data available.

- Women-owned businesses now represent 42% of all companies—nearly 13 million—employing 9.4 million workers and generating revenue of $1.9 trillion, according to the annual State of Women-Owned Businesses Report.[179]
- In addition, over the past five years, the number of women-owned businesses increased by 21%, while all businesses increased by only 9%. In other words, women's contributions to the economy are not insignificant—and we need to foster an entrepreneurial spirit in the next generation of female trailblazers.

ii. #GoalCrushing: Three-Must-Have Ingredients for Success

Goals are what move us forward in our personal lives, and the same can be said for our organization's health. Not all goals are created equal, however. Also, not all goals are within our control. Have you ever heard the common organizational goal challenge of … "do more"?

This is what happens when you have a successful year, and your organization is working on setting your next year's goals. Every organization is trying to improve and push their performance to higher levels.

Beyond SMART goals, consider the following factors when setting key performance indicators to help determine if your goals are appropriate for your business.

1) It's in line with your mission and stokes passion.

What's your *why*? What driving force is behind your product or service? Your goals should take into account your company ethos. For example, say your company is committed to giving back to the community. A goal might be to pledge so many employee volunteer hours each year or make small grants to local organizations to further your organization's passion and interests.

The best goals get people excited and motivated to move past obstacles to achieve success. You want everyone to know that their individual contributions matter and move the needle. This not only creates excitement but also inspires pride.

Stretch goals can also spark excitement on an industry level. As a Harvard Business School article observes, "Super stretch goals are thought to provide inspiration, a sense of mission, for the most capable and adventurous of those seeking to join startups."[180] However, there is and can be a real downside to super stretch goals, including provoking bad behaviors and producing "little communication between the ranks and the top about how they were (or were to be) achieved."[181] You can garner attention when the competition sees you're tackling a huge problem. Regardless of the outcome, you're making waves with your goal setting because you're creating brand awareness by presenting them with a concept that can't be ignored.

2) It scares you.

Sometimes the worthiest of goals instill fear. Fear can be paralyzing, but that forces you to take a leap of faith to get out of a rut. It's these experiences that often lead to innovation. If you ask Tim Ferriss, harnessing our fears can be rocket fuel for moving forward. In his TED talk, Ferriss encourages us to fully envision and write down our concerns in detail, in a simple but powerful exercise he calls "fear-setting."[182] This practice can help you thrive in high-stress environments and separate what you can control from what you cannot.

3) It's tied to a greater good.

Today's consumer is more socially minded than ever. Millennials, especially, are looking for substance from companies they support. They vote with their dollars. This means if your goal is tied to a more significant social good, it humanizes your brand. Customers won't see you as simply a widget—their support for you means they're also making an impact. In other words, they develop a positive association with your brand.

This appeal to the heart (vs. the head) is an added way that customers justify their purchases. Purchases are often driven by instinct. When it comes time for them to make a decision, they'll default to emotion. That's where your social purpose can be the determining factor in driving conversions.

---

iii. Vision and Values ... So What?

Vision and values are great, but they are only a good as the systems that back them up. Without leadership and reinforcement from the top, these guidelines fall flat and become idealist and unmeaningful to people.

Change is constant, but it's possible to keep vision and values consistently active—with the right mindset and actions. Following are three tips I believe companies of all sizes and across all industries can adopt:

1) Be strong—and consistent—in your identity and desires.

Knowing who you are and what you want is one thing but broadcasting that to the world is another animal. And what about your internal messaging? Inconsistencies will no doubt surface and come back to bite you.

A clear and entirely cohesive expression of your vision lays a strong foundation for the values to follow. Building a vision is an opportunity to align vision and values into your business model.

Think of Disney World, for example. There is perhaps a no better example of what it means to empower associates to wow guests—and do whatever it takes (appropriate to the service recovery) to create memories. Vision, values, and execution are all aligned with Disney's customer mantra—creating happiness for people of all ages. They indeed stumble at times, but they strive for perfection and settle for excellence.

2) Lead, train, reinforce—and repeat. Learn from mishaps and service failures.

The most effective companies have leaders who celebrate and highlight successes and reinforce the brand promise by continuously learning and innovating. Such concepts should be infiltrated into regular discussions, coaching sessions, sales meetings, employee evaluations, and more. Values and vision must be part of the company's DNA—not an afterthought.

3) Always be innovating.

If you truly want to retain talent, and your customers, you must reinforce your values with real examples of the desired behavior regularly. Sometimes that might mean evolving the things that define your organization and what differentiates it. Regardless of the direction you take, you must have strong safeguards that keep your vision and values alive so that you can push forward.

---

iv. Hacking Creativity: Start with Solitude

Picasso famously said, "without great solitude, no serious work can be done."

In an experiment, five-year-old children were given a creativity test used by NASA to select innovative engineers. Ninety-eight percent of the children scored in the "highly creative" range, while only two percent of adults who took the same test rated as "highly creative."[183] It should come as no surprise that as we age, we steadily hemorrhage all the creativity out of our veins, and must deliberately exercise the creativity muscles back into shape. Creativity is the ability to look at the same thing as everyone else does, but to *see something different*.[184]

Some of what we are told about nurturing creativity may need to be reframed. Several of our fundamental assumptions and preconceptions may need to be challenged. These include: the best ideas come from group brainstorming, creativity is best nurtured by working in an open office, and there's a gene for creativity—you're either born with it or not. However, these myths may not reflect reality. For instance, in office environments, noise and distractions hamper creativity. On average, workers get interrupted every three minutes, and it can take over 20 minutes to regain your stream of consciousness. The frequency of interruptions is likely higher in open offices[185] and probably why most people wear earbuds to avoid lost productivity.[186]

Moreover, Kellogg professor and author Leigh Thompson observed, "Studies of brainstorming show 75% of a group's ideas come in the first 50% of the time given allocated to them anyway. After that, they run out of steam."[187] Lastly, while genetics do play a role in shaping your creative gifts, much of it can still be learned (think Gladwell's 10,000 hours).

Looking back to the 1960s, Frank X. Barron studied a group of writers, architects, scientists, entrepreneurs, and mathematicians, to see if he could find common themes among these creatives regarding behavior. He concluded that these creative thinkers exhibited certain common traits. Among them were an openness to one's inner life, a preference for ambiguity and complexity, unusually high tolerance for disorder and disarray, and the ability to extract order from chaos. I think the first one is rather insightful. The most creative people know how to sit with their emotions and ideas, no matter how crazy or uncomfortable. I think all of these attributes encompass a crucial dimension of who entrepreneurs are—*they are contrarian thinkers*.

However, is creativity a skill we can cultivate and nurture? For sure—"research suggests that it's possible to prime the mind for creative ideas to emerge."[188] In our hurried and noisy world, how can we train our minds to become more creative? Here are three practical and easy ways[189] to prime the "creative muscle" in our lives:

1) Practice mindfulness.

No longer a phrase only found in textbooks or uttered in yoga studios; mindfulness is something everyone can integrate into his or her lifestyle in a meaningful way. Increased creative thinking is a side effect of the calming of the inner mind during and after meditation.

2) Schedule disruptions.

Working non-stop in a compressed period of time isn't good for our brains or productivity. Get up and take that coffee break or midmorning stretch. Meditate or do yoga at lunch or walk the dog midday. Whatever you do, break up your workflow, so you do not become stagnant.

3) Let your mind wander.

You are probably familiar with the creative benefits of daydreaming,[190] but one of the points often glossed over is the importance of *uninhibited* daydreaming. That means not letting your brain filter the thoughts coming into your head. This can be stifling to creativity—as Barron would argue, it is the full range of emotions that fuel our creativity. When we can quiet our minds, we become more open to exploring things outside of the here and now. Be sure to pause from time to time

---

v. Perseverance Is a Slice of Grit

Some people believe success is a matter of happenstance—something that happens to you and requires no agency. That couldn't be further from the truth. While sometimes fortunate coincidences happen, there are no overnight successes. Startups that make the cut, in the long run, have one thing in common: a persistent business builder behind them who perseveres despite adversity and obstacles (see Chapter 4, section vii. Got Grit?). Here are three ways to make that happen:

1) Find your *Why*—Think purpose + passion.

Passion is good, but it's more surface level. *The purpose* is what gets you out of bed every day. Purpose can encourage us and give us the motivation to prevail when times are tough. The purpose is that the end goal and the mere idea of it fill you with joy. Find that, and from my experience, the rest will follow.

2) Celebrate wins.

It's a jungle out there. You will have failures or false starts—and lots of them, but the goal is never to start out with failure as your strategy. Those who brag about failure are those who seldom had their own skin in the game; typically, they lost someone else's money—friends, investors, or the bank's. Taking time out to bask in success (pause and reflect) can keep you grounded when times are tough.

3) Be your own best friend.

If you need a specific example of how to apply this, try this exercise. Write a letter to your future self. What would you want to hear when you are having a bad day? Then put that letter away until you need it and take those words to heart. In the heat of the battle, we all need encouragement and inspiration. Having a caring and robust support system can combat the loneliness and isolation from being a contrarian (entrepreneurs are by their nature contrarians).

Many of us are looking for the next big thing, and yet when we present ourselves, we aren't positioned to capitalize on it. It is difficult to make things come to fruition, but it is far easier to be prepared when the right opportunity manifests itself.

Perseverance is a slice of Grit, and the other slice is Passion. If you keep improving and keep working hard and smart, it is only a matter of time before things align, and the economic and social dividends of your dream are more fully realized.

---

vi. Three Ways to Embrace Change in Your Business

We live in an age of rapid change and growth. As business leaders, we must stay relevant or face the consequences. History reminds us that adaptability and resilience are the keys to long-term success.

But how? What's the key to reinventing yourself and your business? Here are three strategies for staying and being relevant in the marketplace today:

1) Be picky.

Only about two ideas out of one thousand are typically close to "blockbuster," so you don't have to follow through on every great idea presented to you. Instead, carefully assess each opportunity so you can focus on what you determine will be the most strategic and profitable. If you're spread too thin, it's easy to lose focus and traction. This is a case when being selective is a good thing.

2) Tune in.

It's easy to get caught up in the behind-the-scenes tasks that come with running a business, but don't let yourself become disconnected or out of touch. Look to the trenches and gain customer insights; iterative and ongoing customer discovery and validation are paramount to your long-term relevance and sustainability. Customers need change. We need to evolve *with* our customers.

3) Stay hungry.

Staying on top of the trends and news in your industry is one way to up the ante. Trade publications, industry association meetings, innovisits, blogs, professional education, seeking certifications to professionalize your experiences better, and LinkedIn are all great sources of staying current. You might consider joining a professional trade organization to further network with peers and stay current.

---

vii. How to Foster a Culture of Entrepreneurship at Your Company

It is no understatement that we live in challenging and uncertain times. When I was first out of college and joined the General Electric Company, now called "GE," it was regularly shared that, "Loyalty is 24 hours deep, and on Friday we are even." This is partly why the younger generation tends to change jobs every few years and is likely to have anywhere from thirteen to seventeen careers (not just jobs) in their lifetime. They follow their passion and dreams first. Career progression follows later, if at all. For older people like me, the GE-ism is a clear reminder to "polish your skills" and "sharpen your saw" to stay professionally competitive and personally relevant.

This new "employment context" leaves many companies with two options: accept what is or attempt to get more out of their employees by encouraging their innovativeness, creativity, and entrepreneurial spirit—while at the same time being attentive to the bottom line and staying relevant in the marketplace.

As humans, we are creative by nature. We all have an innate ability to identify problems and patterns, seek opportunities, and find innovative and novel solutions—all skills which lend themselves to entrepreneurship. While I am not a huge fan of the term, in larger companies, it is often phrased as "intrapreneurship."

While the change trajectory may seem steep, there are simple (and gradual) structural and programmatic changes that could help create more internal entrepreneurs or an entrepreneurial mindset while improving communication and bolstering loyalty. Here are a few things you can do in larger organizations to stoke an entrepreneurial culture and spirit in your organization:

1) Encourage structured time to "tinker."

Build cross-functional/multi-disciplinary teams with the objective of various departments/functions to work together and find better ways to innovate for the customer's benefit. Give people "time" to work regularly on their organizational pet projects. Be sure to make sure the physical setting and workplace reflect the best ways for your people to work, learn, and laugh.

2) Dial into your organization's vibe—catalyze the entrepreneurial energy by creating a culture of appreciation, celebrating small wins and successes along the way.

Regularly encourage and nurture the entrepreneurial mindset through lifelong learning, project team participation, and conducting adult field trips (aka *innovisits*—benchmarking organizations outside your industry who are good at something you want to be great at).

Be sure to acknowledge and celebrate employees who take risks—regardless of whether they succeed or fail. Taking chances will drive the organization forward. Create an internal Opportunity Fund to fuel fresh ideas, leverage leadership development opportunities, or put a small group in charge of creating and launching new products and services. By doing so, you will be investing in entrepreneurial capacity building and capitalizing on great ideas flowing through your organization.

3) Develop a cadre of internal storytellers.

Create passionate champions and advocates for sharing your organization's purpose, culture, and ethos. Engage these motivated and capable people as ambassadors in your company (giving company tours, sharing their own stories, etc.). Take the time to invest in this elite group's skills, knowledge, and abilities. You'll find that their enthusiasm is contagious. Also, you will find these efforts will foster and grow the dynamism of your internal entrepreneurial culture efforts. ***The best way to diffuse culture is to immerse people into it.***

The Bottom Line: Change willingly or be changed. If your organization doesn't take it upon themselves to disrupt its own business model and change how it competes and wins in the marketplace, someone smarter and faster will catch you off guard and change the rules of engagement for you. My experience is it is much easier and better to focus on fixing yourself.

---

viii. Banish "The Mondays": How to Stay Engaged at Work

A confession: I have always been jealous of the concept of the *4-hour workweek*[191] popularized by Tim Ferriss. In fact, I have never been able to put into practice his ideas very well. Yet many people have implemented his shortcuts, and they can be life changing. Every year, I try to re-read sections of his book and incorporate some of his practices.

For those of us who can't outsource our lives or take mini retirements, it's easy to fall into a rut. We all have a case of "The Mondays" (or "Monday Blues") from time to time. The antidote is to find ways to stay motivated, productive, and passionate every day on the job so that you don't fall into a downward spiral of burnout and disengagement.

Here are three ways to stay connected at work:

1) Start the day on a high note and keep the end in mind.

The simple pleasures in life can provide some comfort and energy to get you through the day. Maybe it's a cup of coffee, morning jog, meditation, etc. Whatever your pleasure, make sure you carve out enough time in your morning routine to fit it into your day. It truly does set the tone. Rhythm is an essential ingredient in success. While I am not a very relaxed person, I really enjoyed the free ten-day basics of meditation on the Headspace app.[192] I like the notion of living a happier and healthier life, and the science around mindfulness suggests I could live a less stressful life by incorporating these principles into my daily life.

Another aspect to starting off on the right foot is, to begin with, the end in mind[193], as Dr. Stephen Covey suggests. The happiest people have goals they are always working toward. At the beginning of the day or even the night before, make a shortlist of actionable goals you want to hit to move your big "rocks." They should align with your long-term aspirations. That feeling of accomplishment will keep you motivated and on track throughout the day. Covey, an American educator, author, and businessman, suggests having a personal mission statement and asking yourself reflective questions like, "what do I want in life?" and, "will this help get me to where I want to be?"

2) Stay organized to maximize creativity.

Our workspaces reflect and affect our mental state. Is yours a complete mess or tidy? Can you easily retrieve documents? Be mindful of your workflow. Work on one or two tasks at a time instead of taking on everything at once. Depending on your personal "wiring," doing fewer tasks better might work better for you in the end. Some scientific studies suggest having plants, listening to music, specific colors, ergonomic furniture, and lighting can all create a productive and inspired workplace. Pay close attention to what I call the workplace success formula: A^2TF—architecture, artistic expression, technology, and furnishings to create an inspired and productive workplace. While many think remote work will replace place-based learning, I think most people will still prefer to be in a work environment designed for work and to have more physical separation from their workplace and home.

3) Be strategic.

I've discussed this point before. You shouldn't take on just any project or the sake of getting money in the door fast. Clients who want cheap work fast won't get you to your goal. As companies vet candidates for employment, you, too, should vet potential clients or customers to make sure they align with your mission, values, and goals. The right client[194] and project will energize you, while the wrong one will only continue to stress you out and suck the life out of you—and who wants that? It's okay to turn down work. Toxic clients might get you some quick cash, but you will be miserable doing the work and potentially damage your brand in the process.

---

ix. Konmari Method: Spark Joy for Business Success

Chances are, you've probably heard of Marie Kondo. Whether you've watched the Netflix hit, Tidying Up with Marie Kondo, or read her book, *The Life-Changing Magic of Tidying Up*, both highlight Kondo's method of organizing known as the KonMari method. It consists of gathering together all of one's belongings, one category at a time, and then keeping only those that "spark joy."

While many people have been inspired by her thoughtful approach and decluttered their living spaces, the same lessons can be applied to business success. As you take stock of your organization's present and future, consider translating these three relatable concepts into a new way of thinking:

1) Give up things to allow room for others.

On the show, Kondo challenges clients to visualize a clutter-free space. In business, cutting down on clutter can be a placeholder for something that occurs on a deeper level—more time to pursue projects you enjoy, entertain prospects, interact with things and people you value, etc. The key is to identify what is weighing you down. Then make changes to free up time and resources for those that put a fire in your belly. Think: less is more.

2) Stop planning and start doing.

Are you dreading tackling that whale of an item on your to-do list? Take Kondo's advice and conquer smaller projects first. Or divide up that big project into manageable parts. Don't get mired in the quest to follow the complete process (there isn't one)—just do it. Planning without execution is like a hamster on a treadmill. Jim Collins covers this concept[195] well in my favorite book, *Good to Great*.[196]

3) Seek joy.

"Sparking joy" is a catchphrase on the show—and for a good reason. Following Kondo's methodology, a clutter-free environment is a surefire way to keep things around that elicit joy and eliminate those things or people that burden us.

To apply this concept to your work, think of it on multiple levels:

- Consider new habits and how to integrate this thinking into planning activities.
- Think about the customer experience and how you can add "joy" into the mix and surprise and delight your clients or customers.

---

x. Three Lessons from the Founding Fathers

In a way, the founding fathers were among the nation's first innovators, and they offer valuable lessons still relevant today.

1) Don't be afraid to take prudent risks and disrupt the market.

Breaking away from "Mother England" was bold and risky. However, the founders believed it was in the best interest of the people, and they went ahead with issuing the Declaration of Independence. Just think how different life in what we now know as America would be, had they taken the path of least resistance or settled for mediocrity.

2) Think outside the box.

These men weren't afraid of new ideas. When it came time to form their own government, they didn't co-opt Britain's constitution—they came together to draft something that met their needs and sensibilities at the time. You, too, as an entrepreneur, can benefit from thinking more about what could be and less about the limitations.

3) Don't underestimate the importance of autonomy and freedom.

When they declared independence from England, they were sending a message loud and clear that the colonies would no longer be under the thumb of the king. This presented a great opportunity in the form of lawmaking and a say in the structure of their government, among other things. The lesson here? As an entrepreneur, don't be afraid to put your foot down or to push to rewrite the operating rules if you feel restricted by a customer, vendor, partner, etc.

"True freedom in America today is the ability to spend your time and money as you see fit," Infusionsoft CEO Clate Mask explains.[197] "Creating financial freedom for yourself means that you can not only grow your business and pay your employees but to also give your family the quality of life you want for them. Just as importantly, freedom enables you to invest time and money in causes that matter to you, whether that is with your family, friends, or hobbies."

xi. Success, Significance, and Legacy

A colleague of mine has in his office a placard that reads "Success, Significance & Legacy." The placard serves as a reminder that there are three "big" stages you might go through during your career. Even though he is 80 years old, each day, he intentionally thinks about how to build and extend his enduring legacy, and more importantly, how he might add value to others each day.

We all need to occasionally pause and consider what we want out of life and what we want our life to stand for.

If you haven't read Bob Buford's book *Halftime*, you should. In the book, Bob lays it out: "The first half (of your life) is busy with 'getting and gaining, earning and learning,' doing what you can to survive, while clawing your way up the ladder of success. The second half of life should be about regaining control, calling your own shots, and enjoying God's desire ... for you to serve him just by being who you are, by using what he gave you to work with.' What lies between the two is 'halftime?'"[198]

1) If you are chasing success, a business builder may be focused on profitability, growing a customer base, finding outside investment, or adding new employees or buildings. Essentially, this stage is about keeping score and accumulating stuff.

2) If you are chasing significance, a business builder may be focused on how they are paying it forward or how they are making other people's lives better. Essentially, this stage is about surrounding yourself with people who make you better, dreaming big, and becoming the best version of yourself.

3) If you are chasing legacy, a business builder may be driven to make a significant impact. Legacy is about reputation, and what your personal brand promise is to the world and to your family. Across the U.S., serial entrepreneurs are transforming communities (Tony Hsieh in Las Vegas, Jeff Vinik in Tampa) to make the world a better place. Essentially, this stage is about following your passion and being part of a higher purpose. In this stage, it is not about *you* but about the collective *us*.

Another good book is one written by Adam Grant called *Give and Take*, where he describes Givers as "people who perform all sorts of selfless acts with no expectation of reciprocity."[199] Business builders seeking legacy are unequivocally givers.

Entrepreneurs often feel lonely or isolated. These feelings can lead to anxiety, stress, or abandonment. Entrepreneurs need social interactions and networks that can encourage them, inspire confidence, and that can provide emotional support to navigate through the highs and lows of launching and growing a company. Development centers can provide business builders an emotional support system so they can build their social network, create a sense of connectedness and collegiality to reduce isolation and loneliness, and inspire each entrepreneur to stay committed to their business venture. Business builders are courageous individuals and should be acknowledged as such.

Chapter 11: Conclusion

What are you chasing? One of the most critical aspects of inspiration has to do with having a well-prepared foundation upon which to receive it. Rarely (if ever) will something spark entirely out of the blue with a fully formed road map on how to achieve your dreams. Knowing what you want and having an action plan on how to reach your goals will help prime the way for both creativity and inspiration. To quote Thomas Edison once more, "Opportunity is missed by most people because it is dressed in overalls and looks like work." Inspiration is not magic; it comes to those who are already working on making their own success.

Entrepreneurship is Invention + Commercialization. By finding a problem and coming up with a solution. While this sounds simple, today's innovators have often struggled with finding problems that others value enough to pay for it.

Innovators have boundless energy and often channel their creative juices to address systemic industry and customer pain points. By seeing things through different angles, putting disparate product or business model pieces together to address marketplace opportunities, and fostering a passion for making a difference, today's business builders are inspired by people, processes, business models, customer experiences, distribution plays, and brands.

Inspiration is deeply personal. It can be born out of crisis, opportunity, non-linear thinking, and a desire to make things better, simpler, faster, cheaper, and/or smarter. **Where do you do your best thinking?** Figure that out and lean into it, leverage it, and learn from it. By doing so, you will be more connected and fulfilled.

Chapter 11: Questions for Consideration

i. A Pipeline of Female Founders

Are you a female business owner or entrepreneur? Have you considered mentoring? What inspired you to take the path of entrepreneurship, and how can you use what you learned along the way to help others? When you are around young females, try not to talk to them about frivolous things, such as outward appearances, boys, or other stereotypical "girly" things. Instead, speak to them as independent, capable business builders on the verge of a breakthrough.

ii. #Goal Crushing: Three-Must-Have Ingredients for Success

Read this article[200] (refer to the hyperlink in the endnotes) on how to increase your confidence as a business leader by using learning, behavior, and performance goals. Stre.me's strategic boost template[201] can also assist you in setting manageable, actionable, and measurable work plans. Do your goals scare you? Write down all the reasons why and then make counterpoints to each one, how can you face your fear head-on and turn it into a motivating factor?

iii. Vision and Values ... So What?

How does your company put vision and values into account? Are your internal and external messages consistent across the board? If not, how can you take steps to align them? Are successes celebrated and highlighted? Be sure to uphold and reward examples of the company's core beliefs for letting others know what they should strive for. When was the last time you reevaluated the company's defining characteristics? Have they evolved with the times? Maybe it's time to adopt a more modern business DNA.

iv. Hacking Creativity: Start with Solitude

What steps can you take to become more comfortable with solitude and open yourself up for creativity? Where and when do you do your best thinking? Try sitting alone in a room and let yourself experience all your thoughts unhindered for a set amount of time. It may be uncomfortable at first, but with time it will get easier. Once you've mastered that—get moving. Steve Jobs was known for his walks, and for a good reason. Creative output can be increased by as much as 60% when walking, according to a Stanford University study.[202]

v. Perseverance Is a Slice of Grit

You're a reflection of how you spend your time—and with whom, so choose your company wisely. The best social circles, whether personal or professional, stretch you and make you an even better person. For example, if you want to learn sales skills, seek out people who are adept at closing the deal. Over time you will adopt those traits and tendencies which can position you for success. As Jim Rohn famously said, you are the average of the five people you spend the most time with.[203] Who are your top five? What do they add to your life? Is your average improving?

vi. Three Ways to Embrace Change in Your Business

What trends can you capitalize on? Do you have any examples of when you've leaned into a change in your business? How did it help? Are you in touch with your customer's wants, needs, and desires? How can you ensure you are staying up to date and connected to the pulse of the market or industry? Consider holding a customer panel or survey to make sure everyone is on the same page.

vii. How to Foster a Culture of Entrepreneurship at Your Company

Do your employees have time to work on their own projects during regular working hours? In order to encourage and embrace a culture of innovation, you must not be afraid of change or going against conventional ways of doing things, even how the workday is spent. The only constant is change, and you should lean into it, not operate in fear of it. Attempts to hold onto old models will only impede progress. A retired CEO of The Walt Disney Company Bob Iger reminds us, "Don't be in the business of playing it safe. Be in the business of creating possibilities for greatness."[204] How can you build a foundation of risk-taking from a place of courage?

viii. Banish "the Mondays": How to Stay Engaged at Work

A bonus method for engagement inspiration is to surround yourself with trusted advisors and/or an accountability partner. Everyone needs a buddy—in business and life. Join forces with people who support your goals, have a vested interest in your success, and from whom you can get candid feedback and insights. The right person will help you see the bigger picture and celebrate wins alongside you. Make sure you return the favor, too! We often confuse our to-do lists with getting results. Vulnerability and openness are the only straight paths to professional growth and maturation. Simply put, we need to find people who make us better. As Disney regularly asks its cast members, how can we plus things up for our guests? Who pluses you up in your life?

ix. Konmari Method: Spark Joy for Business Success

Have you been putting something off? Sometimes getting started is half the battle, and breaking it into smaller, more manageable pieces can make any task less daunting. Is it possible to add an element of fun to make it more enjoyable? It's okay to reward yourself—give the Pomodoro Technique[205] a chance. What goals could you set your mind to if you cleared out the general clutter? Not sure where to start, use this *Good to Great* diagnostic framework.[206]

x. Lessons from the Founding Fathers

What risk(s) have you avoided taking that might change the trajectory of your business for the better? Are you a glass half full or half empty type of person? What goal shots have you deferred that you should strongly consider moving things forward? As hockey legend Wayne Gretzky reminded us, "You miss 100% of the shots you don't take." Are there any individuals who are negatively influencing your business model? If so, and more importantly, what are you doing about it?

xi. Success, Significance, and Legacy

If you are a business owner, where are you in these three stages (Success, Significance, Legacy), and where would you like to be? Taking all of this into account, what stage are you in, and how satisfied are you with it? Do you have a support center in place to help celebrate each step of your business building? If not, find one today and lock in your network to help guarantee your success and celebration along the way.

20 YEARS OF INSIGHT

i. Lessons Learned From 20 Years at The NIIC

In a way, this entire book is the culmination of everything I have learned at the helm of The NIIC over the past two decades. And yet, even more specifically, working at The NIIC has given me a front row seat to watching organizations elevate their culture to a higher level while simultaneously maximizing team engagement and results while catalyzing internal innovation efforts. By outsourcing corporate innovation responsibilities, I've seen organizations experience greater flexibility and faster results through commercialization assistance, ideation, and other services that help ignite business opportunities.

Although The NIIC is focused on structured coaching and mentor services to bring out the best in other people, at the same time, it has also brought out the best in me. Allow me to illustrate with a brief and personal case story:

I have been enormously blessed to receive three Foellinger Foundation Inspire Grants. This grant gives the non-profit CEO an opportunity to look at adaptive challenges and opportunities in a fresh and transformative way. Through this innovative, capacity building program, I have had opportunities to re-imagine, re-charge, re-create, unlearn, and re-learn key behavioral, leadership, strategic and organizational skills that improve me, my performance, and The NIIC.

My learning journeys have taken me all over the country ...

- to strengthen my higher order thinking skills,
- to learn new success practices,
- to make lasting connections,
- to build resources and organizational capacity,
- to connect dots,
- to grow my own talents, and
- to think and operate differently.

By having these unique, remarkable and memorable experiences, I am able to be more effective, self-efficacious, and more fully engage in The NIICs mission.

That mission includes being a part of other's success. In our years of working with business ideas, business ventures, and passionate people, we've developed considerable entrepreneurial insights, expertise, and a track record that guides individuals in the right direction at every stage and scenario of their business venture. When individuals and corporations work with us, we take them through the assess phase of our three-step proprietary and trademarked process:

ASSESS > DISCOVER > DO

and learn about how well they are "wired" to become a business builder.

Whether it's related to securing capital or talent, connecting with tech mentors, coaches, or services providers (e.g., lawyers, accountants, bankers) or just wondering if an idea is viable, our venture advisory services help advance individuals and their business concept. They work, learn, and laugh (once in a while) with a dedicated team of accomplished business professionals. Individuals with specific skills, capabilities, and industry experience are there for support throughout the thought process and action phase of entrepreneurial passion and vision.

Mentorship

An integral part of business development is seeking advice and guidance from mentors—you can never plan too much, and you don't have to go it alone. That's where our business coaching and business development services comes into play. Having an experienced and trusted advisor, like The NIIC, dramatically increases the likelihood for success, and improves a company's overall approach to managing key enterprise risks when considering scaling up and growing. These include a laser focus on execution, product, financial and market risk.

The NIIC, and similar organizations, are outstanding resources and sounding boards to support analysis and testing of company infrastructure to determine legacy beliefs, market assumptions, validation of new consumers, and identification of opportunities to optimize the launch of new, credible products and services to capture market share.

A credible mentor network can range from serial entrepreneurs and c-suite executives, to subject matter experts and professional service providers. Their involvement is transactional, typically consisting of one-to-three meetings. Continuing the working relationship afterward may occur if you and your mentor consent to do so, and you both realize value out of the relationship.

Good mentors will work with you to provide guidance on mission-critical matters, such as: financial planning, including investment and funding; business development; marketing strategies; human resources; general management; strategic planning; partnership agreements, and networking.

Mentorship programs should be flexible and available at your convenience, at every phase of your venture. The length and frequency at which you seek mentorship are entirely up to you, even if it's a one-and-done meeting to ask, "How can I find a local company to make affordable prototypes?" That's fine too.

Leveraging Innovation

Could your organization use a jump start? By incorporating the use of innovative programs such as the So What, Who Cares, Why Me?™ Program, The NIIC helps drive ideation and action across businesses and organizations. Using WKI's proprietary approach and online toolset, we take teams of up to ten people through a six-week innovation program and utilize psychometric assessments—like Gallup BP-10, Predictive Index, complemented by Matthew Kelly's Dream Manager program, and other life-coaching services, to improve an organization's talent pool in order to bring out the best in people. During this time, teams work together to create a pipeline of great quantity ideas while quantifying the top potential business opportunities of an organization. It is also possible to consider organizations like The NIIC as your outsourced Chief Innovation Officer to help keep culture, systems, metrics, and talent in alignment for innovation success.

If you're serious about an idea (or want to more fully round out your concept with a second opinion of sorts), you need a trusted and credible partner to take you to that next level. Enter The NIIC. We categorize our entrepreneurial resources into four pillars:

Capital, Talent, Workplace, and Networking.

The approach is time-tested with proven results. It's the reason businesses we help start and grow have 91.9% survivability-rate five years after the inception of a new business venture. Simply put, ventures grow faster and stronger with professional guidance and support.

Our experience gives us insight and understanding of the needs of business builders at all levels—pre-company, pre-revenue, start-up, growth, and scale. The knowledge we've gained helps strengthen the ways we serve, continually evolving to better the entrepreneurial experience and your results.

Community and Coworking

Coworking spaces at institutions such as The NIIC can be a crucial element for entrepreneurial success: professional FlexSpace options provide **credibility**—a place of substance for your business and you, **flexibility**—a range of programming options to meet you where you are and more importantly help you get where YOU want to go, and **community**—The NIIC's campus is bustling with motivated entrepreneurs, business builders, and small business owners eager to connect, engage, and bounce ideas off of like-minded entrepreneurs.

The NIIC also offers a variety of opportunities to build "community" through attendance at monthly programming or events we sponsor or co-sponsor. The NIIC is the largest entrepreneurial community under one roof in Northeast Indiana, and the opportunity and resources reflect this status.

I know firsthand, the difference our employees make every day in creating memorable experiences for our clients and guests. They go the extra mile to deliver surprises and delight to advance The NIIC pinnacle customer experience. We are very fortunate to have such capable and energized people looking out for ways to deliver an exceptional customer experience.

Capital

As far as investment, our longstanding partnerships with banks, credit unions, institutional and angel investors make the continuum of capital more transparent and accessible for high-performance companies working with The NIIC.

For high-performance companies thinking about SBA-backed loans, private placement memorandums or dabbling in crowdfunding, having a trusted advisor and financial expert to connect you and your team to these programs can make all the difference in the world.

Capital fuels growth, plain and simple. High-performance companies require constant access to a continuum of capital to ensure stable, long-term success. To capitalize on product introductions, geographic market expansions, strategic acquisitions, and new customer segments, you'll need financial partners capable of growing with you.

There is no downside for seeking outside assistance, don't hesitate to reach out to the local entrepreneurial development center closest to you, and start accelerating your growth today.

ii. Life Lessons Learned from My Mother

My mom passed away in January 2016 after a 25-year courageous fight with Parkinson's Disease. Here are three of the lessons she ingrained upon my heart.

Lesson 1: My mom taught me to be an inspired and engaged learner.

Several months before she passed away, my mom was working with the nursing home where she resided in Massachusetts to get Wi-Fi and computer stations on her wing of the floor. They had Wi-Fi on the first floor but not on her floor. She sought to change the problem that stood in the way of her learning. She wanted to take an online pharmacogenetics course (growing up, she was a nurse and stay at home mom) at the nearby community college. My mom had a "deal" with me growing up that she would buy me any book as long as I read it and discussed it with her. My mom loved and embraced technology. She was a millennial at heart! She spent years doing and assembling a comprehensive genealogy of her family. There is no greater gift to set you up for life than a love for lifelong learning (being an *empowered learner*) and then doing something with what you've learned to be relevant and intentional in the world.

Lesson 2: My mom taught me to advocate for what I wanted.

I told my parents in 7th grade that I was bored stiff in public school and wanted to go to private boarding school. My father's initial reaction was *no way*, and then my mom went back to work as a school nurse to help pay for my private education. She convinced my dad, and I was off to the best experiences of my life. My mom invested in me and bought into my arguments that I wanted to be in an environment that would stimulate me. She often reflected that this was the best investment she ever made in me because it prepared me so well for life. She sacrificed so I could be inspired and encouraged! I am who I am today because of her.

Lesson 3: My mom taught me to be confident and courageous about my career, life, and parenting choices with generosity and caring in every situation.

She always focused on my strengths and how to make them better. She never dwelled on my shortcomings. She didn't inspire me by trying to fix me. She worked hard to make sure I was aware of how to become the best of the version of myself. She loved to challenge my thinking. She set really high expectations of what she felt I could do in my life. She always reminded gently but clearly when I fell short of expectations—not in a negative way but in a motivational way. Sometimes my mom might have been hardheaded and would not take "no" for an answer. I was reminded by JB Bernstein that, "No is the beginning of a negotiation." As she was failing in recent years, I often had to negotiate with her because her intellectual mind far outpaced what her worn out body would allow.

Throughout her entire life, whether it was helping out at church as a young adult, visiting shut-ins at the local nursing home or in their homes or going door to door with her to educate people on smoking and cancer when she volunteered at the local American Cancer Society, she taught me that I had a responsibility to help others and lift them up. **She taught me that giving my time was the most precious gift I could give.** She loved to educate and share with others. She loved to debate with me politics, sports (she knew a lot more than me on this topic!) and religion. She always asked me more about what I was doing, and how I was giving back and was not as interested in any personal success I might have had along the way as she was about the significance and difference I was making in the world. She was intellectually curious, and my best PR agent!

A Stoic Spirit

My mother never defined herself by the enormous limitations (the physical and emotional toll that 25 years of Parkinson's had on her body and her mind) the Parkinson's Disease placed on her life. She never complained—*why me* or had self-pity. She used her disease to impact others. When she was diagnosed with the disease, many of her friends didn't see it as a real chronic illness—like cancer or heart attacks—or thought it was an old person's disease (until Michael J. Fox came along). In response, she set out to educate others, motivating them, and often knew more about the disease than her neurologists or Parkinsonologists—she even started a support group, and studied and read everything available about the disease. She always put others first and loved to share her insights in the nursing home through book club, programs she ran on Parkinson's, and through her art and music talents (none of which I inherited). She had an awesome gift of touching and connecting with other people. After she died, many people, whom I did not know, shared how she impacted their lives.

My mom's life is congruent with an observation made by the Blessed Mother Teresa of Calcutta who said, *"We cannot all do great things, but we can do small things with great love."* It is worth acknowledging that Blessed Mother Teresa was declared a saint in early September 2016. She was right about the difference we can each make in our life if we choose to do so.

iii. Taylor University-MBA Program Indianapolis Commencement Address

Your mountain is waiting …

Dr. Bennett, Dr. Linamen, Dr. Rottmeyer, members of the faculty and MBA staff, distinguished guests, parents, family, friends and

most importantly ... the 2008 graduating class of Taylor University's Indianapolis MBA Program. I am honored to be here and good evening to you all.

This is an especially heartwarming occasion for me, since I was fortunate enough to have played a small part in the original planning efforts for the creation of the MBA program, currently serve on the advisory council, and am an active adjunct professor in the Taylor MBA Program. And now, four years later, to witness the first Indianapolis graduation ceremonies is a gratifying moment for me and a milestone for this innovative and special graduate program.

And you should be especially proud, because you *are* the first – there will never be another "first Indianapolis MBA graduating class," you're <u>it</u>—and you're setting the baseline against which all future graduating class will be compared. You have the first chance to set all the records. What you accomplish with your education, your careers, and your God given talent and lives, will set the bar for all who follow you. I implore you, Set It High! Set records – not only in your career, but in making a difference in the world around you! Make it a real challenge for those who come after you to overachieve the Taylor MBA Class of '08 – Indianapolis!

Speaking of setting records, we have recently seen the passing of two of the world's greatest adventurers – **Steve Fossett** and **Sir Edmund Hillary.**

Each rose to enormous heights, figuratively and literally—Steve in aircraft and hot-air balloons, and Sir Edmund on foot, to the top of Mount Everest.

Each has a lot of "firsts"—Steve, among his many other records, was the first to circumnavigate the globe in a hot air balloon, and Sir Edmund climbed many mountains before anyone else, Everest only being the most famous ... and the highest. These two powerful examples should reinforce in our minds, Hebrews 12:1, "Let us run with perseverance the race that is set before us. God has designed a purpose for each of us – one each of us must *uniquely* and *individually* discover and maximize to our fullest potential for His Glory.

And now I look out before me and see even *more* great adventurers in this room, who join 85 other MBAs over the last four years, who are ready to scale their own heights, set their own records, and make their own mark. It surely must have been you that Dr. Seuss was thinking of when he wrote this classic, *Oh, the places you'll go!* His words are certainly appropriate – and one verse is especially so today, with a bit of paraphrasing:

Be your name Addie, or Brad, or Keva or Ray,

Or Jeff or Nat or Emily ... rising stars of Taylor's MBA

>you're off to Great Places!
>Today is your day!
>Your mountain is waiting.

So ... get on your way!

Throughout your educational career you've been preparing yourself, and now you're ready to ascend the mountain ... the path may be perilous at times, the going rough, and your route to the top not always clear ... but as Seuss reminds us you surely *will succeed*, 98 and ¾ % guaranteed!

And where are all these "Great Places" Dr. Seuss says you're off to? That's up to each one of you; as the good doctor explains, *"You* are the one who'll decide where to go." What a beautiful, exciting opportunity, and at the same instant, what a faith-testing challenge!

Is your destination a life of service, or a life of self-interest?

A man who knew quite a bit about the business world and the Father of Modern Management, Peter Drucker, had this advice: "What we need is the *will* to live more for meaning than for money, status, or applause. We need the *intention* to serve a higher purpose than fulfilling our own selfish wants and needs." Note those particular words, *will* and *intention*—you must have both—the intention to serve a higher purpose is insufficient without the will to follow through and *actually* do it—to *really live* more for meaning than for money, status, and applause.

I call this ***Acting Intentionally***—being "<u>will</u>-intentioned" as opposed to just "<u>well</u>-intentioned"—and it is my first bit of advice that I hope you'll carry away with you tonight—every time you reach a decision point (and believe me, you'll face *thousands* over your business career!), stop and think what it means—what it *really means* to other people—then decide what is right, and *do it!* **Act intentionally.**

There is nothing wrong with material success—I doubt that many of you have pursued an MBA without some hope of achieving success that can be measured at the bottom line—but as I am sure your Christ-centered education here at Taylor has taught you, such rewards are less important in and of themselves; as Christ posed the rhetorical question to his disciples in Mark 8:30, "For what will it profit a man if he gains the whole world, and loses his own soul?"

No, the true value of material success becomes clear only when you recognize that you receive it by Grace, and that you amplify it by acting as a conduit through which God's Grace may flow to others. Step beyond merely acknowledging that you are the *recipient* of Grace and understand that you are called upon to be an *instrument* of Grace, as well. Peter ends his second epistle with a command for us to grow both in grace and in the knowledge of Jesus Christ. Hear Peter's words—

"But grow in grace, and [in] the knowledge of our Lord and Savior Jesus Christ. To Him [be] glory both now and forever." (2 Peter 3:18)

Dr. Scott Peck, author of the timeless classic and seminal work, **The Road Less Traveled,** opined, "Our lifetime offers us unlimited opportunities for spiritual growth until the end. For the call to grace is a promotion, a call to a position of higher responsibility and power. For us to experience one's closeness to God is also to experience the obligation to be the agent of God's power and love. The call to grace is a call to a life of **effortful** caring, to a life of service and whatever sacrifice seems required." *What will you be remembered for? What will you be intentional about today as you embark on this next chapter in your life?*

My second bit of advice is simply this: **Be Courageous.** I share with you now what most of you already know and have experienced. There is a spiritual war out there, and you're going to be faced with fears and doubts that will test your faith to the limits – the uncertainties of world affairs, the clash of cultures, the paradox of religious hatred that pits faith against faith throughout the World. But don't become disillusioned in the face of these fears and doubts. Be strong in your faith – from faith comes courage, the same courage – through-faith displayed by the mother of Moses as she defied the Pharaoh to save his son. **Be courageous.**

The world is awash with anxiety about the unforeseen consequences of environmental change, the spread of new, mutating drug-resistant diseases, technology that is rapidly expanding beyond our ability to understand its future effects, and the globalization that is flattening the world beyond recognition and threatening every economic and social assumption that we've come to rely upon – but don't be paralyzed by the uncertainties that surrounds you. Face them with confidence and **courage**, like Daniel faced the lions' den. **Be courageous.**

Lurking behind every headline is another shock to our spiritual system—an unprecedented erosion of moral values—you're going to be swimming against a rising tide of atheism, secular humanism, apathy, despair and outright hostility to people of faith. The world is a Goliath waging war against faith, daring us to step forward and challenge it. Simply put courage requires us to meet our adversity head-on. As we are reminded by one noted evangelist, "All of these giants and more can be conquered if we have the same <u>faith</u> and <u>courage</u> of David."

Yes, it's going to take a lot of courage to face all that; it's going to take even more courage to do something about it. Be strong in your faith, because through faith you will draw the courage not only to face the world, but to change it. Perhaps you will be as inspired as I have been by the verse that the Bishop of Diocese inscribed in my Bible on the occasion of my confirmation—it was First Corinthians 16, verses 13 and 14—"Be watchful, stand firm in your faith, be courageous, be strong. Let all that you do be done in love." Stand firm. **Be courageous.** Be strong. Be loving.

Be a champion for God in all that you do. The greatest act of courage that you can ever perform and the deepest expression of love that you can ever display is the complete subjugation of yourself to the Will of God. **Be courageous.**

You know, I said earlier that you should use your unique position as the first Taylor MBA – Indianapolis graduating class to set a high bar of achievement to challenge the graduating classes to come. To that I might add, **Set the bar high for yourself.** Don't be happy with today's "microwave mentality" of instant gratification with minimal effort. Set the bar *personally* HIGH, and don't be happy until you clear it, and then when you finally do, *raise it up another notch and try it again* ... the biggest challenges you face in life should be the ones you set for yourself, and that takes *discipline*.

Collins makes an interesting observation about the disciplined thinking that characterized leaders who move their organizations from "good" to "great" ... they do not only have "to-do" lists, they also have "stop doing" lists. They have a remarkable ability to "unplug all sorts of extraneous junk and concentrate on doing significant things." *What can you and I unplug and de-clutter? How do we keep God at the epicenter of our life?* **How do we live THAT life of significance?**

<u>**Imagine for a moment**</u>— "awakening every day trapped in your body, moving slowly, your limbs stiff, your hands shake, and your legs won't do what you want them to, and periodically shuffling instead of taking long strides and periodically freezing, unable to move." Imagine further a life of pain, rigidity, slowness of speech, shakiness, to one day potentially choking oneself to death. This describes my mother's daily battle with Parkinson's Disease. Sixteen years ago she was diagnosed with this disease which was thought to just be an old person's disease—Pope John Paul II, Billy Graham, Muhammad Ali have it, but young people, at the time, like my mother didn't get it (and physicians didn't know much about it!) until Michael J. Fox publicly disclosed he had the disease. My mother is one who inspires me every day. My love of reading and learning comes from her, and she is one of the most courageous and inspirational people I know.

Despite her life-threatening disease, she remains optimistic, hopeful, and daily she rests in God's loving hands. She loves God more today. Today, her faith is stronger, despite her inability to dress herself, to get out bed without assistance, or to make her own meals or to drive her own car. Amazingly so, she still lives at home independently with caregivers delivering the services she needs to maintain her dignity. She still sees the glass as half full and not half empty. She challenges me daily to remember: "to whom much is given, much is required." She reminds me that her love for me is not born out of any success, accomplishments, or credentials I have sought or obtained, but out of the values of living a "good and just" life—loving your family, being kind to others, giving back, inspiring others, living your Faith, and being relevant. She knows a cure for Parkinson's is most likely not in her lifetime, and still she challenges me, in the face of her own great adversity, to do as she has done—be a better person, be a kinder person, be a more patient person, listen more and judge less, advocate for those unable to advocate for themselves, and educate others on this tragic and debilitating disease.

Hers is a life of great significance—to me, and to everyone she touches—*because of the way she lives it!* Hers is a life of continuous spiritual growth, of channeling God's Grace to others, and of *inspiration*—certainly to me—to make my own life one of significance and relevance to others.

Tony Dungy, the **first** African American coach to have a Super Bowl victory and author of the book *Quiet Strength,* explored the role of significance in success. In the final analysis, he says, "God's definition of success is really one of significance—the significant difference in our lives can make in others. The significance doesn't show up in the win-loss records, long resumes, of the trophies gathering dust on our mantels. It's found in the hearts and lives of those we've come across who are in some way better **because of the way we lived.**" Let me repeat this simple but provocative point—it is because of the way we lived. It's up to us, and it's within our control! Remember always—we must live life fully."

Another key leadership influence in my life is Max DePree, author and Chairman Emeritus of Herman Miller, who once remarked, "Human potential is best expressed through love—whether love of people, one's

God, or one's work." Today is the beginning of "polishing your gift" or, as DePree called it, "tuning oneself for life." All the nuggets of knowledge you've mined from your formal education so far are merely "diamonds in the rough" ... they need to be cut and polished with the grit of real-world living before the true value of these gifts comes shining through. That's why we call this "commencement"—it's a beginning, not an end, to quest for life-long learning, relevance, and making a difference. **What "polishing of *your* gifts" can you start to do today?**

Shockingly, on a recent episode of 60 minutes, 94% of students surveyed in college nationwide feel they are overwhelmed and under enormous stress to materially achieve —fancier cars, bigger houses, buying more stuff and high-powered executive Wall Street-like jobs. Don't misplace aspiration for materialism or the American Dream of more is better. Don't mistake fast cars, bigger houses, or lots of money for *real* happiness and contentment.

Harvard University actually has a course called **Positive Psychology: The Science of Happiness.** Over the past four years, this course became the most popular course offered on campus, with 1,400 students attending. A recent study of the pursuit of happiness by an English University ranked the United States 23rd. Denmark places first as the happiest country in the world boasting an average work week of 37 hours, free health care, subsidized child care, elder care, all education is free, you can take as long as you like to complete your studies, and you will receive a minimum of six weeks of vacation a year! Of course, the average person pays at least 50% in taxes—not something that would sell easily in the United States, but I think you see my point that nothing worth doing comes without cost or consequence. There is no free ride.

One of my favorite books recently has been *The Dream Manager* by motivational speaker and writer Matthew Kelly. In it, Kelly encourages the reader to "Connect to your dreams." He says, "A company's purpose is to become the best-version-of-itself. The next question is: What is an employee's purpose? Most would say to help the company achieve its purpose, but they would be wrong. That is certainly part of an employee's *role,* but an employee's *purpose* is to become the best version of him- or herself." Our dreams are the bridge to that "best version" of ourselves. In many ways, we *are* our dreams … or want to be. But people stop dreaming because they get caught up in the hustle and bustle of just surviving, and not really living. And once we stop dreaming, we start living in quiet desperation, and little by little the passion and energy begin to disappear from our lives." The reality is we are driven by our dreams, and "helping people chase and fulfill their dreams is one of the primary functions of all relationships."

Imagine for a moment—someone who understood the importance of dreams better than most was a man whose whole business was dreams—Walt Disney born Walter Elias Disney in December of 1901. Through the magic of animation and movies, Walt built fantastical dream worlds that amused, amazed, and enthralled us all, and then he went further—he created *real* worlds where we could actually step into his dreams and live them on our own! Today, Disney Land, Disney World, and the rest of Walt's Magic Kingdom serve up dreams on demand for every kid who ever "wished upon a star." Walt received sixty-four Academy Award nominations out of which he won on 26 occasions. He holds the record for an individual with the most awards and the most nominations. Walt Disney has also won seven Emmy Awards. According to one of the biographers of Walt Disney, he wrote, "Walt's optimism came from his unique ability to see the entire picture. He was a pioneer and innovator, and the possessor of one of the most fertile and unique imaginations the world has ever known. During his 43-year Hollywood career, he was bankrupt by 22, risked everything three or four times in his life, and his name had become synonymous with the ideals upon which his name represents – imagination, optimism, creation, and self-made success in the American tradition." He was and is for me an inspiration in his pursuit of making life more enjoyable, fun and touching the hearts, minds and emotions of hundreds of millions of people around the globe and changing the face of American culture. And he did it with dreams …

The Master Musketeer had a few things to *say* about dreams, but one statement in particular that Walt made was: "Somehow I can't believe there are any heights that can't be scaled by an individual who knows the secret of making dreams come true. This special secret, it seems to me, can be summarized in four C's. They are **Curiosity, Confidence, Courage, and Constancy** and the greatest of these is Confidence. When you believe [in] a thing, believe it all the way, implicitly and unquestionably … *always remember that this whole thing was started with a dream and a mouse."*

So, I ask you, quite simply, what are your dreams … **and what's your "mouse"?** Make a mental inventory—think of a list of things you would like to do, places you would like to see, things you would like to accomplish have, your relationship with God and others what you would like focus on, and all the "dreams you can find in your heart." Don't fall prey to quiet desperation; instead, **become an "accomplished dreamer"**, a phrase coined by my fellow Taylor colleague and friend Dr. Adkinson, and let your dreams inspire you to a life of constant fascination, intellectual curiosity, and an abundance of God's gifts and blessings. Randy Pausch, a computer science professor, who wrote the book **the Last Lecture** said it best when he said, "It's not about how to achieve your dreams. It's about how to lead your life. If you lead your life in the right way, the karma will take care of itself. The dreams will come to you." **Great advice for us all!**

Imagine for a moment—a seminary for boys and a seminary for girls in Western Massachusetts founded in 1879 and 1881 respectively. Seminary Founder Dwight Moody, one of the best-known Christian evangelists of the 19th century, had a dream of a school that educates the Head, the Hand and the Heart. "Its curriculum would be broad, deep and inclusive, and challenge students to know and value the life of the mind. All students would participate equally in the daily chores of the school by working four hours a week so they would cultivate a respect for the dignity of labor and service to the community, both within and beyond the school." Northfield Mount Hermon School was born of these values of spiritual life and growth, and today—as it did when it was founded *129 years ago*—it vibrantly encourages in each student the "desire to live with purpose and to make a difference in the world." I'm blessed to be a 1983 graduate of this fine, world-class institution and largest coeducational boarding school in America, and I am forever appreciative of "Moody's legacy" of developing, inspiring, and cultivating in me my own voice, through the cultivation of my gifts and talents—"**my** head, **my** heart, and **my** hand." During good times and bad, it has become my spiritual GPS system!

And now, pay close attention, for I am about to utter the words you've all been waiting to hear:

"In conclusion …" let me leave you with a final piece of advice that may just save your sanity in the years to come: **Pause and pause often.** One of the most valuable things I have done for myself, my children, and my family, the past two years is to drive my children to school every day. We commute our three boys to a parochial school that is 30 minutes from our house. Typically, I always have left the house at 5 am to get to the office to try to get some work done before people start arriving at 8 am. For the last two years, I have "paused" to drive my children to school, and you would not believe what I have learned about my kids, their friends, their classes, their spelling and geography tests, their teachers, the Church, their interests, their passion, and their joys, their successes, and their challenges, and disappointments. I would have never learned any of this if I hadn't paused … to look, to listen, to teach, to coach, to support, to inspire and to learn. **Pause, and pause often** … to reflect, to reassess, to reaffirm, and most importantly, to give thanks for the wonderful bounty of God's Grace.

So, if you remember any of what I have shared today, keep in mind Jim Stovall's observation from *The Ultimate Gift:* "Life is full of many contradictions. In fact, the longer you live, the more the reality of life will seem like one great paradox. But if you live long enough and search hard enough, you will find a miraculous order to the confusion."

My suggestions for sorting out these paradoxes are simply these five things—

- **First – Be intentional.** Do His Will. Mother Teresa of Calcutta said: "True holiness consists in doing God's will with a smile and she reminds us that" we cannot all do great things, but we can do small things with great love."

- **Second – Surrendering yourself to God** is a supreme, courageous act, and one from which all other courage flows. We become relevant by being courageous. Be courageous in all that you do.
- **Third – Set the bar high.** Aim high and then set the bar even higher for yourself. Be committed to personal excellence in all you do. Be an empowered, passionate, and engaged life-long learner! We should aspire and strive for no less.
- **Fourth – Become an "accomplished dreamer"** and dream more. "Give yourself permission to dream and enable the dreams of others."
- **And lastly – Pause and pause often.** At this time, let us all be mindful of this weekend as we pause and reflect on the loss of five members of the Taylor University family two years ago in a tragic traffic accident. Today, on the Taylor Upland campus, the Campus community is dedicating a Prayer Chapel that was "built as a call to the university community to prayer and a memorial to Taylor students Laurel Erb, Brad Larson, Betsy Smith and Laura Van Ryn and dining services employee Monica Felver."

Reflecting on her words of unwavering hope, grace and faith, Whitney Cerak's own calling is captured best by her in the Epilogue of the newly released book **Mistaken Identity.** She reminds each one of us God's purpose for us when she wrote,

"I realized that instead of thinking that my life has to be some big windstorm or earthquake for God, perhaps I only have to let him whisper gently through my life. This story made me realize that I don't have to accomplish some giant thing for God … It took a while, but I finally figured out that God's purpose for me is to let Him do whatever He wants in my life, big or small."

Let us reflect on the strong belief that through Whitney's own words, she reminds us that God does have a plan for each of us if we are open to receiving it.

Karl R. LaPan

May the triune God, Creator and Deliverer of all things, continue to bless you and your family today and always, and ... *especially* on behalf of the faculty, I applaud you on your accomplishment today. Congratulations to the graduates of the Taylor University – Indianapolis MBA Class of 2008. We honor each and every one of you tonight not only for your accomplishments, but for the great expectations and plans of things to come. *Your mountain is waiting; now get on your way!*

Thank you, and good night.

CONCLUSION

After over two decades at the helm of the Northeast Indiana Innovation Center (NIIC), I believe more than ever that successful entrepreneurship centers around innovation, inclusivity, and evidence-based solutions. My entire career has been dedicated to imparting these principles to aspiring business builders through trusted advising.

I have had the unique opportunity to shape and build an organization, turning it into one of the top entrepreneurial resource centers in the country with advising at its heart that is hands-on and not just a resource—it's a community.

It is my lifelong goal and commitment to continue expanding my network and ecosystem of thought leaders and help others on their journey to success. This book is a condensed resource of almost every core lesson I've learned throughout my tenure, and it is my utmost hope that you have been able to find some value and insight that will help further along your entrepreneurial path.

In summary, here are the key takeaways from each of the preceding chapters:

Chapter 1: Innovation

Innovation must come from within, both as a business leader/builder and from within the culture of your company. This requires a willingness to lean into the future of work, embracing change and automation. Do not fear failure or the risk required to think differently, sometimes you have to "let go" of the reins a little and allow the qualified people on your team the freedom to push boundaries and make pivots. Never stop learning, and remember—innovation is ongoing work.

Chapter 2: Emotional Well-Being & Self Care

In uncertain times, it is all too easy to be overwhelmed by the unknown. You can manage uncertainty by several means, but most importantly, but cultivating an empathy-driven culture in the workplace. Remove distractions, protect your peace, redefine success, rethink balance, and don't be afraid to ask for help. When you are vulnerable, it helps employees be comfortable with their own vulnerability, allowing for healthy growth which in turn is beneficial for business. Don't isolate yourself, take time to reinvigorate as necessary with like-minded individuals, and always keep your "why" close at heart.

Chapter 3: Connection & Communication

Human capital is arguably one of the most valuable resources of any organization, you must carefully cultivate a people-centric organization that retains quality human interactions and relationships. From the right business partnership, to winning friends and influencing people, communication is key and must be prioritized. Cut out the superfluous jargon, and strive for authenticity and honesty—always. Don't be afraid to go beyond the surface level, and remember, deep connections are instrumental in building and scaling businesses no matter where you are.

Chapter 4: Improvise, Adapt, Overcome

The only constant is change, don't be afraid to pivot and recalibrate at any moment; new facts and information make adaptability essential. In business as in life, you can hope for the best, but prepare for the worst—do your best to ensure your business can weather any storm. When you're feeling stuck, reframe, reconnect, reflect, and recharge in order to push forward. There are bound to be economic ups and downs, but you must lean into failure, hold onto your grit, and practice resilience in all areas.

Chapter 5: Funding

At some point in your entrepreneurial journey, you'll need to figure out where your startup capital is going to originate. Will it be crowdfunding or bootstrapping? Either way you'll need to hold yourself accountable, and likely, work on your sales pitch. What makes you different? Always know your story—and your numbers, and continually invest in yourself, even if it's just reading and networking. Set boundaries, have an "abundance mindset," but always have an out—if you need to, you can always sell the business.

Chapter 6: Networking

No man is an island, and a strong entrepreneurial network and support system can make all the difference in the world. Be prepared to make the most of trade shows, and every networking opportunity by cultivating, investing in, and nurturing relationships. Don't let meetings run away with your time, prioritize and make a schedule so that no time is wasted. In fact, the first seven seconds can be the most crucial—work on nailing your first impression. Embrace the human side of networking, put passion into the process, and find a mentor who can further develop your skills and connect you to a wider group of influencers.

Chapter 7: Optimizing Your Niche

What's your niche? You should know it inside and out and work on capitalizing your unique value-add narrative. Community and customer discovery are core features of the business model search and execution process, take time to tune in. You'll need authenticity, gravitas, personal mojo, stick-to-itveness, and vulnerability in order to carve out your own personal niche. Don't be afraid to start small, and as J.B. Bernstein says, "No is the beginning of a negotiation."

Chapter 8: Competitive Advantage

Competitive advantages are not a laundry list, there may be only one—which is why they are rare and fragile. In order to maximize your potential, you must leverage data in all decision making and enhance value whenever possible. Never rest on your laurels, maintaining a leg up on the competition requires constant innovation and maybe even a little friendly rivalry as a driving force for advancement.

Chapter 9: Sustainability

Running a business is a marathon, not a sprint. In order to stay on top of your A-game, you'll need to delegate, rethink "busyness," stay grounded, and not leave management to chance. Growing pains are unavoidable, prepare for them, adopt the habits of other highly successful business builders, and fortify yourself against "low battery" / entrepreneurial burnout. Growth isn't always a good thing, be sure that your business venture is really what you want and know when to fold 'em.

Chapter 10: Mindset

It takes a special kind of thinking and specific entrepreneurial DNA in order to be able to withstand the unique challenges of business builders. Are you willing to lean into curiosity, challenge the status quo, and dare to create for the sake of creating? If so, goal setting and stoic leadership will become two of your mainstays, along with the right attitude, intentional effort, and recognition of a grateful mindset. Working smarter, not harder takes conscious effort and requires constant vigilance in order to ensure you're not sabotaging your own success. With the right system of support, and continual effort, you can maintain a positive trajectory.

Chapter 11: Inspiration

If it scares you, is in line with your mission, stokes passion, and is tied to a greater good—then it is highly likely that it is an appropriate goal for your business. Be strong and consistent in your identity and desires; lead, train, reinforce—and repeat. Practice mindfulness, schedule disruptions, and let your mind wander. Know your *why*, celebrate wins, and be your own best friend. Start the day on a high note, and keep the end in mind while staying organized and strategic to maximize creativity. Utilize the Konmari Method to spark joy for business success—give up things to allow room for others, stop planning and start doing, and above all else, seek joy.

ENDNOTES

Chapter 1: Innovation

1. Henley, Dede. (2019, January 11). *Four Ways To Unleash Your Creativity In 2019*. Forbes. https://www.forbes.com/sites/dedehenley/2019/01/11/4-ways-to-unleash-your-creativity-in-2019/#50460b5e133e

2. 22nd Annual Global CEO Survey. *CEOs' curbed confidence spells caution*. https://www.pwc.com/gx/en/ceo-survey/2019/report/pwc-22nd-annual-global-ceo-survey.pdf

3. *Apple's net income in the company's fiscal years from 2005 to 2019*. Statista. https://www.statista.com/statistics/267728/apples-net-income-since-2005/

4. *Think Different*. Wikipedia. https://en.wikipedia.org/wiki/Think_different

5. Taylor, Bill. (2011, February 1). *Hire for Attitude, Train for Skill*. Harvard Business Review. https://hbr.org/2011/02/hire-for-attitude-train-for-sk

6. Pradhan, Arun. (2018, March 8). *Learning Agility: Building Learning Organizations*. Learning Solutions. https://learningsolutionsmag.com/articles/learning-agility-building-learning-organizations

7. *3rd Annual 2019 Workplace Learning Report: Why 2019 is the breakout year for the talent developer*. LinkedIn Learning. https://learning.

linkedin.com/content/dam/me/business/en-us/amp/learning-solutions/images/workplace-learning-report-2019/pdf/workplace-learning-report-2019.pdf

8   ISO 9001:2015. https://www.iso.org/standard/62085.html

9   LaPan, Karl. (2017, June 22) *Presentations: Indiana Chamber Connect and Collaborate.* The NIIC. https://theniic.org/newsroom/president-ceo-newsroom/

10 *TED: The Economics Daily.* (2016, July 8). U.S. Bureau of Labor Statistics. https://www.bls.gov/opub/ted/2016/24-percent-of-employed-people-did-some-or-all-of-their-work-at-home-in-2015.htm

11 *The SearchLite.* https://thesearchlite.com

Chapter 2: Emotional Well-Being & Self Care

12 Johnson, Brian. *Optimize Your Life.* https://www.optimize.me

13 Covey, Stephen R. (2016, January 1). *The 7 Habits of Highly Effective People: Powerful Lessons in Personal Change.* Amazon. https://www.amazon.com/Habits-Highly-Effective-People-Powerful-ebook/dp/B01069X4H0/ref=sr_1_3?crid=O1J6HGYKL0CH&dchild=1&keywords=7+habits+of+highly+effective+people&qid=1584907142&sprefix=7+habits%2Caps%2C193&sr=8-3

14 Pomerenke, Joey. (2014, November 6). *Empathy in Business Is Vital to an Entrepreneur's Success.* Entrepreneur. https://www.entrepreneur.com/article/238935

15 Collins, Jim. *Confront the Brutal Facts.* Jim Collins. https://www.jimcollins.com/concepts/confront-the-brutal-facts.html

16   *The Ultimate Wheel of Life Interactive Assessment.* https://wheeloflife.noomii.com

17   Hayes, Adam. (2020, February 6). *Earnings Before Interest, Taxes, Depreciation and Amortization — EBITDA.* Investopedia. https://www.investopedia.com/terms/e/ebitda.asp

18   Chapman, Jake. (2018, December 30). *Investors and entrepreneurs need to address the mental health crisis in startups.* TechCrunch. https://techcrunch.com/2018/12/30/investors-and-entrepreneurs-need-to-address-the-mental-health-crisis-in-startup-culture/

19   Kelly, Matthew. (2007, August 21). *The Dream Manager: Achieve Results Beyond Your Dreams by Helping Your Employees Fulfill Theirs.* Amazon. https://www.amazon.com/dp/B000WHVS0C/ref=dp-kindle-redirect?_encoding=UTF8&btkr=1

20   Bruder, Jessica. (2013, September). *The Psychological Price of Entrepreneurship.* Inc. https://www.inc.com/magazine/201309/jessica-bruder/psychological-price-of-entrepreneurship.html

21   Chan, Nathan. (2016, April 28). *89: The Power of Embracing Vulnerability as an Entrepreneur with Brené Brown.* Foundr. https://foundr.com/brene-brown-embracing-vulnerability

22   Doane, Beth. (2018, June 20). *5 Mental Health Rules for Entrepreneurs.* Forbes. https://www.forbes.com/sites/yec/2018/06/20/5-mental-health-rules-for-entrepreneurs/#79afd7037784

23   Visit the link for a free assessment to see how well-balanced your life is at this moment. *The Ultimate Wheel of Life Interactive Assessment.* https://wheeloflife.noomii.com

24   Scott, Susan. (2004, January 6). *Fierce Conversations: Achieving Success at Work and in Life One Conversation at a Time.* Amazon. https://www.amazon.com/Fierce-Conversations-Achieving-Success-Conversation/dp/0425193373

25 Kelly, Matthew. (2015, July 5). *Off Balance: Getting Beyond the Work-Life Balance Myth to Personal and Professional Satisfaction.* Amazon. https://www.amazon.com/Off-Balance-Work-Life-Professional-Satisfaction/dp/1942611331/ref=sr_1_1?ie=UTF8&qid=1499256004&sr=8-1&keywords=off+balance

Note: Be sure to take the satisfaction assessment on pages 48-59 of the book to get a baseline measurement.

26 Gladwell, Malcolm. (2007, April 3). *Blink: The Power of Thinking Without Thinking.* Amazon. https://www.amazon.com/Blink-Power-Thinking-Without-ebook/dp/B000PAAH3K/ref=tmm_kin_swatch_0?_encoding=UTF8&qid=1588803741&sr=8-1

27 Schoeffler, Benjamin. *Overcoming Imposter Syndrome—Sub 007.* BrilliantSide. http://www.brilliantside.com/overcoming-impostor-syndrome-sub-007/

28 *Understanding the Johari Window model.* (2013, November 10). Self-Awareness. https://www.selfawareness.org.uk/news/understanding-the-johari-window-model

29 *Use of the Third Place Policy.* (2018, May 19). Starbucks Stories & News. https://stories.starbucks.com/stories/2018/use-of-the-third-place-policy/

30 *Sheryl Sandberg Gives UC Berkeley Commencement Keynote Speech.* (2016, May 16). YouTube. https://www.youtube.com/watch?v=iqm-XEqpayc

31 Sinek, Simon. *How great leaders inspire action.* (2009, September). TED. https://www.ted.com/talks/simon_sinek_how_great_leaders_inspire_action?language=en

32 Sinek, Simon. *Start with Why: How Great Leaders Inspire Everyone to Take Action.* (2009, September 23). Amazon. https://

www.amazon.com/dp/B002Q6XUE4/ref=dp-kindle-redirect?encoding=UTF8&btkr=1

Chapter 3: Connection & Communication

33   Reisinger, Don. (2019, January 10). *A.I. Expert Says Automation Could Replace 40% of Jobs in 15 Years*. Fortune. https://fortune.com/2019/01/10/automation-replace-jobs/

34   Newman, Daniel. (2014, April 10). *The Role of Influence in The New Buyer's Journey*. Forbes. https://www.forbes.com/sites/danielnewman/2014/04/10/the-role-of-influence-in-the-new-buyers-journey/#2a441e45585d

35   Richards, Robbie. (2017, October 3). *Sales and Marketing Alignment: 45 Experts Explain How to Connect the Dots*. SnapApp. https://www.snapapp.com/?p=5453

36   Grenny, J., McMillan, R., Patterson, K., & Switzler, A. (2011). *Crucial Conversations: Tools for Talking When Stakes Are High*. Amazon. https://www.amazon.com/Crucial-Conversations-Talking-Stakes-Hardback/dp/B00FKYP0LU/ref=sr_1_4?crid=1FPECIYJNK5HQ&keywords=crucial+conversations&qid=1556155580&s=gateway&sprefix=crucial+con%252Caps%252C195&sr=8-4

37   Carnegie, Dale. (1936). *How to Win Friends & Influence People*. Amazon. https://www.amazon.com/How-Win-Friends-Influence-People/dp/0671027034/ref=sr_1_4?ie=UTF8&qid=1543867201&sr=8-4&keywords=how+to+win+friends+and+influence+people+by+dale+carnegie

38   Carnegie, Dale. (2012, December 25). *How to Win Friends & Influence People in the Digital Age*. Amazon. https://www.amazon.com/How-Friends-Influence-People-Digital/dp/1451612591

39   Booher, Dianna. (2015, January 5). *9 Reasons Communication Fails*. Fast Company. https://www.fastcompany.com/3040332/9-reasons-leaders-fail-to-communicate-and-what-to-do-about-it

40   *Most Annoying Business Jargon*. Forbes. https://www.forbes.com/pictures/ekij45gdh/most-annoying-business-jargon/#3bce4f1d546a

41   Dizik, Alina. (2017, August 15). *Good start-ups have great networks*. Chicago Booth Review. https://review.chicagobooth.edu/entrepreneurship/2017/article/good-start-ups-have-great-networks

42   Ng, Serena. (2016, March 10). *Laundry Detergent From Jessica Alba's Honest Co. Contains Ingredient It Pledged to Avoid*. The Wall Street Journal. https://www.wsj.com/articles/laundry-detergent-from-jessica-albas-honest-co-contains-ingredient-it-pledged-to-avoid-1457647350

43   Ng, Serena & Terlep, Sharon. (2017, March 16). *Honest Co. Replaces Its CEO With a Clorox Veteran*. The Wall Street Journal. https://www.wsj.com/articles/honest-co-to-replace-ceo-lee-with-clorox-executive-vlahos-1489697157

Chapter 4: Improvise, Adapt, Overcome

44   Whiteman, Doug. (2020, January 21). *45 Retail Chains Responsible for Many of This Year's Record 9,300 Store Closings*. Yahoo! Finance. https://finance.yahoo.com/news/25-retailers-already-announced-close-132806255.html

45   *Office of Veterans Business Development (OVBD)*. SBA. https://www.sba.gov/business-guide/grow-your-business/veteran-owned-businesses

46   *How Frequent Is My Type?* The Myers & Briggs Foundation. https://www.myersbriggs.org/my-mbti-personality-type/my-mbti-results/how-frequent-is-my-type.htm?bhcp=1

47 *Wing & Control Surface Rebuilding.* Airframe Components by Williams Inc. http://www.airframecomponents.com

48 PEST Analysis: Identifying "Big Picture" Opportunities and Threats. MindTools. https://www.mindtools.com/pages/article/newTMC_09.htm

49 Karnjanaprakorn, Michael. (2010, October 22). *Take a Bill Gates-Style "Think Week" to Recharge Your Thinking.* Life Hacker. https://lifehacker.com/take-a-bill-gates-style-think-week-to-recharge-your-t-5670380

50 Hoque, Faisal. *Want to Lead? Enable Others to Flourish.* (2015, June 29). HuffPost. https://www.huffpost.com/entry/want-to-lead-enable-other_b_7681046

51 Duckworth, Angela. (2016, May 3). *Grit: The Power of Passion and Perseverance.* Amazon. https://www.amazon.com/Grit-Passion-Perseverance-Angela-Duckworth/dp/1501111108/ref=sr_1_1?ie=UTF8&qid=1498657838&sr=8-1&keywords=grit

52 Duckworth, Angela. *Grit Scale.* Angela Duckworth. https://angeladuckworth.com/grit-scale/

53 Rosen, Amy. (2015, August 7). *Why "Grit" May Be Everything for Success.* Entrepreneur. https://www.entrepreneur.com/article/247840

54 Lapowsky, Issie. (2013, January 24). *Arianna Huffington's Rule for Success: Dare to Fail.* Inc. https://www.inc.com/magazine/201302/rules-for-success/arianna-huffington-dare-to-fail.html

55 Danner, John. (2015, January 1). *How Smart Leaders, Teams, and Entrepreneurs Put Failure to Work—The Other F Word.* Amazon. https://www.amazon.com/Smart-Leaders-Entrepreneurs-Failure-Hardback/dp/B00VYV6K9E/ref=sr_1_3?ie=UTF8&qid=1486060435&sr=8-3&keywords=failure+the+other+f+word

56 Cain, Susan. (2012, January 24). *Quiet: The Power of Introverts in a World That Can't Stop Talking.* Amazon. https://www.amazon.com/Quiet-Power-Introverts-World-Talking-ebook/dp/B004J4WNL2/ref=tmm_kin_swatch_0?_encoding=UTF8&qid=1589084593&sr=8-1

57 James, Jeff. (2018, October 30). *Why Innovative Organizations Must Fail in Order to Be Successful.* Disney Institute. https://www.disneyinstitute.com/blog/why-innovative-organizations-must-fail-in-order-to/

Chapter 5: Funding

58 *Business Crowdfunding Experts Since 2012.* Crowdfund Better. https://www.crowdfundbetter.com

59 *Women outperform men in seed crowdfunding, according to analysis by PwC and The Crowdfunding Centre.* (2017, July 11). PWC Global. https://www.pwc.com/gx/en/news-room/press-releases/2017/women-outperform-men-in-seed-crowdfunding-according-to-analysis-by-pwc-and-the-crowdfunding-centre.html

60 Gorbatai, A,. & Nelson, L. (2015, August). *The Narrative Advantage: Gender and the Language of Crowdfunding.* Berkeley.

http://faculty.haas.berkeley.edu/gorbatai/working%20papers%20and%20word/Crowdfunding-GenderGorbataiNelson.pdf

61 *Away Lifetime Limited Warranty.* Away Travel. https://www.awaytravel.com/warranty

62 *Make It Right.* Hilton. https://embassysuites3.hilton.com/en/about/make-it-right.html

63 Dagostino, Mark. (2019, October 22). *The Power of WOW: How to Electrify Your Work and Your Life by Putting Service First.* Amazon. https://www.amazon.com/dp/B07ZHMQVPX/ref=dp-kindle-redirect?_encoding=UTF8&btkr=1

64   *Zappos.* https://www.zappos.com

65   Michels, David. (2019, June 17). *The Trust Crisis In Business.* Forbes. https://www.forbes.com/sites/davidmichels/2019/06/17/the-trust-crisis-in-business/#4f6388744a6a

66   *Moving Closer to the 2025 Horizon.* Indiana Chamber. https://www.indianachamber.com/wp-content/uploads/2019/06/IN-Vision2025-2PageNarrative.pdf

67   Ahmed, Mona. (2018, July 5). *How 997 people can make American great again.* Ewing Marion Kauffman Foundation. https://www.kauffman.org/currents/how-997-people-can-make-america-great-again/

68   *Percent of population that starts a new business.* (2019, September 23). Kauffman Indicators of Entrepreneurship. https://indicators.kauffman.org/indicator/rate-of-new-entrepreneurs

69   Hwang, Victor. (2019, May 9). *Three reasons why entrepreneurship isn't just an American Dream.* Ewing Marion Kauffman Foundation. https://www.kauffman.org/currents/3-reasons-why-entrepreneurship-is-not-just-an-american-dream/?utm_source=newsletter&utm_medium=email&utm_campaign=iaw_05_09_2019

70   MacBride, Elizabeth. (2019, May 31). *Is Entrepreneurship Becoming the Purview of Upper-Class Men?* Forbes. https://www.forbes.com/sites/elizabethmacbride/2019/05/31/is-entrepreneurship-becoming-the-purview-of-upper-class-men/#1f151fbbd594

71   Magistretti, Bérénice. (2018, January 29). *SVB: 71% of startups don't have women on their board of directors.* VentureBeat. https://venturebeat.com/2018/01/29/svb-71-of-startups-dont-have-women-on-their-board-of-directors/

72   Hart, Kim. (2020, January 15). *Venture capital slowly seeps outside of Silicon Valley.* Axios. https://www.axios.com/venture-capital-midwest-growth-13ac8514-e8e2-498f-98b7-71026277e826.html

73 *Leaders are Readers. Go, Leader, Grow!* https://goleadergrow.com/2018/08/23/leaders-are-readers/

74 Wilson, Fred. (2017, December 3). *The Early State Slump.* AVC. https://avc.com/2017/12/the-early-stage-slump/

75 Ovans, Andrea. (2015, January 23). *What Is a Business Model?* Harvard Business Review. https://hbr.org/2015/01/what-is-a-business-model

76 Feldstein, Martin. (2017, April 20). *Why the U.S. Is Still Richer Than Every Other Large Country.* Harvard Business Review. https://hbr.org/2017/04/why-the-u-s-is-still-richer-than-every-other-large-country

77 Maurya, Ash. (2012, March 13). *Running Lean: Iterate from Plan A to a Plan That Works.* Amazon. https://www.amazon.com/Running-Lean-Iterate-Works-OReilly/dp/1449305172

78 Zimmerman, Angelina. (2016, August 12). *Discover the 7 Key Traits of an "Abundance Mindset."* Inc. https://www.inc.com/angelina-zimmerman/discover-the-7-key-traits-of-an-abundant-mindset.html

79 Block, Peter. (2011, March 15). *Flawless Consulting: A Guide to Getting Your Expertise Used.* Amazon. https://www.amazon.com/Flawless-Consulting-Guide-Getting-Expertise/dp/0470620749

Chapter 6: Networking

80 *Optimize Your Life.* Optimize. https://www.optimize.me

81 Kelly, Matthew. (2015, July 5). *Off Balance: Getting Beyond the Work-Life Balance Myth to Personal and Professional Satisfaction.* Amazon. https://www.amazon.com/Off-Balance-Work-Life-Professional-Satisfaction/dp/1942611331/ref=sr_1_2?keywords=off+balance&qid=1583409526&sr=8-2

82   Osterwalder, Alexander. (2017, May 12). *Value Proposition Design*. inUseExp: YouTube. https://www.youtube.com/watch?v=bX18bmpHaw

83   *Build a more diverse, inclusive and stronger team*. Diverse Talent Strategies. https://diversetalentstrategies.com

84   Martin-Books, Alison. (2016, March 16). *Learning to Lead Through Mentoring: 8 Mentoring Lessons to Help You Pursue Meaningful Mentoring Relationships*. Amazon. https://www.amazon.com/Learning-Lead-Through-Mentoring-Relationships-ebook/dp/B01CYGKEV2

85   Osterwalder, A., Pigneur, Y., Bernarda, G., Smith, A. (2015, January 28). *Value Proposition Design: How to Create Products and Services Customers Want*. Amazon. https://www.amazon.com/dp/B06X429CJH/ref=dp-kindle-redirect?_encoding=UTF8&btkr=1

OR, for a quick view/summary and chart:

What is the Value Proposition Canvas? B2B International. https://www.b2binternational.com/research/methods/faq/what-is-the-value-proposition-canvas/

86   Wiens, Jason. (2016, October 17). *International Entrepreneur Rule: The good, the bad, and the unknown*. Ewing Marion Kauffman Foundation. https://www.kauffman.org/currents/international-entrepreneur-rule/

87   Intuit Inc. *The Golden Age of Small Business*. (2016, October 20). Business Wire. https://www.businesswire.com/news/home/20161020005548/en/Golden-Age-Small-Business

88   *What Is Blue Ocean Strategy?* Blue Ocean. https://www.blueoceanstrategy.com/what-is-blue-ocean-strategy/

89   Kelly, Matthew. *The Off-Balance Assessment*. Floyd Consulting. https://www.floydconsulting.com/off-balance-assessment

90 Hull, Patrick. (2013), December 6). *Don't Get Lazy About Your Client Relationships*. Forbes. https://www.forbes.com/sites/patrickhull/2013/12/06/tools-for-entrepreneurs-to-retain-clients/#4829b3e72443

Chapter 7: Optimizing Your Niche

91 Schomer, Stephanie. (2020, January). *#7 on the Franchise 500: Planet Fitness Knows You Don't Want to Go to the Gym*. Forbes. https://www.entrepreneur.com/article/344514

92 *About Planet Fitness*. Planet Fitness. https://www.planetfitness.com/about-planet-fitness

93 *Now Available Nationwide*. Impossible. https://impossiblefoods.com/burgerking/

94 Drayer, Lisa. (2019, August 14). *They might be better for the planet, but are plant-based burgers good for you?* CNN. https://www.cnn.com/2019/08/09/health/plant-fake-meat-burgers-good-for-you-or-not/index.html?no-st=1565798554

95 Fromm, Jeff. (2018, June 14). *Why Storyliving Brands Win with Gen Z*. Forbes. https://www.forbes.com/sites/jefffromm/2018/06/14/why-storyliving-brands-win-with-gen-z/#74a508ee7d72

96 *May restaurant sales continue roller coaster ride*. (2019, June 6). Nation's Restaurant News. https://www.nrn.com/finance/may-restaurant-sales-continue-roller-coaster-ride

97 Butler, Sarah. (2018, July 23). *Quorn invests £7m into R&D on back of veganism boom*. The Guardian. https://www.theguardian.com/business/2018/jul/23/quorn-invests-7m-r-and-d-veganism-boom

98 *About Us: The History of Earth Day*. Earth Day. https://www.earthday.org/history/

99   Weiler, Stephen. (2017, March 16). *Six charts that illustrate the divide between rural and urban America*. The Conversation. https://theconversation.com/six-charts-that-illustrate-the-divide-between-rural-and-urban-america-72934

100 Godin, Seth. (2012, August 20). *The race to the bottom*. Seth's Blog. https://seths.blog/2012/08/the-race-to-the-bottom/

101 Kaltenbaek, Ben. *Lean Startup: How to Test a New Product*. Boot Start. http://www.boot-start.com/en/blog/lean-startup-test

102 Vuittonet, Alice. (2015, September 20). *30 Women Who Have Revolutionized A Male-Dominated Industry*. TechCrunch. https://techcrunch.com/gallery/30-women-who-have-revolutionized-a-male-dominated-industry/

103 *With their clever dishes and savvy social media food trucks have emerged as important vehicles for economic opportunity and growth jump-starting a $2 billion-plus industry in cities across America*. Food Truck Nation. https://www.foodtrucknation.us

104 Gallo, Amy. (2014, October 29). *The Value of Keeping the Right Customers*. Harvard Business Review. https://hbr.org/2014/10/the-value-of-keeping-the-right-customers

105 Reichheld, Fred. *Prescription for Cutting Costs*. Bain & Company. https://media.bain.com/Images/BB_Prescription_cutting_costs.pdf

106 *Insights with J.B. Bernstein*. The NIIC. https://theniic.org/insights/insights-j-b-bernstein/

107 Fernandez, Mary. (2019, October 16). *How to Create a Concrete Buyer Persona (with Templates & Examples)*. OptinMonster. https://optinmonster.com/how-to-create-a-concrete-buyer-persona-with-templates-examples/

Chapter 8: Competitive Advantage

108 Porter, Michael. (1998, June 1). *Competitive Strategy: Techniques for Analyzing Industries and Competitors.* Amazon. https://www.amazon.com/Competitive-Strategy-Techniques-Industries-Competitors/dp/0684841487/ref=sr_1_1?keywords=Michael+porter&qid=1581080193&sr=8-1

109 Collins, Jim. (2001, October 16). *Good to Great: Why Some Companies Make the Leap and Others Don't.* Amazon. https://www.amazon.com/Good-Great-Some-Companies-Others/dp/0066620996/ref=sr_1_3?keywords=good+to+great&qid=1581080090&sr=8-3

110 *Chuck Surack.* Wikipedia. https://en.wikipedia.org/wiki/Chuck_Surack

111 *The Sweetwater Difference.* Sweetwater. https://www.sweetwater.com/about/the-sweetwater-difference/

112 Hamm, John. (2002, December). *Why Entrepreneurs Don't Scale.* Harvard Business Review. https://hbr.org/2002/12/why-entrepreneurs-dont-scale

113 *Top 250: The Ranking.* (2020). Restaurant Business. https://www.restaurantbusinessonline.com/top-500-chains

114 *Explore the Elements of Value.* Bain & Company. www2.bain.com/bainweb/media/interactive/elements-of-value/

115 Fowler, Damian. *The hype machine: Streetwear and the business of scarcity.* BBC. https://www.bbc.com/worklife/article/20180205-the-hype-machine-streetwear-and-the-business-of-scarcity

116 Devinney, Michele. (2019, August 8). *Craft beer comes to a head.* WatzUp. https://whatzup.com/events/northern-indiana-brew-trail-craft-beer-comes-to-a-head

117 *Fat Tire Colorado U.S.A.* New Belgium. https://www.newbelgium.com/beer/fat-tire

118 Loudenback, Tanza. *Why employee-owned New Belgium Brewing gives workers bikes, travel vouchers, and paid sabbaticals on their work anniversaries.* Business Insider. https://www.businessinsider.com/new-belgium-brewery-employee-perks-2016-6

119 *5 Reasons Why Competition Is Good For Your Business.* Forbes. https://www.forbes.com/pictures/emjl45fhdh/5-reasons-why-competition-is-good-for-your-business/#79ec3c761f97

120 Porter, Michael E. (1996, November-December). *What is Strategy?* Harvard Business Review. https://www.instituteofbusinessstrategy.com/strategy.pdf

121 Sachs, Jonah. (2017, February 24). *Pixar's Ed Catmull On How Collaborative Competition Drives Success.* Fast Company. https://www.fastcompany.com/3068491/pixars-ed-catmull-on-how-collaborative-competition-drives-success

122 Andersson, Mae. (2019, February 1). *Super Bowl ads often fumble their message.* The Journal Gazette. https://journalgazette.net/business/20190201/super-bowl-ads-often-fumble-their-message

123 Su, R. & McDowell, E. (2020, February 2). *How Super Bowl ad costs have skyrocketed over the years.* Business Insider. https://www.businessinsider.com/super-bowl-ad-price-cost-2017-2

124 McSpadden, Kevin. (2015, May 14). *You Now Have a Shorter Attention Span Than a Goldfish.* Time. https://time.com/3858309/attention-spans-goldfish/

125 Godin, Seth. (2009, November 12). *Purple Cow: Transform Your Business by Being Remarkable.* Amazon. www.amazon.com/Purple-Cow-New-Transform-Remarkable/dp/1591843170

126 Chafkin, M. & Bergen, M. (2016, December 8). *Google Makes So Much Money, It Never Had to Worry About Financial Discipline—Until Now.* Bloomberg. https://www.bloomberg.com/news/features/2016-12-08/google-makes-so-much-money-it-never-had-to-worry-about-financial-discipline

127 Molloy, Margaret. (2015, November 9). *Why Simple Brands Win.* Harvard Business Review. https://hbr.org/2015/11/why-simple-brands-win

Chapter 9: Sustainability

128 Otar, Chad. (2018, October 25). *What Percentage of Small Businesses Fail—And How Can You Avoid Being One of Them?* Forbes. https://www.forbes.com/sites/forbesfinancecouncil/2018/10/25/what-percentage-of-small-businesses-fail-and-how-can-you-avoid-being-one-of-them/#65432b8b43b5

129 *The World's 50 Most Innovative Companies 2019.* Fast Company. https://www.fastcompany.com/most-innovative-companies/2019

130 Andre, Annie. (2017, November 1). *7 Leadership Quotes on Delegation to Inspire You to Greatness.* Prialto. https://blog.prialto.com/inspirational-delegation-quotes

131 Jackley, Jessica. (2011, April 21). *The Pregnant Entrepreneur and The VC Who Wouldn't Fund Her.* Forbes. https://www.forbes.com/2011/04/21/pregnant-entrepreneur-ceo-and-the-venture-capitalist.html#4ba906bf47cb

132 Cohen, Jennifer. (2020, January 12). *Reasons Why We Don't to Achieve New Year's Resolutions.* Forbes. https://www.forbes.com/sites/jennifercohen/2020/01/12/reasons-why-we-dont-achieve-resolutions/#4c7fa07641a8

133 Happy or Not. https://www.happy-or-not.com/en/

134   de Meza, D., Dawson, C., Henley, A., & Arabsheibani, G.R. (2019, January). *Curb your enthusiasm: Optimistic entrepreneurs earn less.* Science Direct. https://www.sciencedirect.com/science/article/abs/pii/S0014292118301582?via%3Dihub

135   Collins, Jim. (2001, October 16). *Good to Great: Why Some Companies Make the Leap and Others Don't.* Amazon. https://www.amazon.com/Good-Great-Some-Companies-Others/dp/0066620996/ref=sr_1_1?keywords=good+to+great&qid=1553165425&s=gateway&sr=8-1

136   Grove, Andrew. (1999, March 16). *Only the Paranoid Survive: How to Exploit the Crisis Points That Challenge Every Company.* Amazon. https://www.amazon.com/Only-Paranoid-Survive-Exploit-Challenge/dp/0385483821

137   Twin, Alexandra. (2019, September 5). *The 4 Ps.* Investopedia. https://www.investopedia.com/terms/f/four-ps.asp

138   Covey, Stephen. (2013, November 15). *The 7 Habits of Highly Effective People: Powerful Lessons in Personal Change.* Amazon. https://www.amazon.com/dp/B00GOZV3TM/ref=dp-kindle-redirect?_encoding=UTF8&btkr=1

139   Khateeb, Omar. (2017, November 29). *The 4 Stages to Technology Adoption Inside the Chasm.* Medium. https://medium.com/@omarmkhateeb/the-4-stages-to-adoption-inside-the-chasm-6c9c19e4375

140   Ranta, Kristian. (2019, February 22). *Mental Health Hacks for Entrepreneurs.* Forbes. https://www.forbes.com/sites/theyec/2019/02/22/mental-health-hacks-for-entrepreneurs/#325a0bf6513d

141   Clarkson, Natalie. (2015, September 9). *Richard Branson: Why entrepreneurs should practice mindfulness.* Virgin. https://www.virgin.com/entrepreneur/richard-branson-why-entrepreneurs-should-practise-mindfulness

142   Speights, Keith. (2017, May 21). *Success rate: What percentage of businesses fail in their first year?* USA Today. https://www.usatoday.com/story/money/business/small-business-central/2017/05/21/what-percentage-of-businesses-fail-in-their-first-year/101260716/

143   Lou, Michelle. (2019, March 6). *There's now only one Blockbuster left on the planet.* CNN. https://www.cnn.com/2019/03/06/business/last-blockbuster-on-the-planet-trnd/index.html

144   Schellinger, Mark. (2018, March 23). *In Business, You're Either Growing or You're Dying.* Forbes. https://www.forbes.com/sites/forbeslacouncil/2018/03/23/in-business-youre-either-growing-or-youre-dying/#3cb6aa83400d

145   Schwantes, Marcel. (2018, January 18). *Warren Buffett Says This 1 Simple Habit Separates Successful People from Everyone Else.* Inc. https://www.inc.com/marcel-schwantes/warren-buffett-says-this-is-1-simple-habit-that-separates-successful-people-from-everyone-else.html

146   Umoh, Ruth. (2018, March 11). *Arianna Huffington says she became successful after she quit one common bad habit.* CNBC. https://www.cnbc.com/2018/03/11/arianna-huffington-became-successful-after-she-started-sleeping-well.html

Chapter 10: Mindset

147   Harter, Jim. (2018, August 26). *Employee Engagement on the Rise in the U.S.* Gallup. https://news.gallup.com/poll/241649/employee-engagement-rise.aspx

148   *Optimize Your Life.* https://www.optimize.me

149   Stilwell, Bobby. (2020, February 25). *First Lego League: More than just robots.* WHNT. https://whnt.com/news/stem/first-lego-league-more-than-just-robots/

150   Wolny, Nick. (2020, February 24). *Identifying Your 'Curiosity Type' Is the Key to Getting More Done*. Entrepreneur. https://www.entrepreneur.com/article/345981

151   Frye, Lisa. (2018, June 1). *More People Are Taking Time Off, and That's Good for Business*. SHRM. https://www.shrm.org/resourcesandtools/hr-topics/employee-relations/pages/workers-taking-more-vacation-.aspx

152   *The Ultimate Wheel of Life Interactive Assessment*. Noomii. https://wheeloflife.noomii.com

153   *Wheel of Life Template with Instructions*. The Coaching Tools Company. https://www.thecoachingtoolscompany.com/products/wheel-of-life-coaching-tool/

154   Carranza, Anthony. (2020, May 4). *7 Clever Goal Tracker Apps to Keep You on Track in 2020*. Lifehack. https://www.lifehack.org/798999/goal-tracker

155   Coventry, Petrina. (2016, May 30). *Six ways the ancient philosophy of Stoicism can help business entrepreneurs*. The Conversation. https://theconversation.com/six-ways-the-ancient-philosophy-of-stoicism-can-help-business-entrepreneurs-59890

156   Holiday, Ryan. (2016, October 18). *The Daily Stoic: 366 Meditations on Wisdom, Perseverance, and the Art of Living*. Amazon. https://www.amazon.com/Daily-Stoic-Meditations-Wisdom-Perseverance/dp/0735211736/ref=sr_1_3?keywords=stoicism&qid=1581373923&sr=8-3

157   Holiday, *The Daily Stoic*, February 10th.

158   Kreiss, Taylor. *Stoicism 101: An introduction to Stoicism, Stoic Philosophy and the Stoics*. Holstee. https://www.holstee.com/blogs/mindful-matter/stoicism-101-everything-you-wanted-to-know-about-stoicism-stoic-philosophy-and-the-stoics

159 *Shawn Achor.* GoodThink. http://goodthinkinc.com/speaking/shawn-achor/

160 Duszyński, Maciej. (2020, April 23). *Pareto Principle—All You Need to Know About the 80/20 Rule.* ResumeLab. https://resumelab.com/career-advice/pareto-principle?gclid=CjwKCAjwqpP2BRBTEiwAfpiD-yJEISMFj43u5SoJs4qPvbgZjACbLC7F24eHUiOYd3eGie0UA6LWYxoCVr4QAvD_BwE

161 Areitio, Andy. (2018, December 13). *What is a startup and how is it different from other companies (new and old)?* Medium. https://medium.com/theventurecity/what-is-a-startup-and-how-is-it-different-from-other-companies-new-and-old-428875c27c29

162 Valinsky, Jordan. (2019, November 7). *Bad time to be a CEO: 170 top executives left last month.* CNN Business. https://www.cnn.com/2019/11/06/investing/ceo-departures-october-record/index.html

163 Valinsky, *Bad time to be a CEO*, 2019.

164 *On moral courage.* (2015, June 1). Lehigh News. https://www2.lehigh.edu/news/moral-courage

165 Thomas, Joseph J. *The Four Stages of Moral Development in Military Leaders.* USNA. https://www.usna.edu/Ethics/_files/documents/Four%20Stages%20of%20Moral%20Development%20Thomas.pdf

166 LaPan, Karl. (2018, August 16). *Are you a Compassionate & Conscious Capitalist?* The NIIC. https://theniic.org/insights/are-you-a-compassionate%E2%80%8B-conscious-capitalist/

167 Healy, Maureen. (2016, November 23). *Why Gratitude Matters.* Psychology Today. https://www.psychologytoday.com/us/blog/creative-development/201611/why-gratitude-matters

168   Cummings, Carol. (2015, June 8). *Being Grateful*. Brookdale. https://www.brookdalenews.com/being-grateful.htm

169   Rath, Tom & Clifton, Donald O. (2004, July 8). *The Power of Praise and Recognition*. Gallup. https://news.gallup.com/businessjournal/12157/power-praise-recognition.aspx

170   *14 Famous Businesses That Launched with Less Than $10,000*. (2020, January24). Entrepreneur. https://www.entrepreneur.com/slideshow/344211

171   Say, My. (2013, December 3). *5 Powerful Exercises to Increase Your Mental Strength*. Forbes. https://www.forbes.com/sites/groupthink/2013/12/03/5-powerful-exercises-to-increase-your-mental-strength/#1c21e9174cda

172   Kukolic, Siobhan. (2017, July 21). *Shoot for The Moon*. Huff Post. https://www.huffpost.com/entry/shoot-for-the-moon_b_59721cd0e4b06b511b02c2c9

173   Bahcall, Safi. (2019, March 19). *Loonshots: How to Nurture the Crazy Ideas That Win Wars, Cure Diseases, and Transform Industries*. Amazon. https://www.amazon.com/dp/B07D2BKVQR/ref=dp-kindle-redirect?_encoding=UTF8&btkr=1

174   *Between the Stimulus and the Response*. Daily Stoic. https://dailystoic.com/between-the-stimulus-and-the-response/

175   Roumeliotis, Ioanna. (2015, April 23). *Shawn Achor's 6 exercises for happiness*. CBC News. https://www.cbc.ca/news/health/shawn-achor-s-6-exercises-for-happiness-1.3040937

176   Toren, Matthew. (2015, September 17). *4 Warning Signs Your Team Is Working in Silos, and How to Destroy Them*. Entrepreneur. https://www.entrepreneur.com/article/250477

177   Ghadimi, Pejman. *Why You Should Compete in a Saturated Market.* Business Collective. https://businesscollective.com/why-you-should-compete-in-a-saturated-market/index.html

Chapter 11: Inspiration

178   Castrillon, Caroline. (2019, February 4). *Why More Women Are Turning to Entrepreneurship.* Forbes. https://www.forbes.com/sites/carolinecastrillon/2019/02/04/why-more-women-are-turning-to-entrepreneurship/#47362dc3542a

179   *The 2019 State of Women-Owned Businesses Report.* American Express. https://about.americanexpress.com/sites/americanexpress.newshq.businesswire.com/files/doc_library/file/2019-state-of-women-owned-businesses-report.pdf

180   Heskett, James. (2019, July 1). *Are Super Stretch Goals Only for the Very Young?* Harvard Business School. https://hbswk.hbs.edu/item/are-super-stretch-goals-only-for-the-very-young?cid=wk-sm-li-sf104808262&sf104808262=1

181   ibid

182   Ferriss, Tim. (2017, May 15). *Fear-Setting: The Most Valuable Exercise I Do Every Month.* The Tim Ferriss Show. https://tim.blog/2017/05/15/fear-setting/

183   Thompson, Charles. (2011, April 15). *What a Great Idea! 2.0: Unlocking Your Creativity in Business and in Life.* Amazon. https://www.amazon.com/What-Great-Idea-2-0-Creativity-ebook/dp/B004WTB6GC

184   Charles, Thompson. (1992, January 1). *What a Great Idea! The Key Steps Creative People Take.* Amazon. https://www.amazon.com/What-Great-Idea-Creative-People/dp/0060553170/ref=tmm_hrd_swatch_0?_encoding=UTF8&qid=&sr=

185   Davis, Tim. (1984). *The Influence of the Physical Environment in Offices*. Academy of Management Review. https://www.jstor.org/stable/258440?seq=1

186   James, Geoffrey. (2017, May 18). *Open-Plan Offices Kill Productivity, According to Science*. Inc. https://www.inc.com/geoffrey-james/science-just-proved-that-open-plan-offices-destroy-productivity.html

187   *Creativity: better alone or in groups?* CreativeHuddle. https://www.creativehuddle.co.uk/creativity-better-alone-or-in-groups

188   Barras, Colin. (2014, March 13). *Can you learn to be creative?* BBC Future. https://www.bbc.com/future/article/20140314-learn-to-be-creative

189   Cooper, Belle Beth. (2014, April 2). *10 Surprising Ways to Transform Your Creative Thinking*. Forbes. https://www.fastcompany.com/3028465/10-surprising-ways-to-transform-your-creative-thinking

190   Davis, Josh. (2015, May 27). *The Hidden Benefits of Daydreaming*. Forbes. https://www.fastcompany.com/3046172/the-hidden-benefits-of-daydreaming

191   Ferriss, Timothy. (2009, December 15). *The 4-Hour Workweek: Escape 9-5, Live Anywhere, and Join the New Rich*. Amazon. https://www.amazon.com/4-Hour-Workweek-Escape-Live-Anywhere/dp/0307465357/ref=sr_1_1?ie=UTF8&qid=1501158115&sr=8-1&keywords=4+hr+work+week

192   *Be kind to your mind*. Headspace. https://www.headspace.com

193   Covey, Dr. Stephen R. *Habit 2: Begin with the End in Mind*. FranklinCovey. https://www.franklincovey.com/the-7-habits/habit-2.html

194   McHale, Curtis. (2016, September 8). *Want great clients? You need to be picky.* HuffPost. https://www.huffpost.com/entry/want-great-clients-you-need-to-be-picky_b_57d18e1de4b0f831f707166a?guccounter=1

195   Collins, Jim. (2017). *How Do You Do "Stop Doing?"* Jim Collins. https://www.jimcollins.com/media_topics/StopDoing.html

196   Collins, Jim. (2001, October 16). *Good to Great: Why Some Companies Make the Leap and Others Don't.* Amazon. https://www.amazon.com/Good-Great-Some-Companies-Others/dp/0066620996/ref=sr_1_1?ie=UTF8&qid=1547645108&sr=8-1&keywords=good+to+great

197   Mask, Clate. (2016, January 28). *Money Isn't What Really Drives Your Business. It's These 3 Things.* Inc. https://www.inc.com/clate-mask/money-isn-t-what-really-drives-your-business-it-s-these-3-things.html

198   Buford, Bob P. (2015, October 6). *Halftime: Moving from Success to Significance.* Amazon. https://www.amazon.com/Halftime-Significance-Bob-P-Buford/dp/0310344441/ref=sr_1_1?ie=UTF8&qid=1496943772&sr=8-1&keywords=halftime

199   Grant, Adam. (2014, March 25). *Give and Take: Why Helping Others Drives Our Success.* Amazon. https://www.amazon.com/Give-Take-Helping-Others-Success/dp/0143124986/ref=sr_1_1?ie=UTF8&qid=1496943806&sr=8-1&keywords=give+and+take

200   *How Goals Can Increase Your Confidence as a Business Leader.* (2020). STRE.ME. https://stre.me/uncategorized/how-goals-can-increase-your-confidence-as-a-business-leader/

201   *How to Create Value with Confidence, Focus, and a Clear Vision of Success.* (2020). STRE.ME. https://stre.me/strategic-boost-template/?utm_source=blog-cta&utm_medium=three-ways-to-increase-confidence&utm_campaign=strategic-boost-v01

202 Garnett, Laura. (2018, April 2). *This Is the Scientific Reason Steve Jobs Went for Walks*. Inc. https://www.inc.com/laura-garnett/this-is-scientific-reason-steve-jobs-went-for-walks.html

203 Groth, Aimee. (2012, July 24). *You're the Average of The Five People You Spend the Most Time With*. Business Insider. https://www.businessinsider.com/jim-rohn-youre-the-average-of-the-five-people-you-spend-the-most-time-with-2012-7

204 Scipioni, Jade. (2019, October 23). *10 principles for great leadership, according to Disney's Bob Iger*. CNBC. https://www.cnbc.com/2019/10/23/disney-ceo-bob-igers-principles-for-great-leadership.html

205 Cirillo, Francesco. *The Pomodoro Technique*. Francesco Cirillo. https://francescocirillo.com/pages/pomodoro-technique

206 Collins, Jim. *Where Are You on Your Journey from Good to Great? Diagnostics Tool*. Jim Collins. https://www.jimcollins.com/tools/diagnostic-tool.pdf

CPSIA information can be obtained
at www.ICGtesting.com
Printed in the USA
LVHW041957280422
717483LV00002B/137

9 781665 524551